D0452312

RIDING ROUTE 94

RIDING ROUTE 94

An Accidental Journey
through the Story of Britain

David McKie

PIMPERNEL
PRESS LTD
www.pimpernelpress.com

Journalist and author **David McKie** grew up in London and Leeds, and read history at Oriel College, Oxford. After the *Keighley News* and *Oxford Mail* he joined the *Guardian*. Thereafter he turned to writing books, which have included *Jabez: the Rise and Fall of a Victorian Rogue* (shortlisted for the Whitbread Biography Award); *Great British Bus Journeys*; and *McKie's Gazetteer*. David McKie lives in south-west London.

Pimpernel Press Limited
www.pimpernelpress.com

Riding Route 94
An Accidental Journey through the Story of Britain
© Pimpernel Press Limited 2017
Text © David McKie 2017

David McKie has asserted his right to be identified as the author of this work in accordance with the Copyright, Designs and Patents Act 1988 (UK).

All rights reserved. No part of this publication may be reproduced, stored in a retrieval system or transmitted, in any form, or by any means, electronic, mechanical, photocopying, recording or otherwise, without prior permission in writing from the publisher or a licence permitting restricted copying. In the United Kingdom such licences are issued by the Copyright Licensing Agency, Barnard's Inn, 86 Fetter Lane, London EC4A 1EN.

A catalogue record for this book is available from the British Library.

Designed by Anne Wilson
Typeset in Apollo

Cover illustration (also on title page and page 231) adapted from an image by Iwona Wawro/Shutterstock

ISBN 978-1-910258-34-7
Printed in the UK by CPI Books Ltd.

9 8 7 6 5 4 3 2 1

CONTENTS

HOLD ON TIGHT, PLEASE!

THIS IS NOT A BOOK ABOUT BUSES; it's a book about where they take you. Nor was it designed as a state of the nation book – there are plenty of those. I have called it an accidental journey through the story of Britain because I wanted to avoid being able to choose where I visited. George Orwell went to Wigan, Sheffield and Barnsley in search of what he expected to find. The same purpose colours J.B. Priestley's account of his *English Journey*. I tried to find some device that would produce an entirely random, unpremeditated sequence of journeys. In this sense, I have followed the not often praised or emulated example of the ninth-century Welsh monk Nennius, who in his *Historia Britonnum* described his method of historiography in the notable and painfully honest sentence: *coacervavi omne quod inveni*: 'I have made a heap of all I have found.'

The device I chose was this. I would travel the land using only buses which had identical numbers. So the sequence of places through which I journeyed would be entirely arbitrary. Even then, some themes would emerge, especially the contrast between the fate of communities that grow and prosper (though they may not always have done so) and those apparently set on a course of irreversible decline. Inevitably much of the North would tend to produce one kind of picture and much of the South another. For this reason, I start with two journeys which link the fate of winners and losers: Blewbury on the Berkshire Downs and Middlesbrough. That should also serve to indicate that this is not a travelogue. No one in search of enchanting scenery would be likely to head for Grangetown, on the edge of Middlesbrough, a community called into being for the making of iron and steel and now – even before the closure of the Redcar plant in 2015 – shorn of that purpose and struggling.

But what bus routes should I use? If I picked 12 as my magic route number, I'd have far too much to choose from. A higher number, though – say 312 – would restrict the supply and rule out too much of the country. Eventually I settled for the range 90 to 99, then whittled it down to the two most promising: 93 and 94. That 94 prevailed may have had something to do with the minor allure of that number, as evident in the regularity with which it occurs in *Private Eye*. But it also involved a perhaps indefensibly personal calculation: the 93 bus in London is one I've used and grown incurably used to over the past forty years.

To make sure of my regional spread, I included some routes where a 94 has a local prefix. For example, the book's second journey, out of Middlesbrough, involves a 794, but that's because it's a council-subsidized Boroughbus, all of which have numbers that start with a seven. Likewise my 94 on the Isle of Mull is a 494, the four a reminder that it's subsidized by Argyll and Bute Council. Some of my plans were foiled by local government cuts. Routes I'd expected to go on – one in my old home town of Leeds – were struck down. Though they did not obliterate the 94 bus from Carlisle to Brampton, cuts in subsidy reluctantly imposed by Cumbria Country Council reduced it to one journey a day from Carlisle to Crosby, with the only journey back to Carlisle on the same bus leaving ten minutes later. Two other journeys perished: Wrexham right across Wales to Barmouth, now a T3, and a bus through East Anglia, which would have picked up deeper purple-coloured UKIP territory than anything I was able to sample; that's now an X1. Others I did manage to take were axed soon afterwards.

Curtailments and cuts are multiplying and more will inevitably follow as the local authorities who keep threatened services going find their funds no longer run to it. The think tank IPPR calculated in 2015 that council spending on local transport services fell by almost 20 per cent in 2013–14, with Cumbria topping the list with cuts of 44 per cent. John Harris wrote in the *Guardian*: 'Buses are a vital requirement for young people and most Britons on limited incomes. Around 40 per cent of people over 60 use a bus at least once a week; one of the many certainties that comes with an ageing population is an increased demand for public transport. Everyday reality, however, is headed in the opposite direction.' Yet the issue commands only scant attention; and that, as Harris says, may be due to the fact that the London bus world is thriving and cuts in the capital are relatively few. Elsewhere, Harris wrote, there is 'slow and stealthy decline as timetables shrink, bus shelters slowly crumble, and in far too many places buses simply disappear.'

My game plan worked in the sense that it took me to towns and villages that would never have found a place in a carefully chosen itinerary: Tunstall, Staffordshire, where the local football team once fielded a side whose goalkeeper and four defenders had a combined age of around 300; Frog Island, a former industrial area on the edge of Leicester, which may not be there for much longer; stricken townships like Tyldesley in Lancashire and Felling in County Durham, marooned by change; pretty, unassuming Dervaig and barely perceptible Calgary on the Isle of Mull; St Columb Major, charmingly cloistered in Cornwall. It also introduced me to a clutch of intriguing people I'd never heard of: Sir Goldsworthy Gurney, the wickedly plotted-against pioneer of the steam omnibus; Hodgson Casson, battling evangelist, and the One-Eyed Captain, the Hallelujah Giant and the Converted Sweep who followed him in Gateshead; O.G.S. Crawford, dyspeptic airborne archaeologist and author of a tirade called *Bloody Old Britain*; and the one I most cherish – Julie Outhwaite, aged ten, who wrote an account of her native place which seems to express what thousands in the grimy grimness of industrial towns must also have longed for, touching on the danger that where squalor and shabbiness go, sociability often disappears with it, which recurs throughout these pages.

Some of what I have chanced on is centuries old. So, into the story have come, without deliberate planning, the Norman Conquest and its bloody aftermath, medieval ways of life that flourished, then failed, the Wars of the Roses, Henry VIII's break with Rome, the Civil Wars, the Industrial Revolution, the rise of religious dissent, the sometimes inspired and sometimes sadly mismanaged reconstruction that followed the Second World War, and so on through to the present day.

Inevitably some conclusions have nosed their way into individual chapters. But most are encapsulated in the last, which homes in, as so much always does in this lopsided land, on London. That Britain voted in June 2016 to get out of Europe came as a huge surprise to many: less so to anyone who in the previous year had travelled the country and picked up the burgeoning sense of dispossession, the upsurge of alienation from government at all levels that Brexit dramatized: with Brussels, yes; but even more crucially, here, with London.

I

BLENDING BLEWBROUGH

94 Blewbury–Didcot
794 Middlesbrough–Grangetown–Eston–Middlesbrough

SOON AFTER DAWN in Blewbury, Oxfordshire, and the village is coming to life. There's a hint of early sun away down the A417 towards the Thames Valley and the horses will no doubt soon be out on the Berkshire Downs to the south (these are still the Berkshire Downs, though forty years ago Blewbury was part of a tract taken from Berkshire and awarded to Oxfordshire). At Linnets and Beavers, Rose Cottage and Dragonwyke, down Westbrook Street where Kenneth Grahame came to live after completing *The Wind in the Willows*, in Church Road and Church End, in Berry Lane, Eastfields and Dibleys, the day is beginning. The air is full of birdsong. And outside the Load of Mischief, three people, of whom I am one, await the day's first 94 bus to Didcot.

I thought the Load of Mischief would be a pub, but it isn't. It's a private house adorned with a little plaque that celebrates its previous life. Like two others before it, this one has gone out of business, leaving only the Red Lion and the Barley Mow. That's part of a process which has seen the village transformed from a community where in the mid-nineteenth century more than half the working population were employed in the farms and fields to a pleasantly prosperous place where most people find their employment at some distance. Where once they set out on foot for a day's work with the plough or harrow or tractor, it's now more likely to be the four-mile journey for Harwell and the Atomic Energy Research Establishment or the ten miles to Culham, where the Centre for Fusion Energy is home to the JET (Joint European Torus) and MAST (Mega Ampere Spherical Tokamak). And sometimes the journey is still more ambitious, to the City of London, for instance: seventy miles away.

Look here upon this picture, and on this. Well before dawn, a week later, I am in Grangetown, east of Middlesbrough, on a road that leads to the coast at Redcar. The night is still deep dark, but the sky is lit by the gushes of flame which flare day and night from industrial works which can never sleep. Grangetown is close to the Tees, and the birdsong here is mainly the mournful cries of seagulls. Outside the Magnet Hotel, two people, of whom I am one, await the day's first 794 Boroughbus to Middlesbrough.

I thought the Magnet would be a pub. But it isn't: it's more the shabby wreck of a pub which after a time of trouble and turbulence closed down, perhaps for good. An air of defeat hangs over it. Disconsolate boards say it's for sale, but only the bravest of souls is likely to buy it.

It's a very cold morning in March. Alongside me at the bus stop is a figure so comprehensively swaddled up that I cannot tell if it's a man or a woman. The bus is due at 5.37. After five shivering minutes it hasn't arrived. But a voice which emanates from the swaddling clothes is reassuring. 'It's usually late,' she says. 'But it always comes.' At 5.45, it suddenly does, signalled by a thrilling blaze of light as it hurries out of the northern darkness towards the Magnet, to sweep us down towards the Eston Hills.

The sky is blue-grey now, streaked in the east by an almost industrial red that seems to promise (and will indeed deliver) a glorious morning. This was, long ago, rural England, as Blewbury, for all the change that's come over it, still is today. A 'venerable village', Blewbury had already been termed in a tenth-century charter. Later it became, like others around it, a wool town, but that trade faded away. You can get some picture of what it was like in the middle years of the nineteenth century from the census of 1861, when the men were predominantly agricultural labourers, and most of the working women domestic servants. This, like many others before the railways came, was a self-contained community where 60 per cent of the people were Blewbury born, and the great majority of those denied that privilege came from nearby villages.

Five family names – Herridge, Aldridge, Corderoy, Martin and Belcher – accounted for one in five of those in the village; ten family names covered almost a third. The Herridges and Aldridges mostly worked on the land; the Corderoys were big farmers, people of power and influence.

Then change came, especially when the railway arrived in the 1880s. Today almost all the village's shops have gone, and Blewbury lost its railway in 1962. Apart from the A417 racing across the southern edge, all feels calm and settled. Streams run through it, which made it a place of watercress beds. At its heart is the church of St Michael and All Angels, Grade I listed, celebrated for a chancel window designed and created by J.F. Bentley, who built Westminster Cathedral.

You won't find an estate agent's office in Blewbury, but there are plenty in Didcot, whose windows demonstrate that houses round here don't come cheap. But then there's plenty that makes Blewbury feel like a fine place to live. There are favourite walks on the Downs and below them you can choose the ancient Icknield Way or the older, higher Ridgeway.

The poet Edward Thomas came here to write a book called *The Icknield Way*, published in 1913, calling in for a while at the Load of Mischief and deconstructing at length the sign that still hung there (the 'load' was a large obstreperous woman being carried by a crushed-looking man.) There is easy access to Thames-side villages, which mattered to Kenneth Grahame, who had been living for years before close to the river.

The contingent aboard the 94 this morning is not what I had expected. I'd assumed there would be people heading for jobs in the City, but not so. People of this persuasion prefer their cars, as the car parks around Didcot station – some already full when we get there at twenty to eight –will shortly attest.

So most of those aboard this morning are students or workers in Didcot shops. Only the driver, a local man recently returned from years in New Zealand, who greets most of his passengers by name, is conspicuously chatty and cheerful. It's a route, consistent with the unhurried nature of Blewbury, on which not much happens. Beyond East Hagbourne, a gentle and privileged-looking village, there is hardly a notable sight till you come to the outskirts of Didcot, and then to its centre, and beyond it, that potent magnet, the railway station.

'Didcot-change-for-Oxford' people in Oxford used to call it, since this was what the porters bawled out on the station platform, where so many tedious minutes were spent awaiting the trains that would carry them on to their dreaming spires. The Didcot you saw from the train in those days looked like a drab little town, an impression soon confirmed if you got out and gave it a closer inspection. The line had only taken this course because more lordly Abingdon had been aghast at such an impertinent infiltration and told Brunel to take his project elsewhere. Indeed, there were some in Oxford who tried to resist the railway. 'It would, so the greybeards thought, place awful distractions in the way of undergraduates,' Jan Morris writes in her book about Oxford: 'it would disturb the metabolism of the place, vulgarize the learned setting, and bring hordes of common strangers into the city.'

Though the coming of the railway set Didcot growing, that progress was augmented by the army arriving here at the start of the First World War. It was the army, even more than the railway, the local historian Brian Lingham says, that fashioned modern Didcot. Maybe: but it's the railway that is helping to refashion it now. Didcot station has been uplifted to 'Didcot Parkway'. When the 94 puts you down at the end of the 15-minute run from Blewbury, the station concourse is thronged and here awaiting your patronage are trains for a generous range of destinations: four in the next hour for London Paddington; a fast train to Bristol Temple Meads and another to Malvern by way of Oxford; one for Cardiff and one for Cheltenham. Yet at no little cost: the expenditure needed here has reached a level unimaginable to people in a place like Grangetown. The cost of a weekly season ticket to London Paddington (45 minutes on faster trains) was increased at the beginning of 2016 to £123.70, while the price of an annual season ticket was raised to £4,832.

Despite that, the gateway status of Didcot has made it increasingly sought after, helping it expand from a village to a town of 25,000, and growing. Big Sainsbury's, big Tesco, of course, and since 2005, the Orchard Centre, which marshals the PC Worlds, Argoses, Nexts and other near-essential ingredients in the way we shop now. There is also a five-screen cinema; and the Cornerstone arts and entertainments centre, completed in 2008 at a cost of £8 million; as well as a tourist lure in the Didcot Railway Centre, which trades both on rail nostalgia and on modern childhood addictions like Thomas the Tank Engine. A shop-cum-office, occasionally open, on the edge of the Orchard Centre, makes much of other local successes: notably, the famous scientific achievements at Harwell and Culham and new adventures in science and technology now under way – with still more to follow.

Didcot acquired additional claims to fame with the building in the 1970s of a mighty power station featuring six drum-like towers, 375 feet high, whose design (by Sir Frederick Gibberd) collected awards, though *Country Life* magazine named it the UK's third-worst eyesore. Three of these towers were demolished at 5 am on a Sunday in July 2014. Though warned to stay away, thousands turned up to watch, including one enthusiast who told a reporter that Didcot had not seen a day like it since its football team won the FA Vase. The other towers remain, but seem likely to go within a decade. And the area won't on the whole be sorry. When the plans to build the complex were unveiled, the *Oxford Mail* solicited local opinion and found a strong sense of outrage. This power station, one woman complained, was all wrong for this part of the world: it was going to make it look 'like somewhere up North.'

Like Middlesbrough, perhaps?

*****

By the middle of the nineteenth century Middlesbrough was establishing itself as one of the wonders of modern Britain. It wasn't just Middlesbrough which thought so: William Gladstone, then Chancellor of the Exchequer, had come to the town in 1862 and, addressing one of those monstrous banquets in which prosperous citizens in Victorian England so delighted, had described it as 'this remarkable place, the youngest child of England's enterprise' and 'an infant Hercules'.

A mere thirty years earlier there had been next to nothing here. In 1801 there were only four houses and two dozen people. Then in 1829, Joseph Pease, one of the Darlington family who had created the Stockton and Darlington railway, and a group of his Quaker businessmen colleagues saw that a tract of low-quality land here on the banks of the Tees, to which the railway could be extended, could furnish the ideal location for the transportation of coal from the South Durham coalfields, where the Peases were major owners, to London and expanding markets elsewhere. The settlement they created then was north of the railway: small and compact, but a place of some ambition, as you can see from the sad remains of some of the buildings that survive: the now abandoned town hall, the Greek Revival Custom House of 1837. By 1831, the little town had a hundred and fifty inhabitants. Ten years later it had five thousand. Yet this in a sense had been a false start. Other claimants, notably Hartlepool, fourteen miles up the coast, began to erode Middlesbrough's apparent success.

Then, just as the coal trade faltered, a new technology came to Middlesbrough's rescue. The agents of innovation, enthusiastically backed by the Peases, were Henry Bolckow, from Mecklenburg in north Germany, who would one day become the town's first mayor and its Liberal MP, and John Vaughan, born in Worcestershire of Welsh parents – not only business partners but neighbours who had married a pair of sisters. It was they who became the agents of the matchless success that Gladstone honoured. By 1870, Middlesbrough and its Teesside hinterland would produce from its more than forty blast furnaces around 15 per cent of the world's iron output. People talked of the town as 'Ironopolis' and compared it to Ballarat and the Klondyke. This was not the only British town to have suddenly sprung up from nothing. Barrow-in-Furness, Hartlepool, Crewe and Birkenhead were conspicuous others. But this one beat the lot.

Yet even in its glory days, the place was stocking up problems. Housing was run up at speed, dirt cheap and basic, to accommodate the new work force – housing which would become the next generation's slumland. The town's population was overwhelmingly male, since initially those drawn there by the prospect of work either had no families or chose not to bring them. That made for aggression and drunkenness. And the Irish, who came in large numbers as they had to other booming British towns and cities, were the subject of resentment, which sometimes turned to violence. In 1871 Irish incomers made up 9 per cent of the town's population, well

below the figure for Liverpool but a match for Manchester's 9 per cent
and far greater than the mere 2.5 per cent in Birmingham. Many of these
arrivals would not stay in Middlesbrough long: but while they did, they
were hardly a force for peace and stability. And Middlesbrough, though it
also had shipbuilding and ship repair, was all along ominously dependent
on the fortunes of a single industry. In 1861, almost half of those at
work in manufacturing were employed in ironworks, though that figure
had eased down to 33 per cent ten years later. But in general, the town
lacked diversity: 85 per cent of the male workforce were employed in
manufacturing, with only one in ten in the commercial sector.

Yet none of that was allowed to detract from the town's pride in its
historic success and the mark it had made across the civilized world. The
iron it supplies, said the Middlesbrough newspaper editor H.G. Reid,
'furnishes railways to Europe; it runs by Neapolitan and Papal dungeons;
it startles the bandit in his haunts in Cicilia; it streaks the prairies of
America; it stretches over the plains of India; it surprises the Belochees;
it pursues the peggunus of Gangotry. It has crept out of the Cleveland
hills, where it has slept since the Roman days, and now, like a strong and
invincible serpent, coils itself round the world.'

In 1889 the Prince and Princess of Wales, who came to open the new
town hall, the grandest building the town had yet seen, with a clock tower
designed to echo Westminster's, were greeted to a characteristic deluge of
self-adulation from the mayor, Raylton Dixon, an old Etonian shipbuilder.
In his great book *Victorian Cities*, Asa Briggs quotes Dixon's response to
the flattering address of the Prince: '"His Royal Highness owned he had
expected to see a smoky town. It is one, and if there is one thing more
than another that Middlesbrough can be said to be proud of, it is the
smoke (cheers and laughter). The smoke is an indication of plenty of work
(applause), an indication of prosperous times (cheers) – an indication that
all classes of workpeople are being employed, that there is little necessity
for charity (cheers) and that even those in the humblest station are in a
position free from want" (cheers).'

Yet even as they stood to toast the town, and themselves, there were
signs that the boom years might soon be over. What had made the
Middlesbrough industry so dominant by 1880 was the discovery thirty
years earlier of a seam in the Eston Hills near-perfect for the making of
iron. Yet by 1880 iron was losing ground to the new technologies of steel-
making. Middlesbrough might have been Ironopolis, but Sheffield seemed
set to overtake it as the city of steel. By 1880, Bolckow and Vaughan were
both dead, and their successors could not avert what began to look like

irreversible decline. There would be later boosts in times of war, and with the establishment of new enterprises at Wilton, on the south side of the Tees, and especially at Billingham, on the northern side, contiguous with Middlesbrough though in no sense part of it, where chemical manufacturing – originally developed for wartime purposes – began and expanded and came in the 1940s under the high command of Imperial Chemical Industries (ICI). But here too, from the late 1970s onwards, once booming industries began to falter, even to disappear.

The decline of Teesside inevitably blighted communities like Grangetown, where my 794 Middlesbrough Boroughbus journey begins at the Magnet Hotel. After years in the care of successive local authorities, Grangetown has since 1974 been part of what is now known as Redcar and Cleveland. The original community here was called Eston Grange, taking its name from the village of Eston, sheltering under the hills where Vaughan and his geologist friend John Marley discovered their seam. Eight streets were run up, on a grid pattern, designed to contain 768 houses. This was a characteristic Middlesbrough settlement. The 1881 census shows a community utterly dominated by the jobs which first iron, then steel, had created. Some 72 per cent of people in work here were earning their money from iron and steel.

It was clearly a place without deep local roots. Of the heads of households – all male, bar one widow – and their spouses, just two had been born in Eston, and four more in Middlesbrough or adjacent communities. Twenty-five had been born further afield in Yorkshire. But twenty one – almost a quarter – had been born in Ireland, and five in Wales or Monmouthshire.

Thirty years on, this Grangetown would develop into a community of more than 5,000 people. All down its central street, Whitworth Road, there were shops, more than forty in all: seven classed as grocers and provision merchants, five as 'shopkeepers' or general dealers, with six butchers, four shoemakers, three drapers, a greengrocer and two fruiterers, two hardware shops and two confectioners, a post office, a baker, a chemist, a newsagent, a hairdresser, a decorator, a milliner, a watchmaker and, at the end, a pawnbroker. At first there had been no pub, but local magistrates had become so concerned with the extent of shebeening that they called for one to be provided. In photographs this Grangetown looks dark and unprepossessing and overshadowed by industry; pollution hung over it, visible, unavoidably breathable and even tasteable. The local doctor, John Glen, who lived on Whitworth Road, was grieved and alarmed by the circumstances of his patients and warned where living in such conditions might lead. Yet it seems to have been quite a contented community, not

least because for many who had long gone without it, even lost hope of it,
it provided stable work.

A local poet – Julie Outhwaite, aged ten – wonderfully caught the balance:

> Grangetown has a smoky atmosphere
> Chimneys belching forth their cloudy dust
> From the iron and steel works that stood so near
> Without these mills our families would be lost
> Our feet unshod our larders bare.
> We'd like to see them go, and yet the cost
> To old and young alike, would be unfair.
> It would be good to see a fertile plot
> Where flowers and trees would blossom for all time,
> To know the joys of nature we have not
> Amid our dusty streets and dirt and grime!
> But some of us its homeliness does prove
> It could never be the same, where else we move.

That Grangetown has gone. The land it used to occupy is now Bolckow
Park – a park not in Julie Outhwaite's sense of flowers and trees blossoming
for all time, but of that increasingly prevalent twentieth-century
phenomenon, the industrial park. Some of the street names survive, but
little else. The Grangetown which replaced it – creating, it was said, a
garden city in place of the dusty streets, dirt and grime of its predecessor
– is south of the A66, where the old one was north of it, and stretches
down towards Eston. Its street names spell out its creators' aspirations:
the main road running north–south, where the Magnet uncertainly stands
– bisected at this point by the Broadway, a section of the main road from
Middlesbrough to Redcar – is called Birchington Avenue. Others around
it equally hint at the joys of alluring holiday destinations: Sandringham,
Arundel, Dovedale, Coniston, Derwent Water, Harlech, Tenby.

The intention that this new Grangetown should be a kind of Teesside
garden city was to some extent achieved. The houses have room around
them; there are good green spaces, generous playing fields and a brightly
painted primary school. It is far better ordered and more salubrious than
the shattered streets of a district like the Gresham ward of Middlesbrough,
where, to much local complaint, the council has allotted many near-
derelict terrace houses to asylum seekers. The planners might well have
claimed that they'd taken account of Julie Outhwaite's aspirations. Yet this
new world does not seem to provide chances to meet and exchange the

news and the gossip, as Whitworth Road used to do. And though today's Grangetown has a sports and social club, there isn't any obvious homely replacement for the Magnet as a place to gather and reminisce. 'I think everyone in Grangetown went to the Magnet pub Friday and Saturday nights,' one old habitué told a local website. 'George would play the organ and lads and lasses would get up and give a song. I cannot remember trouble. Everyone had a good night out.'

A government assessment in 2015 put Middlesbrough among the authorities with the highest proportion of deprived neighbourhoods in England. South Oxfordshire (the authority for Blewbury and Didcot) was among the least. Grangetown itself was listed seventeenth among the most deprived wards in England. In the specific instances of levels of income, employment, health, education and crime, it was scored in the lowest category among 32,482 wards, though it was found to be better than 62 per cent of them for living environment and higher still for access to services. An analysis by Experian rated Middlesbrough – a town heavily dependent on public sector employment – as the local authority most vulnerable to cuts in public spending.

*****

But you don't need the statistics to tell you that Grangetown is quite unlike Blewbury. You only need to have looked out of the windows of the 94 to Didcot, and now through those of 794 to Middlesbrough as it hurries on towards the inviting backdrop to much of this journey, the Eston Hills. Eston village has a richer and livelier mix than Grangetown, as demonstrated in its Square (in fact a triangle), where a sense of aspiration (banks, building societies, Thomson Travel) mingles with hints of desperation (Bargain Booze, fast food takeaways, Ramsdens, pawnbrokers).

Here at last the bus stops travelling south and turns westward on a road running above a valley that opens up a generous, even majestic, panorama of industrial Teesside with its lights and flares against a now lightening sky. Near Normanby, the bus takes a further deviation, down a lane between green fields and into the hills, turning back at a place called Norman Conquest, which proves to be a garish-looking pub. We return to Middlesbrough through South Bank, once a scene of teeming activity, housing the works of the two great Teesside companies, Bolckow and Vaughan, and Dorman Long, and shipbuilding on the river. Much of the old South Bank has been swept away, and much of what's left looks near derelict. Of all the places I see on my journeys, this is one of the saddest. And now at last we are into Middlesbrough, and half an hour on from Grangetown the 794 has reached its journey's end, the borough's well-ordered bus station.

This dip into two strikingly disparate places cannot pretend to be a scientific contribution to the long debate over what is misleadingly termed the North–South divide. Blewbury and Didcot cannot fully sum up the South, nor are Middlesbrough and Grangetown pure epitomes of the North; and indeed, as will become clear in subsequent journeys, the whole concept is flawed. There are areas within rampantly prosperous London – as also in Cornwall and other parts of the allegedly cosseted South – where deprivation exists on a truly 'northern' scale. Yet ask yourself at which end of the country you'd expect to find a parking space on offer at £400,000; or which region has the fastest rate of growth in England and Wales (five times faster than in the rest of the country); or whether it was the North or the South which in 2014 housed all the ten areas where people were most heavily dependent on anti-depressants. (Clue: the Redcar and Cleveland Primary Care Trust, which looks after Grangetown, came second only to Blackpool in prescribing anti-depressants.) Every time the answer makes the South the more desirable. 'We are all in this together,' the then Chancellor George Osborne declared when austerity politics began, but that is not one imagines how it would have been seen in the bar at the Magnet, Grangetown – had the Magnet been spared extinction.

Middlesbrough has rarely been able to take much pleasure in what visiting writers have made of it. 'Why indeed, the cynical might ask, should any children be born in Middlesbrough at all, considering the more than dismal picture which investigation discloses of existence in that feverish industrial centre?' the usually enlightened and generous Liberal MP and social commentator C.F.G. Masterman asked in 1911. J.B. Priestley called it 'more like a vast, dingy conjuring trick, than a reasonable town'. Douglas Goldring, in the mid-1920s, made the place sound like an exhibit in a freak show. 'Until recently, in my ignorance, I had no idea such places existed,' he confessed. 'And yet, even Middlesbrough, by accident as it were, has a kind of frightful loveliness which the eyes of the younger generation, trained by the Cubists, will be able to appreciate better than we can. Its miles and miles of ironworks, with their belching chimneys and enormous blast furnaces, their fantastic pipes and tubes and monstrous retorts, their sudden bursts of flame and rising columns of smoke – white brown or densest black – have a strange and dreadful beauty, macabre and terrifying.'

But that, apart from its celebrated transformer bridge, was the only beauty to be found there: 'All else is mean with a meanness that has to be seen to be believed.' The town's best future might be to waste away. In

2013 the *Economist* magazine argued in its superior way that it was time for governments to stop wasting money on trying to revive places like Burnley, Hull, Hartlepool and Middlesbrough, which were now beyond all hope of revival.

But Florence Bell, novelist, playwright, writer of children's books, and second wife of the Middlesbrough ironmaster Hugh Bell, knew the town from within. In her candid and honourable book *At the Works: A Study of a Manufacturing Town*, published in 1907, she did not attempt to conceal the very serious problems it had with ill-health and poverty, dangers at work, drunkenness, gambling and other indulgences, but even so she defended most of its people for doing their best to cope with their circumstances, the women especially. High-minded disapproval was never likely to cure or even alleviate poverty, she told those of her social equals who were harsh in their judgements on working-class families and eager to give them lectures on the values of thrift. Her own arithmetic told her that many families lived on the edge, and one serious setback could ruin them. Why, she asked, were they so much scrutinized and condemned when other social classes were not? 'It has come to pass', she wrote, in lines that reverberate still, 'that the working class is used, so to speak, as the unit of the moral investigation, until we well nigh believe that this class is the chief repository of the vices and virtues of the nation.'

Also, while aware of the ugliness of the town, she also saw in its industrial landscape, by night especially, an unexpected beauty. And to get a fair balance now, I think there are things that ought to be noticed about disparaged, even vilified, Middlesbrough that I haven't yet said. Perhaps the right place to assess them is a walk that begins near the Norman Conquest pub at the Flatts Lane Woodland Country Park visitor centre. From here you can climb up to Eston Nab, a segment of the Eston Hills that the landowners sold in January 2014 to a voluntary organization called the Friends of the Eston Hills. Now you can see two essential aspects of Middlesbrough. To the north, the often dramatic landscape of industry; to the south, a fine sweep through to Yorkshire, and especially a panorama of Roseberry Topping, an endearingly oddly shaped hill, and one of this region's most treasured landmarks. Through the valley below it runs the route of the 93 bus from Middlesbrough through to Whitby, which I know from previous visits here to be one of the most beautiful bus journeys in the land.

The sense of these two contrasting sides to Middlesbrough and Teesside around and beyond it was wonderfully caught at the end of the 1970s by the Lincolnshire aristocrat, schoolmaster and topographer Henry

Thorold, in his *Shell Guide to County Durham*. He smuggled this judgement
into an entry on Billingham, since strictly the southern side of the Tees
was outside his remit. 'From the foothills of the Cleveland Hills behind
Middlesbrough,' he wrote, 'from a bedroom window at Ormesby Hall at
night, the whole industrial world along the banks of the Tees comes to life
in an extraordinary way, brilliant with a thousand lights, the great girders
of the Transporter Bridge dark in silhouette: a magic city.' Has anyone else
called this landscape, which seems above all to mean Middlesbrough, 'a
magic city'? Probably not. Even Mayor Raylton Dixon, that proud lauder
of Middlesbrough smoke, did not rate it as highly as that. But looking out
from here, up high on the Eston Hills, I think it's deserved.

2

SERVING REBELLION

94 Oxford–Charlton-on-Otmoor–Bicester

ON THE OUTSIDE WALL of the Crown public house in the village of
Charlton-on-Otmoor, six miles from Oxford, there's a plaque that says:
'Rebellion served here'. As an emblem for the place it adorns, it could
hardly be more fitting. The word 'moor' has two conflicting meanings: a
bleak, intimidating tract of high land of the kind where you might expect
to encounter Heathcliff, or Rochester, or the Hound of the Baskervilles; or
a low, marshy, boggy fenland – more Hereward's country than Heathcliff's.
The 4,000 acres of Otmoor belong to the second category. Remote,
inaccessible and hard to traverse, this was always a place identified with
nonconformity. Nineteenth-century Otmoor had its own institutions, its
local practices, its particular kind of cattle disease, known as the moor-
evil; even, observers noted, its own way of walking, best described as a
slouch, apparently designed to cope with the wet conditions.

Otmoor people, it was said, were born with webbed feet. They were
sturdy and independent, ever ready to challenge authority. A sense of
that persisted into the following century. 'To write or walk there in an
autumn twilight', wrote the Scot John Buchan in 1940, 'is to find oneself

in a place as remote from man as Barra or Knoydart.' People in Charlton, a village whose very name – the tun of the ceorl – spoke of a place outside the habitual feudal order, used proudly to claim that they'd never had a lord of the manor. When rebellion came, Charlton was at the heart of it; and at the heart of Charlton, the chosen place where rebellion was plotted and organized, was the Crown.

My 94 bus starts at a place which seems worlds away from Otmoor: the university city of Oxford. The journey begins in St Giles, outside the Ashmolean Museum, close to the Martyrs' Memorial commemorating Hugh Latimer, Nicholas Ridley and Thomas Cranmer – their own kinds of rebel, executed in 1555 and 1556 for heresy, for refusing to abandon their Protestant beliefs. Across the street is the gate of St John's College; mighty Balliol is just round the corner on Broad Street. But St Giles has another side to it. This was (and is) the scene of an annual fair, a time when respectable townspeople trembled at the thought of the riff-raff descending on Oxford, and anarchy ruling. And St Giles was the scene of the most spectacular moment in the Otmoor rebellions of 1829–35.

The people of Otmoor had risen up against enclosure: the legal extinction of common land which poor people could use to graze their cattle and turn out their geese. The exercise was carried out in the name of agricultural efficiency, on the calculation that big landowners could make the land productive as the poor could never do. Even before the enclosure campaign, the commoners' rights had been eroded by landowners: the earls of Abingdon, the most powerful of such interests on Otmoor, employed an official called a moor-driver, who would round up the cattle he found on the common and hold them until they were claimed; those unclaimed became the property of the Abingdons and were branded with their mark.

But systematic enclosure came late to the moor and its 'seven towns' – really no more than villages: the two biggest in 1830, Charlton and Beckley, housed only around 350 people. Elsewhere across England enclosures had been widely applied since the sixteenth century, sometimes sparking local rebellions. But on Otmoor the main proprietors, some of whom rarely went near the place, had made no sustained effort to carry it through. That changed when in 1777 a clever and determined young man called Alexander Croke inherited his Otmoor estate, Studley Priory. He was only nineteen, and still an undergraduate at Oriel College, Oxford, but he quickly saw the advantages – for himself, of course, but also, as he argued, for the local and indeed the national economy – of enclosing the moor, draining its wetlands and making it productive. That would cost, he calculated with unlikely precision, £1,812, 1s 8½d, but would quickly pay for itself by yielding an annual income of £4,000.

That he made only limited progress was partly because he could not persuade the most powerful of Otmoor's landowners, Willoughby Bertie, 4th Earl of Abingdon, to join his crusade. Abingdon was a maverick: a patron of music who was one of the sponsors of Haydn's London concerts. He was also that rare phenomenon, a radical peer, and he set his face against Croke's intentions, publishing a pamphlet noting that 'for the poor and miserable wretches, who, if this Bill be carried into execution, are totally deprived of their Rights, not the smallest notice is taken, not the least provision made.'

Thanks to his intervention the enclosure Bill was blocked in the Lords. But, sadly for the poor and miserable wretches of Otmoor, death deprived them of the fourth earl in 1799, and his successor was more in tune with Croke's way of thinking. Dr Croke (who would shortly become Sir Alexander) had in the meantime been away running Nova Scotia, and making himself unpopular for his imperious and inflexible behaviour, but in 1815 he was back, and soon a fresh Bill was being pushed through Parliament.

Villagers petitioned against it, but their petition was ruled to have reached their lordships too late. 'In this way', wrote Bicester historian John Dunkin, 'was Otmoor lost to the poor man, and awarded to the rich, under the spurious idea of benefitting the public.' Or, in the words of a rhyme much heard where enclosers went to work: 'The law locks up the man or woman/ Who steals the goose from off the common/ But leaves the greater villain loose/ who steals the common from the goose.' Dunkin noted, too, that though a scheme of compensation for the commoners was included in the Bill, that was only open to those who would pay a share of the cost of drainage and the cost of erecting fences, which few could afford.

At first the operations of the enclosers sparked little protest. The first signs of rebellion came not from the poor and wretched, whose long-established rights were now under threat, nor even against enclosure, but against the drainage operations essential to Croke's endeavours. On 5 June 1830, a contingent of farmers began to break down the embankments the enclosure commissioner had been building along the new course he had engineered for the River Ray. The winter had been a wet one even by Otmoor standards and now they found that their fields were extensively flooded, in part because of the new embankments. Should the problem persist, as they judged it was certain to do, they would surely be ruined. So they hacked the embankments down: a response which *Jackson's Oxford Journal* considered natural, though 'not very legal'.

Two local landowning parsons – Rector Philip Serle of Oddington and Theophilus Cooke, perpetual curate of Beckley, both of whom were magistrates – took out a warrant for the farmers' arrest, and in July twenty-two of them (some accounts say twenty-three) were put on trial at Oxford. But much to the chagrin of the ministers, Mr Justice Park directed the Oxford jury to acquit them, holding that the commissioner had gone well beyond his remit in diverting the river and building the embankments, and finding that the farmers had in that case every right to do what they'd done.

In legal terms, the effects of this judgement were limited. Yet this was the signal for Otmoor to rise against its oppressors. The common people of Otmoor thought the acquittal signalled something very much broader: an endorsement of their contention that their rights had been stolen from them. From now on, enclosure became the grounds of the conflict. The farmers had fought for their legitimate interest; the humbler people of Otmoor would do the same.

They began by cutting down all the ironmongery of enclosure. With faces blackened and wrapped around with scarves, some dressed in women's clothes, they began nightly excursions to break down prohibitive fences. The campaign began at the end of August, in a mood that suggested a celebration, with the chanting of slogans (most of all, 'Otmoor for ever') and the sounding of horns to signal action.

The two great proprietors, Croke and the 5th Earl of Abingdon, took counsel with the Revd Serle and the Revd Cooke. They stationed men – perhaps two dozen of them – on nightly watch. Accordingly, on 3 September, the campaign of destruction was focused on the private properties of Serle and Cooke and finally of Sir Alexander too. One of his sons, Wentworth Croke, was among the watchmen, and he now produced a pistol and made to shoot, at which point a fence-breaker struck him on the head with an axe, the most violent moment in the disturbances so far. The Oxford Militia was summoned along with Lord Churchill's Yeomanry.

Three days later the trouble intensified. Some 500 people – backed by supporters, some from outside Otmoor who, some estimates said, swelled the numbers to a thousand, or even, one London newspaper claimed, 4,000 – met to perambulate the moor, both the areas to which they believed they had justified access and others where they did not, arming themselves, the *Oxford Journal* reported, with reaphooks, bill-hooks, hatchers and duckets, and cutting down such barriers as stood in their way. Asked what justification they had for their actions, they merely replied: 'Otmoor for ever!' All this was done in daylight, without any disguise. The purpose was not just destruction, but what they now called possessioning. Sixty-six men were seized, of whom forty-four were taken to Islip, an ancient town just off the moor, to be conveyed by wagon next day to Oxford prison. That journey would provide the rebels with a spectacular triumph.

The day's events were witnessed by reporters from the *Journal*. The two wagons containing soldiers and their prisoners on their way to the gaol in Oxford Castle took them through St Giles in the midst of the fair. The *Journal* reported:

> As soon as they had entered Oxford, the cries of 'Otmoor for ever!' in the wagons were speedily and lustily responded to from without. The prisoners were cheered and the soldiery irritated. The ebullition of feeling was simultaneous and appeared to pervade all classes, not, however, directed so much against the yeomanry, who behaved most patiently, as against the cause that had sent the men there as prisoners. Sticks, stones, brickbats and mud were plentifully thrown in all directions, which the soldiers warded off pretty successfully till they turned from Beaumont Street towards the castle. Here they were forced one by one from their posts. The officer and privates rode off at full speed to the castle, to get open the gates for the captives and to alarm the governor, Mr Grant, of the danger of the gaol being stormed. The populace increased in number, and redoubled their perseverance in pelting. The prisoners, less and less securely guarded, slipped out, one after another, at the tails of the wagons, till all were released; and the overpowered residue of yeomanry fled from the unequal combat, and escaped from the unmerciful missile attack in the direction of Botley.

The outcome could easily have been uglier, especially if the soldiers had used their weaponry – though they must have known that if they did so, they might be slaughtered. The soldiers retired to lick their wounds; Otmoor was all celebration. The *Journal* appended to its report of the St Giles rescue a second account of events, inserted it said, at the request of the 'gentleman of rank' who had provided them with it. The fair at St Giles, he said, had attracted 'vast numbers of the worst description of people', whose numbers were swollen in time to several thousands and 'many' of the yeomanry had been seriously injured by the desperate assaults to which they had been subjected.

The following week a much longer contribution, again designed as it said to correct the record, found space in the paper. It began by repudiating, at times even ridiculing, the moor people's claim that enclosure had robbed them of ancient rights. They purported to believe that these rights were traceable back to a grant of common land by some unnamed lady to the poor of the Otmoor towns; yet the claim had been searched and found to be groundless – and was anyway 'too silly for any but old women and children to believe'. They claimed they had a right to the soil of Otmoor, but that belonged by law to the Earl of Abingdon as Lord of the Manor. They believed they had a right to turn out cattle on the common, but that only applied if they had enough land of their own to sustain them, which they plainly did not.

The rights, in any case, this authority asserted, were hardly worth having. Because of floods the land was mostly unfit for pasturage and unhealthy for cattle. Sheep were subject to rot; the moor-evil prevailed among the larger cattle. The cattle were mostly half-starved; the benefit the poor could enjoy from keeping geese and collecting dung was small and in practice exercised only by a few higglers who drove off the geese and cattle of others to feed their own. So little benefit accrued from these rights that the inhabitants were ragged and penniless, and in looking after a brood of goslings, a few rotten sheep, a skeleton of a cow or a mangy horse, they lost more than they might have gained by their day's work, and acquired habits of idleness and dissipation, and a dislike to honest labour, 'which has rendered them the riotous and lawless set of men which they have now shewn themselves'.

It was customary for enclosers to argue that their system would benefit not just themselves but the whole community. But this advocate went further, representing enclosure as selfless philanthropy. Not only were they rescuing the miserable wretches of Otmoor in all the ways he had listed, they were conferring benefits on the country at large, right down to these poor inhabitants, 'without benefit to themselves, and without injury to anyone'. As production increased, the nation would no longer have to depend for supplies of corn on the nation's enemies; the price of corn would fall – and all this without any benefit to the proprietors themselves, whose expenditure had far exceeded their profits. This diatribe was signed 'An Otmoor proprietor'.

Otmoor responded to this record of altruism with its usual ingratitude. The disruptions continued. Many who took no part in the fence-breaking gave the rebels aid and comfort. A file in the Oxfordshire History Centre contains anguished letters that flew back and forth between the proprietors, an influential figure called William Henry Ashdown, who had recently been MP for the county and was chairman of its Quarter Sessions, and, in many cases, the Home Secretary, Lord Melbourne, to whom this assembly kept saying, although in rather more respectful language: stir yourself; we need help, and we need it immediately.

In March 1833, two and a half years after St Giles and the events on the moor that had preceded it, the magistrates received a bleak reply to their latest entreaties, which had requested the stationing of a permanent military presence at Islip. Lord Melbourne regretted he could not sanction such a course. The magistrates must try to protect property on the moor 'with the means which are at their disposal'. In fact, though, they had drawn on all the support they could find, and it had not worked.

One reason for that was the general sympathy across Otmoor for the protestors. A farmer called Thornton, almost the only informer the authorities could find, described a characteristic scene in the Crown – or Higgs's beer-house, as it was then often known – where the plotters assembled and picked up donations from the wider community. 'I remember Saturday the Second of February last,' he reported in 1833:

> Between nine and ten o'clock on that night I went to the Crown Public House at Charlton (which is kept by Thomas Higgs) in order to see the Overseer, Mr Richard Priest, who I was informed was there. I went in, and Mr Priest said to me, 'Sit down, and I'll attend to you presently' (or words to that effect.) The House was nearly full of Men (to the number of Forty or Fifty, including those who were just outside the House) all of whom were dressed in shabby old jackets and Smock-frocks and otherwise disguised by their faces being blacked or veiled with black scarves over them so that though some of them may have been intimately known to me I could not recognise anyone unless he happened to speak . . . Mr Priest said to the Landlady Give the Men a shilling's worth of Beer . . . There were at this time about twenty men in the Room & Mr Priest said to them, as soon as he ordered the Beer, 'Go into Otmoor, and cut it all down if you can, but mind you are not caught'. The men were all armed – some with Guns, some with Bill-hooks, some with Forks, and some with great-Sticks . . . I stopped there till the men all went out of the House. They went together down the Lane which leads to the Moor.

With this mood prevailing, appeals for the enrolment of special constables brought no response. Offers of quite substantial rewards went unheeded. Again in March 1833, notices were posted across the moor, warning that further depredations would be met with severe punishment, and offering a reward of £50 – the equivalent now of £1,250 – for any information leading to convictions for felony, riot and or conspiracy, or for the instigation or encouragement of such crimes 'either by words, or by giving Money or Beer' (as was known, and not only from Thornton's testimony, to be happening regularly at the Crown in Charlton). What was more, the King had been pleased to offer his most gracious pardon to any who had been accomplices in these, together with a further reward of £100. There do not seem to have been any takers.

Croke and his friends also tried appeals to the courts, but here too they were disappointed. The penalties available were in any case, as they had told the Home Office, too slight to serve as deterrents. Formerly, such offences had been treated as punishable by transportation. But now they had been relegated to the status of misdemeanours, which would lead to small fines or brief imprisonment. Even then, cases they expected to win went against them.

Yet in time, without the intervention that was begged for, the trouble began to subside. Some villages, especially Charlton, remained militant; others seemed to lose their taste for the fight. And the better-off, 'respectable' farmers began to see that enclosures could bring benefits for them too, especially when the authorities made provisions to entice them. The cottagers had more to lose: without their frail independence they would have to resort to waged labour. The farmers ceased to support the insurrection, and gradually began to enlist on the other side. The heart went out of the protest. There were stray outbreaks of disruption, even into the 1840s, and surveyors who came on to Otmoor to plot the line for the Buckinghamshire railway got a taste of the treatment once meted out to enclosers. But otherwise the spirit of rebellion abated. And from 1851, when the railway came, the old cohesiveness of a community born on the moor, married within the moor, and schooling its children in moor traditions, began to fracture.

So the enclosers could congratulate themselves on their eventual triumph. Except that there was no triumph. The moor remained damp and soggy and unproductive. As Bernard Reaney says at the end of his excellent pamphlet, *The Class Struggle in 19th Century Oxfordshire: The Social and Communal Background to the Otmoor Disturbances of 1830 to 1835*: 'The Otmoor commoners, like others who attempted to defend themselves against landowners and capitalists, were eventually defeated. But in this case where the common people had failed nature took some revenge. The moor reaped for its enclosers neither capital nor rents, as they had fondly imagined, but only a legacy of mounting costs . . . The unconquerability of the moor mocked the bold schemes of the 1780s, and the lifelong dreams of the avaricious Croke.'

*****

My bus to Otmoor is empty, except for me. The driver says this one, leaving Oxford around 11, rarely gets many passengers. We ease out through salubrious north Oxford, bisecting the raging bypass to edge round sprawling Kidlington. Then on to Islip – 'Islip, please drive slowly', says a sign at the boundary, but given its narrow, congested streets, you could hardly do otherwise.

But Islip still isn't Otmoor. The first destination on this route that qualifies is Oddington, a small enough place, that scored low among Otmoor 'towns' in the nineteenth-century census returns, but houses a church which hints at a more significant past. And now we are into Charlton, the capital, so far as it has one, of the moor. It's the sort of place that's replete with signs of what used to be here: The Old Post Office, The Old Stores, The Old Bakery, The Old Dairy, Cobblers Cottage, and The Old Smithy, tucked away in Blackberry Lane. There's also the old George and Dragon, now a private residence, but once another den of Otmoor conspiracy.

Charlton still has its church, its school and its pub, though the fourth requisite for a complete village, a shop, is gone. And here, across the road from the church, is the Crown, with its dark conspiratorial history. Beyond it, where the bus turns north towards the Bicester road, there's a modest road running east that takes you to Charlton's old satellites, nowadays spelled Fencott and Murcott. And here, among the fields on the northern side, the story begins of another rebellion, this time directed not against aristocrats bent on enclosure, but against the forces of government intent on building a motorway by the most convenient route, and – apparently – damn the environmental consequences; an endeavour which resulted in defeat for the mighty, and another proof, perhaps, of what Reaney called 'the unconquerability of the moor'.

The line for the motorway drawn on the government's map, though acceptable to the county council and the local MP, caused dismay across the territory when people first saw it in 1980, resolved as it seemed to be with little respect for the moor's reputation for quiet remoteness and sanctuary, for wildlife as well as for traditionally minded people, set to provide the fastest, straightest possible journey between junctions 8a (Wheatley, Thame) and 9 (Bicester, Chesterton, Kidlington), but cutting off about a tenth of the moor from the rest. The outrage was echoed well beyond the bounds of the moor. James Lees-Milne, architectural historian, saviour of threatened houses for the National Trust, diarist and dedicated aesthete, didn't deny that the motorway deserved to be built; yet Otmoor, he protested, was 'an oasis of medieval England of that exceptional beauty peculiar to flat fenland'. It was also the haunt of rare flora and fauna, while Beckley Park was 'one of the most unspoilt and romantic little great houses in the home counties'. 'The very idea of eliminating Otmoor and destroying the setting of Beckley either by a motorway or by a reservoir [another mooted proposal] is absolutely beyond my comprehension. If the Ministry of Environment [an invention of Edward Heath's Conservative government, designed to establish its commitment to green values] does not at once turn down both these threats unequivocally, and direct its attention to alternative sites, then the conservationists may as well pack up, abandon England to the Philistines and emigrate.'

But this was Otmoor, and conservationists here knew they would have to take practical action. The government seemed unmoved even when the inspector who had held an inquiry which lasted 117 days recommended that Otmoor should be sympathetically dealt with. A man called Joe Weston, who lived in the village of Forest Hill, two miles or so from the edge of the moor, was at this time serving as co-ordinator of the Friends of the Earth in nearby Wheatley. He had started his working life as a van driver, but took a degree course at the Oxford Polytechnic and would in time become a lecturer there – by then it was Oxford Brookes University. He was still a student when he launched himself into the M40 campaign. He would later recall how, sitting one evening in an Oxfordshire pub with a group of like-minded people, he began to think of obstructions which might be placed in the way of the government juggernaut in the hope of saving the moor and, especially, safeguarding a notable sanctuary for butterflies known as Bernwood Forest.

So they hatched an ingenious plot. A farmer called Terence Holloway, staunchly opposed to the projected motorway route, owned land on the Charlton–Murcott road. He had planned, at their suggestion, to take the case to the European Court of Human Rights, but found the prospect daunting. So Weston and his fellow protestors made him a proposition. They would buy his land from him, and then sell it on: sell it on to hundreds of small investors, attracted by the chance of stopping the project, creating such a pattern of multiple ownership that to try to carry through compulsory purchase in every case would be beyond the wit and resources of the Department of Transport, the route's principal sponsors. In a further piece of inspired ingenuity, he thought of a name for this land. It was here, according to local legend, that Lewis Carroll, who in his Oxford days knew Otmoor, first imagined the chessmen characters moving about the board in *Alice Through the Looking Glass*:

For some minutes Alice stood without speaking, looking out in all directions over the country – and a most curious country it was. There were a number of little brooks running across from side to side, and the ground between was divided up into squares by a number of hedges, that reached from brook to brook.

'I declare it's marked out just like a large chessboard!' Alice said at last.

To some of those who wanted the M40 built as simply and swiftly as possible, the Alice's Meadow venture seemed as bloody-minded and purely destructive as Croke and his allies had found the Otmoor disruption of a 150 years before. Tony Baldry, the recently elected Tory MP for Banbury, the constituency that covered Otmoor, and president of the M40 Support Group, vowed to take action in Parliament to prevent such operations. Yet when in December 1984 the rest of the M40 route was approved, the fate of the Otmoor section was left undecided. That sounded like a good omen, and sure enough, in November 1985, the government surrendered. A new route had been found, east of the original line just as the opposition had always suggested – subjecting the M40's motorists to the biggest bend on any British motorway. 'The Otmoor kink', people called it.

In 2008, the law was changed to prevent this tactic being used ever again to frustrate a government's planning intentions. Maybe Weston, had such an occasion arisen again, might have thought up other forms of defence. But three years later, during one of the bonfire night parties he staged every year at his home in Forest Hill, he suffered a heart attack and died. He was 58. He left, as well as thousands of grateful beneficiaries on and off the moor, his widow, Anna, a son, Michael, and a daughter – Alice.

*****

Leaving Charlton, my 94 bus ducks under the mighty M40, signalling in effect the end of one's Otmoor experience, and soon reaches the village Merton, where it stops outside a pub called the Plough, like so many countryside pubs, sad and abandoned. Estimates in 2015 put the prevailing rate of closures at around thirty a week, with suburban pubs the most vulnerable. Some of the causes are indisputably good, the smoking ban especially. But the supermarkets, whose influence on culture and society resonates repeatedly through these journeys, are shaping it too by making it so much cheaper to drink at home rather than in some hostelry. George Orwell saw this coming; 'the whole trend of the age', he wrote back in 1943, long before the age of the supermarket, and indeed of the Internet, 'is away from creative communal amusements and towards solitary mechanical ones. The pub, with its elaborate social ritual, its animated conversations and – at any rate in the North of England – its songs and week-end comedians, is gradually replaced by the passive, drug-like pleasures of the cinema and the radio. This is only a cause for rejoicing if one believes, as a few Temperance fanatics still do, that people go to pubs to get drunk.' RIP, the Plough at Merton, and so many valued others.

After Merton comes more substantial Ambrosden, which has several shops, a post office and a pub called the Turner Arms, named for one of the principal local families. Some of these 94s now deviate to tiny Piddington and Blackthorn, but mine presses purposefully on to Bicester: once best known as a military town, and second to that perhaps for hunting, but even more celebrated now as the home of a shopping outlet village which it's said that your truly plugged-in overseas visitors nowadays add to their itineraries alongside Oxford, Stratford and Blenheim.

This final stage of my journey has echoes of further threats to Otmoor even after it had it won its fight over the M40 route. There might have been a great reservoir; there might have been a national cycleway; there might also have been a Weston-Otmoor ecotown, proposed in 2008 by a company called Parkridge Holdings, to be based on the upmarket village of Weston-on-the-Green, well off the moor but dragging in parts of Otmoor too. This time local opinion was almost uniformly hostile. Local opinion including the county and district councils and that former defender of the original M40 plan, Tony Baldry MP, rallied against it. So, usefully catching the eyes of journalists, did the tennis player Tim Henman, whose family lived on this territory and whose father was prominent in the campaign. The project was dropped in the following year in favour of an ecotown based on Bicester. Otmoor was saved again.

Today, much of the moor remains open, green – and wet; indeed its very wetness is now regarded as one of its virtues. In 1997 the RSPB, in partnership with the Environment Agency, bought a thousand acres of farming land and, reversing the ambitions of the enclosers, restored it to wetland, establishing a nature reserve on Otmoor which is home to wildfowl and waterfowl. The skylark, lapwing, hobby, little egret and tufted duck are listed as its star species, but remarkable eruptions of starlings, especially at twilight, have been filmed and enshrined on YouTube. As for Alice's Meadow, you may find it close to Moorman's Farm on the northern side of the road from Charlton to Fencott and Murcott, not far short of the set of white gates which tell you you're entering Murcott. There is nothing much to mark its significance: only a noticeboard which when I was there mentioned neither Alice nor Joe Weston. Such self-effacement is no doubt a sign of the quiet virtue of the Otmoor community.

Meanwhile, I thought as I said goodbye to Charlton, there is always that sign on the wall of the Crown to carry the message 'rebellion served here'. Except that this is not really what it means. Rebellion in this context is not what on these occasions welled up on Otmoor, but a beer brewed in Marlow, Bucks.

3

A JOURNEY FROM GURNEY TO GURNEY

94 Cheltenham–GCHQ–Churchdown–Gloucester

THIS, IN A SENSE, is where it all started. It started with Goldsworthy Gurney (later, Sir Goldsworthy): Cornishman, general practitioner, surgeon, chemist and, above all, multipurpose inventor of everything from a musical organ, an oxygen blowpipe, and an experimental technology that would lead to wireless telegraphy, to a bus driven by steam. Born in 1793, Gurney grew up in Truro, which brought him into the presence of Richard Trevithick, the great pioneer of steam. Little that entered his clever head was forgotten or left unexplored. In the 1820s, settled in London, he rented a workshop in Oxford Street and set to work on the prototype of a steam-driven vehicle which would dispense with the need for horses.

In 1825 he took out a patent. Since no one showed much interest in exploiting his discoveries, he set up a factory in Albany Street, Regent's Park, and began to build his engines himself. Before long they were notching up horse-beating speeds of as much as 20 mph on test runs. Even his limitless ingenuity, though, was not quite enough. He needed a sponsor with money and influence, and found one in Sir Charles Dance, the son and grandson of eminent architects, but himself a military man who had fought in Wellington's army and been wounded (though only slightly) at Waterloo. With Dance's backing, Gurney succeeded in running a steam engine from London to Bath and back, at an average speed of 14 mph. And with that achievement behind them, they were ready in February 1831 to establish the first regular steam-powered service on the route (most of which was helpfully flat) between Cheltenham and Gloucester, a journey of nine and a half miles, running four times a day, with the hope, indeed expectation, that it might be extended in time to Bristol and even Birmingham.

Gurney's contraption found some ferocious opponents. Some of these had turned out at Melksham in Wiltshire in the hope of disrupting the run from London to Bath, when the steam bus was stoned, by unemployed millworkers in some accounts, by fairground workers in others. Its stoker was injured. But that was merely an early rehearsal for the twin-track campaign of sabotage that would be launched against his Cheltenham–Gloucester service.

Local interests saw a disastrous threat to their livelihoods. Stagecoach proprietors foresaw the death of their businesses. Owners of horses feared ruin. Farmers quailed at the thought that the phasing out of the horse would imperil their market for provender. Ostlers and grooms from coaching inns joined the agitation, while people who lived on the chosen route wrote to the press alleging that hideous accidents were sure to occur. Powerful railway interests were on the warpath too. The local turnpike trustees were persuaded to condemn the steam carriages as 'a public nuisance'. I cannot believe', Dance told them, 'that the enlightened body of gentlemen who I now have the honour to address seriously resolve to obstruct such an undertaking, sanctioned as it is by the King and encouraged by the first people in the country.' But as he would have known, the trustees were no friends of steam. The most vociferous in denunciation was Joseph Rea, a horse dealer.

Dirty tricks on the highway followed. Steam coaches were halted and blocked; crushed granite was dumped on the road to thwart their progress. But even more damaging was the machination of hostile interests at Westminster. Provisions were written into appropriate bills to ramp up the cost of tolls for steam vehicles to three times the level charged for those drawn by horses.

The forces of progress, as they classed themselves, were not slow to retaliate. A select committee, chaired by a steam enthusiast, Charles Jephson, enthusiastically endorsed the new enterprise, saluted Gurney as the first in the field, denied that his bus was either nuisance or safety hazard, and demanded immediate legal protection for steam operations. The chairman himself drafted an appropriate bill.

The House of Lords, however, was a stronghold of the agricultural interest and much less persuadable. It set up its own select committee, which rarely met, and did all it could to ensure that nothing much happened. Dance at this point could see no chance of settled progress, and despite his earlier vow that he'd never let his opponents bully him off the road, he announced in late June that the Cheltenham–Gloucester service, which had carried some 3,000 passengers on journeys amounting to 4,000 miles, would now be abandoned. Backers pulled out; other clients of Gurney's became fearful and broke their links with him; the money sustaining his workshops in Albany Street ran out. He closed them down, wound up his business, and filed for bankruptcy, with debts running to £232,000 -- the equivalent of £11 million today. From then on he devoted his ingenuity to less contentious forms of invention. All of which helped account for the knighthood belatedly bestowed upon him in 1863, shortly before paralysis struck him down. But the sense of his defeat on the Cheltenham–Gloucester road never left him.

Some have speculated that had he succeeded, the road, not the railway, might have remained the conventional way to travel, that the runaway expansion of the railway might never have taken place. In a book called *The Suppression of the Automobile: Skulduggery at the Crossroads*, David Beasley argues that road transport was more potentially profitable, and failed only because powerful political interests were determined to stop it. 'If the steam carriage proponents in Parliament had forged a lasting alliance between the radical Whigs and Conservatives,' he says, 'the railways would have been stopped in their tracks. By 1833 the innkeepers, stagecoach owners, and their employees recognized that the railway was ruining them and that the steam carriage was their only hope to keep road traffic alive. Canal proprietors saw the steam carriage as their natural ally against the railway.' They might also have mobilized support from small title-holders 'ruthlessly thrown off their lands', owners of great estates subjected to serious disruption, agricultural interests and associations of artisans. As it was, the railway interests prominent in the Lords saw the railway as their high road to profit; and the steam-powered bus, on the basis of that conclusion, was steamrollered into oblivion.

*****

It is therefore the railway, not the motor coach, which has brought me to Gloucestershire to sample the Gurney project's successor, the 94 Stagecoach. On my bus from Cheltenham station, the driver is asked by two women for tickets to the city centre. He sighs loudly enough for most of his cargo to hear him. 'I'm afraid we are not a city,' he says, 'only a town.' Gloucester, he explains, is a city. Gloucester has a cathedral, whereas Cheltenham has only a parish church – though recently (this thought seems to cheer him) the parish church had been elevated to the status of minster.

This confession seemed to me an unusual event. It must be rare to hear Gloucester extolled over Cheltenham (especially in Cheltenham), rather than the other way round. Nowadays Cheltenham more often than not comes first when the names are coupled together, from the Cheltenham and Gloucester Building Society to the Cheltenham and Gloucester branch of the Gloucestershire Beekeepers Association. Yet Gloucester is by far the older (as well as the bigger) community, a significant local ingredient (as Colonia Nervia Glevensium, handily abbreviated later to Glevum) of Roman Britain, and a far more dominant player in events thereafter. There was, from 1385, and still is today, a Duke of Gloucester. Was there ever a Duke of Cheltenham? Never.

So Gloucester had for centuries been a place of great consequence, when Cheltenham was a mere village. But then came the Spa. 'The town,' the county's historian, the Reverend Thomas Rudge, rector of St Michael's, Gloucester, wrote of Cheltenham in 1802, 'which consists of one long street, and is now filled with handsome buildings, was formerly of no great account. The discovery of a medicinal spring, first drew the attention of the public in 1740 . . . [it] owes its present appearance to Mr Henry Skillicorne, who in 1738 bought the premises, built a dome over the well, and erected a convenient room for the accommodation of company. It then received the name of Cheltenham Spa and, the great credit the waters have obtained for the relief of scorbutic affections, together with the salubrity of the air, and the pleasantness of the surrounding country, have made it a place of great resort.' And one which quickly grew to a place of some 3,000 people when Rudge was writing to a population that in the 1820s was nosing ahead of Gloucester's, and by 1861 would be 5,000 ahead.

To some of Gloucester's citizens, Cheltenham was a mere upstart: 'a very shouldering, unpliant neighbour', the Reverend Thomas Fosbroke complained in 1819. Gloucester too had its spa, tucked away in the south-west corner of today's city, but it was always a meagre affair compared with the glories of Cheltenham. Nowadays Cheltenham has a wealth of festivals, luring in visitors from all over Britain and overseas, the most famous of which is probably horse racing: 'the capital of racing' it calls itself. Gloucester used to have racing too, but meetings ceased in 1876. Cheltenham has a celebrated cricket festival every summer. Gloucester still stages county cricket, but not every season. Gloucester takes its turn every three years in hosting the Three Choirs Festival (the venues in other years are Worcester and Hereford) and puts on an annual festival devoted to rhythm and blues, but Cheltenham upstages that with one of the country's top literary festivals, with gatherings devoted to poetry, classical music, jazz and science. It also cashes in every year with a festival devoted to that ever more ravening British obsession, food. (On the other hand, there isn't a Cheltenham cheese, but there is a Double Gloucester.)

The centre of Cheltenham also possesses a grace and elegance few British cities can match. The 94 starts its journey on the town's best shopping street, the Promenade, the kind of dreamily tree-lined street created to be strolled along, and particularly to be strolled along by the kind of expensive and elegant shoppers, svelte and suspiciously thin, who feature in artists' impressions of future shopping developments.

The 94, as befits a bus permitted to start in such a location, is no run-of-the-mill vehicle: it's a Stagecoach Gold – one of a fleet they've established up and down the country in the hope of reassuring middle-class passengers that service buses are decent enough for them to ride in. They have stitched leather tip-up seats, metallic paint, free Wifi, drivers in special livery and a general aspiration to an opulence undreamed of by Goldsworthy Gurney's jolting customers. From the Promenade it embarks on a route which might have been chosen to illustrate the essential appeal of Cheltenham: stately mansions, stately terraces, stately parks, stately private and public buildings. It treats passengers to Imperial Square and the Montpelier Gardens, which of course has what such parks demand: a gleaming bandstand. Here too we are shown what used to be known as the Queen's Hotel, though today the sign says just Queen's. Afternoon teas, I see, are served from noon onwards, and will set you back £16.

Even then, you won't see all the characteristic allurements of Cheltenham in the course of this journey, all those buildings which seem to cry out: 'Just look at me!' You won't, for instance, see the contingent of stately stone ladies, well rounded though lacking arms, who hold up the upper stories of Ask Italian and Flax on Montpelier Walk. But the message is unmistakeable. This place has bagfuls – designer bagfuls – of style.

Ten minutes on towards Gloucester, just beyond an enormous roundabout, those on the top deck catch their first glimpse of a building now familiar to anyone who watches the TV news. It is very large, cylindrical, dome-like and doughnut-like, though less sinister than you might expect with a place so packed with secrets. This is GCHQ, Benhall, whose presence and meaning are no longer concealed: indeed there are buses that run out of Cheltenham whose destination boards simply say GCHQ, a name once never pronounced in public by those who worked there for fear of frightful consequences.

Why was Cheltenham chosen for its location? Years ago there was a common assumption that Cheltenham was largely made up of old military men, especially Indian Army military men, returned with their memsahibs and settled in a town famous for being healthy and perhaps for prolonging lives. John Betjeman liked to attribute the popularity of the spa town – a place he preferred even to Bath as gayer and more original – to the reputation of the waters as a cure for exactly the kind of liver troubles brought on by expatriate life in the East.

In fact the selection of Benhall had nothing to do with that. It happened, as such things so often do, largely by chance. A new home had to be found for the super-intelligent intelligence people of Bletchley Park. A staff member on the lookout for sites found two in the outskirts of Cheltenham, one here and one at Oakley, once requisitioned for used by government departments in case they might need to move out of London in wartime, but taken over for clandestine purposes by the Americans later on in the war. British Intelligence commandeered them, without at that stage revealing their purpose, and eventually they were merged, again with no hint of what they were there for. Local people called them the Foreign Office. It was only a spectacular spy scandal – the unmasking of Geoffrey Prime, employed officially by GCHQ but unofficially, and more enrichingly, by the KGB also – that brought the truth about the Cheltenham site into the light of day.

I am here by chance on 5 November, two days after the place's director, Robert Hannigan, launched a fiery attack on social media sites such as Facebook and Twitter, which he said had become 'a command and control network for terrorists' – so fiery, indeed, that I rather expected to see a vast bonfire erected, perhaps on the roundabout, with an effigy of Mark Zuckerberg on top. To get to the gates, which are guarded by conventional block posts with no outward sign of being armed to the teeth, you use Hubble Road, which may or may not refer to the most powerful optical instrument ever devised by man, capable of picking up images invisible to ordinary mortals. You can get quite close to the perimeter fence, which has notices of a forbidding kind, prohibiting the use of cameras. Oddly, some of these relate to the 1911 Official Secrets Act, which went out of use in 1989, as if some in the security services feared there might still be a few of the Kaiser's agents lurking around.

Yet I found the place disappointing. It lacked the sense of menace that a nest of spies – more than 5,000 people work here, which is quite some nestful – ought to generate. In the same sense I scrutinized those (there were only two) who got off my 94 bus from Cheltenham here, in the hope of detecting some dark intent. A tiny voice, much like that of the gnat in *Alice Through the Looking Glass*, seemed to whisper: 'Is this woman a secret agent?'

But no, the word that best described those leaving the 94 was less 'menacing' than 'innocuous'.

*****

Leaving the doughnut behind it, the gold 94 deserts the main road and takes to the B4063 through a tract of Gloucestershire known as the Golden Valley. Here we enter a kind of conditional countryside, some of it open, green and bounded by pleasant hills, but some punctuated by burst of prefabs – not unsightly, but scarcely rural – and various manifestations of industry. Staverton, which comes next, is home to Gloucestershire airport, from where you may fly to the Isle of Man, Belfast and Jersey, or elsewhere by special arrangement. It is here because the Gloucestershire Aircraft Company manufactured its planes here and flew them out of its company airfield. Later the name was simplified: Gloucestershire was judged too much of a mouthful for foreign use and Gloster was adopted instead. The Gloster Gladiator flew in the early years of the Second World War, and Gloster were given the contract to build Britain's first jets. One up to Gloucester perhaps? But, oddly enough, the enterprise started in Cheltenham.

There's a pretty ring of hills southwards beyond the airport, but there's also in the vicinity a crop of the kind of industrial sites that cluster round every airfield. Churchdown village, or at least the slice you see from the bus, isn't that villagey, either; a straggle of buildings, many quite recent, and an Esso shop'n'drive. You would hardly deduce that this was once the resort of a colony of writers, artists and musicians, but so it was – especially for a spot called Chosen Hill, south of the village.

Gloucestershire is a county of composers: Vaughan Williams, Gustav Holst, Herbert Howells and the doomed composer-poet Ivor Gurney were all born here. Gurney, walking with Howells and looking up at this hill, said to his companion: 'I wish you'd write a tune that shape.' Howells's Piano Quartet of 1916, dedicated to 'the Hill at Chosen and Ivor Gurney who knows it', was in part his response. But perhaps the composer most moved by this landscape was the London-born Gerald Finzi, who knew it only because he had come here for holidays with his mother. There's an ancient church, St Bartholomew's, perched on this hill, but what moved Finzi most was a tiny cottage, once the home of the sexton, where he had once spent Christmas Eve – a night which, according to his biographer Stephen Banfield, brought him to write *In Terra Pax*, a choral work based on St Luke's version of the Christmas story, framed by poems by Robert Bridges which put the birth of Jesus in an English setting; a work that Banfield says 'contains the best and most of him'.

In September 1956, during the Gloucester festival, Finzi and his wife, Joy, brought Vaughan Williams to see Chosen Hill. Finzi knew by now he had not long to live; he had been diagnosed five years earlier with Hodgkin's Disease, and given ten years at most. But this expedition denied him even that. A day or two later there were signs of further deterioration. Shingles set in, then chickenpox. His doctor sent him to the Radcliffe Hospital in Oxford, where on 26 September he was able to hear a radio performance of his Cello Concerto. He died the following day. He was fifty-five.

And now our bus ends its allegedly rural phase and rejoins the A40, the main route between the towns. And here on the brink of Gloucester is the Oxstalls campus of Gloucestershire University. It is unsurprising to find that where Gloucester has one of its campuses, Cheltenham has two; or that this institution evolved from an earlier Cheltenham and Gloucester College of Higher Education. And here a skyscape encouragingly stocked with tall spires looms up ahead, and we enter the ancient cathedral city.

*****

Jacob, the book of Genesis tells us, was a smooth man and Esau a hairy one. There is something of that distinction here. Cheltenham – or its centre, which is what most people see (some of the outlying suburbs tell a different story) – looks smooth and privileged. The route into Gloucester bus station, through a dismal jumble of charmless buildings with a view of a wretched 1970s railway station, tells you at the outset that where Cheltenham is smooth Jacob, Gloucester is hairy Esau. The centre of Cheltenham speaks of ease and grace; the centre of Gloucester, more of endeavour. Cheltenham is full of premeditation, the premeditation of gifted planners and architects, the chief among them John Buonarotti Papworth, who created Montpelier and designed its Rotunda, based on the Pantheon in Rome (and nowadays Lloyds Bank). Gloucester looks more like a place where things just happened, came out of improvisation, sometime for good, sometimes not.

One looks at it now and wonders what Papworth might have done with it. Gloucester is drenched in history, some 2,000 years of it since the Romans came; its superb cathedral dates from the eleventh century. Cheltenham's by contrast is a tale swiftly told. Cheltenham is about displaying things, Gloucester more about making them. It's not hard to pick up appropriate resentments. For many in Gloucester, Cheltenham is posh, superior, snooty. It is said that the use of the term 'chavs' to categorize and disparage working-class people began at Cheltenham Ladies' College, whose very building seems to suggest that education here is some kind of religious experience. No one calls Gloucester posh or snooty.

To knock Gloucester for not being Cheltenham is like disparaging chalk for not being cheese. They are there for quite different reasons. Yet Gloucester is a place that has often bred disappointment – ever since the visit of Dr Foster, who as children learn at an early age went there in a shower of rain, stepped in a puddle right up his middle, and never went there again. Its most potent failure is the place that should be one of its glories: the junction of the four principal streets, Northgate and Westgate, Eastgate and Southgate. David Verey in the *Shell Guide to Gloucestershire* calls it 'a most unworthy centre for any town anywhere'. The great topographer Ian Nairn, who usually favoured the rugged over the smooth, aired his dismay in a *Sunday Times* column in February 1981: 'Gloucester is crucified on its cross. Eastgate, Westgate, Northgate, Southgate, meet at nothing more uplifting than a set of traffic lights. There is a medieval church tower on one corner, but that's all. The (Victorian) church that went with it was demolished in the 1950s to make room for part of a new shopping centre.'

A famous High Cross stood at this point until 1871. Thereafter, a toll house, and then a bank, gave it some focus. Not now. Nairn found things to savour in Gloucester, especially the cathedral, though also the galleried fifteenth-century courtyard of the New Inn in Northgate Street. But a city needed a heart, so the problem of Gloucester Cross had to be solved. Gloucester, he said, should close the cross, pave the space over, and build on it some structure that would tell the whole story of this extraordinary and long-suffering site.

And Gloucester did indeed close the cross to traffic, and devote it to the safe transit of people. Yet the disappointment remains. What's here is a dull confluence of streets which offer on their four corners the offices of mobile network operators and Internet service providers; a stall selling covers for mobiles; the church tower now turned heritage centre; the offices of the bank HSBC – the only building here of any distinction – and a Vodafone branch with the usual garish frontage. No sense of occasion, no sense that this is the fulcrum of a truly historic city. What it needs is some flavour of Gloucester's unique and individual heritage; and that can't be supplied by merely opening a heritage centre.

Too much else has been lost. You could have heard that complaint in Gloucester as far back as 1828, when local historian John Britton lamented the loss of picturesque antiquities: 'its old gate-houses, walls, castle, bridges, and most of the timber houses [in which] it formerly abounded have disappeared and given place to formal brick elevations, expanded streets, and a bridge of one wide arch across the river.' 'The medieval city', wrote David Verey midway through the following century, 'has almost completely disappeared.'

Stand at the point where the High Cross used to be and contemplate your four options. Westgate is the most enticing, with an easy curve as it eases down to the river. That's also the best way to reach the close and then the cathedral, where Edward II is buried. That made Gloucester a place of pilgrimage. Edward, the record suggests, was not celebrated in life for his saintliness, so maybe the ghastly way he was put to death had something to do with it. But I choose to set off instead down Eastgate in search of a more authentically Gloucester figure: the composer and poet Ivor Gurney.

*****

Of Gloucestershire's quartet of notable twentieth-century composers, Vaughan Williams was born at Down Ampney, close to the southern border with Wiltshire, and Herbert Howells at Lydney, on the Severn Estuary not far out of Wales. Holst, born in smooth Cheltenham, had a relatively tranquil life, much of it as a teacher at St Paul's Girls' School. He came from a comfortable middle-class family with a tradition of music. He volunteered at the start of the First World War, in the year he turned forty, but was turned away on medical grounds. What set him back thereafter stemmed from his greatest success: the *Planets Suite* of 1918, so striking on its originality and its immediate impact that the world from then on largely dismissed all he wrote as not up to that achievement.

For Gurney, born in less favoured Gloucester, life was always a turmoil, with bouts of mental illness, which in time became continuous. Both his music and his poetry were long undervalued. Where Holst was spared the experience of the First World War, Gurney, inexplicably as it seems in the light of his medical history, was passed fit and served on the Somme. He was gassed at St Julien, near Passchendaele, though his psychological troubles long predated that. After the war he was so far out of control that in 1922 his family had him sectioned. First confined in a Gloucester hospital, Barnwood, he was transferred after three months to another in Dartford, Kent, 140 miles away, where he interspersed composing and writing verse with pathetic appeals, mainly to the Metropolitan Police, for release from his unjust imprisonment. That was never granted: he died in 1937, having lived forty-seven years.

As a student and in subsequent occupations Gurney spent much of this time in London, but he always yearned for Gloucester. Later, as he grew more and more disturbed after the war, he would, says his biographer Michael Hurd, '[think] nothing of walking from London to Gloucester, sleeping out in barns or under hedgerows when the weather was good,

earning a few pence by singing folksongs in country inns, burdened with
little more than his pipe and baccy pouch, pencils and notebook ready to
jot down music and poetry as it occurred to him.'

It was not just the county and its countryside that drew him, but his
city, too. The poet Patrick Kavanagh, in a preface to a book of Gurney's
verse, found a resonance here that had earlier been noted by their fellow
poet Edmund Blunden.

'The towers of the cathedral, the towers and spires of other churches,
St Nicholas, the 'two Maries' and so on, imposing yet homely, had, as
Blunden suggested . . . much to do with Gurney's sense of form . . .
Gloucester has hills on one side, and the Severn River on the other,
where his father came from. An easy walk out of the town – across
the bridge at Over – and you are at Maisemore, [to Gurney] 'sacred'
Maisemore, on the river; nearby are Ashleworth, Hartpury, Framilode
and other places whose names are the litany Gurney recited in France
and during the years he was out of sight of them in his asylum . . .
As a boy, if he put his nose out of his front door, he saw, one way, the
famous Cross of Gloucester – not a stone cross, but the place where the
four main streets have met since the foundation of the town – and if he
looked the other way, down Barton Street, he saw at the end of it (the
effect is still theatrical) his mother's country, the green Cotswold hills
. . . Gurney was not really a country boy, as his middle class London
friends thought . . . He was a town boy, loving the town, but also
dreaming of escape, and escape was within eye-shot.'

These places – the city streets, the familiar, cherished villages, these
landscapes full of longing, were as precious to him as the dearest of
companions. The Severn, too. In March 1917, in wartime France, he both
wrote these words – the book in which they were included was called
Severn and Somme – and set them to music:

> Only the wanderer
> Knows England's graces,
> Or can anew see clear
> Familiar faces.
> And who loves joy as he
> That dwells in shadows?
> Do not forget me quite,
> O Severn meadows.

Gurney was born in Queen Street – the house disappeared long ago – and lived thereafter in Barton Street, which begins where Eastgate ends as you leave the city. There is said to be a plaque to Gurney somewhere along this street, but I failed to find it. Today's Barton Street is very different from his. Bismillah supermarket and halal butcher, Europe Booze, Ex-Catalogue, Fried Chicken, Polski Slep and a string of others much like them are names undreamed of in Gurney's day. The Vauxhall Inn remains in all its old ostentatious exuberance, though it's now a grocery supermarket and halal butcher's too. And yet on this day one can get some sense of the place as it once was. The window of a framery shop is displaying a picture of Barton Street, taken from an old postcard, as it was in 1906, the year when Gurney turned nineteen. It was all shops and agreeable bustle then, ladies in sweeping hats and eager children scurrying about them: a place that looked pleased with, even proud of, itself. But today on Barton Street and the drab side streets that run off it, there's a prevailing sense of dejection. Huge poster, stuck on a wall on this street: 'Expand Heathrow, and the benefits will extend all over Britain.' What, even to Barton Street? That takes some believing.

*****

Something else according to Kavanagh fed the boy from Barton Street's love for this city: 'Gloucester is a docks as well as a county town; they are decayed now, but they still impart to the streets a sense of the sea, of being in touch with distant places. You can hear seagulls.' The 94 bus does not go as far as the docks, but other buses do, so as the light begins to fade from the November sky, I take one and ask to be put down at Quayside. A middle-aged woman sitting beside me has lived all her life in the city, but she says this without enthusiasm, so I ask why. Gloucester is not what it was, she tells me. For years it has been steadily going down. In what sense, exactly? But I know the answer before she delivers it, since it's one that was so often at the core of this kind of discontent even before UKIP made itself a vehicle for it: the sense among older inhabitants that their town has been taken from them. They are the dispossessed. 'Too many foreigners,' she says, dropping her voice.

The Quayside development, blazoned about as the city's great new shopping and entertainment experience, doesn't do much for her either. 'All Next and Gap and that kind of thing,' she says. And looking around I can see what she means. What's been confected here on Gloucester's waterside is much the same as has been, or is being, or if it hasn't will shortly be, created in every town of any size across the nation. It's standard late twentieth-century issue, spiced up with additional twenty-first-century glitz. 'Made in Glitzerland,' I've begun to say to myself, wandering through them. And here is Gap, sure enough, and Next, and M&S, which carry the Glitzerland label of 'outlet' to excite shoppers all the more. And alongside them on the malls, Calvin Klein and Clarks and L.K. Bennett and Cotton Traders. Across the way, further names in neon light up the evening. Pizza Hut, Sainsbury's.

Leave the glitz for a moment, and push on to the bridge that spans the Gloucester–Sharpness Canal, and here you get a taste of the dockland when it was still in business. Cheltenham has nothing like this. The first old industrial building is today in a state of advanced dereliction; much of the fabric gone, trees growing through the roof: the sort of scene that is nowadays invariably billed as offering 'investment opportunities'. Turn north-eastwards along the canal and things brighten. There are houseboats and barges here. There's a 'historic lightership' called the *Sula*, which at appropriate times serves tea and coffee on deck. It's for sale, but one shouldn't therefore see it as a project that failed, but rather, as the notices say, 'an ideal and very unique opportunity'.

That appeal can be seen to have worked elsewhere: there's a sequence of refurbished buildings, with Cineworld lurking behind them, under tonight's enormous moon, and a spanking new gym alongside the Llanthony Bridge, with a fine display through its windows of people improving themselves, pedalling away with apparent enjoyment, one woman seeming almost to dance as she does so. Beyond that, in a region designated as 'historic docks', is a slightly tarted-up congregation of survivors from the heyday of Gloucester docks, displaying their names as proudly as they did then: Albert Warehouse, Reynolds Warehouse, Vinings Warehouses, subsequently put to different uses (the Albert for a time housed the Robert Opie Collection of Packaging) and now parcelled up into apartments.

And here, on the way back to the shopping malls, is a sequence which, a sign outside Zizzi says, offers 'delicious dining to go with your outlet shopping'. Little in this sector of 'historic Gloucester' answers to Gloucester culture, Gloucester values, Gloucester history. Yet the place, even though this is midweek, is decently busy and the families that pass by my restaurant window look contented enough. It may not be to the taste of my woman on the bus or her coeval old Gloucestrians, but it seems to be a formula that young Gloucester, a population that keeps expanding, is happy with. Yes, it's true that the city is not what it was; but there's every sign that some of the citizens prefer it that way. The centre of Gloucester may be a disappointment to people like Nairn and me. But we, as it says in a corner square of the Monopoly board, are merely 'just visiting'. And for those who yearn for something smarter, sweeter, smoother, more Jacob than Esau, there's always, every ten minutes, the gold 94 to Cheltenham.

4
BIRMINGHAM STAMPED ALL OVER IT

94 Birmingham–Saltley–Hodge Hill–Chelmsley Wood

CITIES EVOLVE, sometimes through deliberate choice, sometimes through sheer force of circumstance. That truth is written all over Britain's second city – second in size though not, since the renaissance of Manchester, second in reputation. Birmingham, and the greater Birmingham that has grown out of it, were created largely by circumstance, but they also reflect the legacy of two remarkable men who took the heart of Birmingham to pieces and put it together again, very much in their own image.

The first was Joseph Chamberlain, who had come here at the age of eighteen to take charge of his father's business – the manufacturing of wood screws – in 1854. A force of nature, people called him, who knew what he wanted and knew how to get it. When he died, in 1914, having made a second reputation as a restlessly turbulent national politician, the Liberal prime minister, Herbert Asquith, called him in a Commons tribute: 'Vivid, masterful, resolute, tenacious', a judgement which few who had worked with him, or against him, could have been moved to dispute.

He was born in Camberwell, then just outside London, but for most of his life was everywhere recognized as a Birmingham man: first as a manager and employer, but soon as a force in the politics of the town, one of the powerful exponents of what came to be known as the civic gospel – a gospel which at heart owed as much to Nonconformist religious commitment as to the hope of shaping a new kind of democratic community. Robert William Dale, one of the Nonconformist ministers who formed the philosophy which Chamberlain mobilized and transformed into action, summed up its essence: 'Towards the end of the 'sixties, a few Birmingham men made the

discovery that perhaps a strong and able Town Council might do almost as
much to improve the conditions of life in the town itself as in Parliament
. . . they spoke of streets in which it was not possible to live a healthy and
decent life; of making the town cleaner, sweeter and brighter; of providing
gardens and parks and a museum.'

Their revolution could not have occurred had not Birmingham, through
evolution, grown prosperous. This had been a town of small enterprises
– a world away from places based on one monolithic industry, like
Manchester ('Cottonopolis'), Bradford ('Worstedopolis') or Middlesbrough
('Ironopolis'). Its success was attributed sometimes to its sheer diversity,
sometimes to a matchless talent for innovation. The growth of the town
was spectacular. In 1801, some 73,000 people lived in what then was
Birmingham – 40 per cent more than in 1785. By 1831 there were almost
150,000; by 1861, almost 300,000; by 1901, half a million; and by 1921,
over 900,000, though much of that increase was due to extensions of the
city's archaic boundaries.

But until Joe Chamberlain's day, Birmingham's aspirations had failed
to grow with it. The town had remained in the control of a group who
were known as economizers, whose main concern at all times was to keep
down the rates; and this in a place the imagination and determination
of whose radicals had been decisive in attaining the parliamentary
reform of 1832. The Chamberlain radicals developed a new form of party
organization that could seek out supporters and mobilize their power at
the ballot box: the Birmingham caucus system, as it came to be known.
With the power that this brought, they were able to fashion a form of what
would come to be known as municipal socialism, taking over the gas and
waterworks companies (gas, despite the apprehensions of economizers,
was soon turning in substantial profits). Their medical officer of health – a
post whose creation the economizers had long opposed as unnecessary –
helped shape a further agenda, defining an area of 'narrow streets, houses
without back doors or windows [that's to say, back-to-backs] . . . confined
yards; courts open at one end only, and this one opening small and
narrow; the impossibility, in many instances, of providing sufficient privy
accommodation; houses and shopping so dilapidated as to be in imminent
danger of falling, and incapable of proper repair.' Thomas Street, Lichfield
Street, Buck Street, John Street, close to today's suavely manicured Priory
Queensway, where my journey begins, were about the most squalid of all.

All this, the reformers determined, must be swept away. But
Chamberlain's ambitions had another dimension. He wanted to make this
a town to compare with those he had seen and admired abroad, Paris

especially. Birmingham must have boulevards, streets with a swagger about them. And as mayor for three years in succession, 1873-5 – a job with more executive clout in those days than in the years that followed – he was perfectly placed to get what he wanted. One of the key ingredients in his improvement scheme was the driving of a great new street, Corporation Street, through the line of some of these slums.

It did not take Chamberlain long to accomplish his dream. Even while his designs were still taking shape he left Birmingham politics. As he wrote to a colleague: 'I think I have now almost completed my municipal programme and may sing *nunc dimittis.*' Despite his long subscription to the belief that a municipal politics could do as much if not more to enhance the life of the average citizen as anything instigated in Whitehall and Westminster, he was persuaded to move to the national stage. In a by-election in 1876 he was returned unopposed as an MP for Birmingham, and remained one through various changes of party allegiance till his last re-election, though by now he was greatly debilitated by the effects of a stroke, in December 1910. In line with his oldest and firmest loyalty, he was buried, at his own request, in Birmingham rather than Westminster Abbey.

*****

The second great radical amender was not a man whom Birmingham had elected, but a council official. Herbert Manzoni, son of an Italian-born sculptor, joined the city engineer's department in 1923, the year of his twenty-fourth birthday, and worked his way up through the ranks until, at thirty-six, he became its chief. Much of Asquith's evocation of the then lately dead Chamberlain – 'vivid, masterful, resolute, tenacious' – applied to Manzoni too; one might also have added (for both of them): a certain ruthlessness in pursuit of their aspirations.

Manzoni's compelling preoccupation was with the motor car – then the emblem of the city's prosperity and success. The car, he is often alleged to have said, was now king. That inspired him to propose the great inner ring road in which the twentieth century's Priory Queensway is one episode. Traffic was choking the city: this ring road (or 'concrete collar', as others called it) would let it circulate freely, as a kind of liberated expression of the city's life. But Manzoni's remit went much further. He had not been appointed the city's principal planner, but that in effect was what he became. The Second World War served his purpose, as did the post-war Town and Country Planning Acts, opening the way to the sweeping central development schemes that he favoured. Plans had been laid before 1939 for a radical reordering of Birmingham. Areas close to the centre were singled out for redevelopment, with some of the space assigned to factories and the rest reserved, by rigorous zoning, to accommodate flats and maisonettes, allowing workers to live close to their workplaces – but not, as before, among them.

Once the war was over, that could be made to happen. Manzoni had contemplated the still cluttered, overcrowded and ill-housed streets of 1930s Birmingham and seen two solutions. Some people should continue to live in the core city; others could be decanted. Both deserved to have space and green vistas around them. In the city, that meant building high, giving a breathing space around the tower blocks. And outside the centre, land could be acquired where whole new communities could be brought into being: again with green space and high buildings.

As a corporation official, Manzoni needed the backing of elected councillors, and that he was consistently given, even if they sometimes became uneasy about what he was driving through. Clearly, he wanted the best for the people of Birmingham, though he rarely sought out their opinions. 'How much better it would have been', the Birmingham historian Professor Carl Chinn told the *Birmingham Post* when it marked the fiftieth anniversary of Manzoni's retirement, 'if slum clearance had been more thoughtful and if working-class people had been asked for their views . . . if houses had been built and not flats and the needs of the elderly, young families and others had been taken into account more sensitively?'

He seemed, too, to have little interest in history, to have found the past an impediment. 'I have never been very certain', he once said, 'as to the value of tangible links with the past. They are often more sentimental than valuable. As for Birmingham's buildings, there is little real worth in our architecture. As for future generations I think they will be better occupied in applying their thoughts and energies to forging ahead, rather than looking backward.' That approach did for the library of 1882; it did for the old Bull Ring, a bustling, populist sort of place under the censorious scrutiny of St Martin's Church above and behind it; it almost did for A.N.W. Pugin's Roman Catholic cathedral, St Chad's, reprieved by only one vote when the city council debated its fate. These were Victorian buildings, and the climate of the times despised the Victorians: architecture venerated today was then written about with contempt. James Roberts, the Birmingham architect who built its iconic Rotunda in the 1960s, has said of Manzoni: 'He had no interests in architecture at all, aesthetics at all, he wasn't interested in people or pedestrians. It was cars, lorries, getting things through and out again and so he did considerable damage to the heart of Birmingham.'

And as to high flats, Manzoni did not go unwarned. Indeed, as far back as 1919, the *Birmingham Post* reported that the city's medical officer of health, Dr Robertson, had strongly advised that the old city back-to-backs must not be replaced by blocks of flats, which he feared might in time become more unwholesome than courtyard cottages. By 1988, the city had 428 tower blocks. In 1958, the city housing manager, John P. Macey, warned the council that at least 80 per cent of Birmingham flat-dwellers disliked their homes.

Herbert Manzoni was city engineer for twenty-eight years; he died with a knighthood and many honours; distinguished societies made him their president. But thereafter his reputation sharply declined and his legacy with it. A new phase of radical amendment began. His ringway was modified. The car, the city resolved, was no longer to be king. The man who had demolished the ancient Bull Ring did not live to see his own replacement Bull Ring replaced, or, as part of that process, the elimination of the splash of recuperative green space he had created there, to which the city had given the name Manzoni Gardens.

*****

The 94 begins its journey through Aston, once a large independent parish, best known in recent years for the football club Aston Villa, and nowadays reputed to be the home of Aston University and Birmingham City University, though in fact the map says they are both in Birmingham. Across the road from this complex there's a ruined factory building: the old, dead Birmingham face to face with the new.

But Aston is only a moment's experience before we come upon Nechells, a name that derives from an Old English word meaning land tacked on to a village or estate, and a place that introduces one of the characteristic themes of Birmingham as shaped by sheer force of circumstance: immigration. This tract of the town was one of the chosen destinations for immigrants from Ireland lured to Birmingham by the prospect of work. The Irish contingent here was never as large as those of Liverpool, London or Manchester, though at peak they made up around 4 per cent of Birmingham's population. As so often occurred in big towns where the Irish were concentrated in one or two places, they were not always welcome, and on occasion, persecuted: notably in the events of 1867, which became known as the Murphy riots, after an itinerant preacher who had converted from Catholic to Protestant and begun to whip up animosity against his former co-religionists.

Though that agitation diminished, uneasy relations persisted, and welled up again when in November 1974 twenty-one people were killed and close to 200 injured by IRA bombs in the city centre, among them several who were Irish or Irish-born. Irish homes and businesses were firebombed; airport workers boycotted flights to Ireland. The annual St Patrick's Day parade was cancelled because of fears of retaliation. But in time fences were mended; the parades resumed, and the ferment died. When such tensions arose again, it would be a different immigrant group that was targeted.

Most of the houses that the first Irish arrivals occupied disappeared long ago in redevelopment schemes. And not before time. A woman who lived there in the 1930s described the lives of people in homes like hers: 'It would have slept eight people at least. There was me mum, my sister, my two elder brothers, they shared a room, and meself, but Mum also had two lodgers, young men lodgers, becos of not having a husband, she needed the extra money to keep the house going.' Twenty years on there were still homes without electricity or running water, with an unpleasant and inescapable smell for much of the time from the place's two gasworks. All that was drastically altered in the 1960s, when a new road driven through Nechells divided it into two parts and some of the worst streets on either side were cleared. Many Irish families had by now moved further out of the city.

And here now is Saltley: a name that evokes a further turmoil involving incomers, remembered today for the battle of Saltley Gate in February 1972. The National Union of Mineworkers had gone on strike in protest against a pay offer of 7 per cent where they had called for increases which, according to different estimates, would be worth from 35 to above 40 per cent – reflecting, they said, a long decline in their pay rates compared with those of comparable workers abroad. But supplies were still getting through, thanks to stockpiles at various sites, one of which was the Saltley coke depot. A Yorkshire contingent headed by the then little known Arthur Scargill came to Birmingham to mount a blockade, with workers from across the city joining them. And they won. On 10 February, setting off huge celebrations, the police ruled that in the interests of safety the gates should be locked. That moment was instrumental in the miners' eventual success in winning a rise of 20 per cent.

The anniversary is still celebrated at the site of Scargill's triumph, though the coke depot has gone, along with the public toilets from whose roof he harangued his irregular army. You can still pick out the location from the 94 bus if you look for a wall which bears the legend:

E

O S M N

since that, as the sign on the door reveals, is the Sportsman pub, much in demand, not least from thirsty reporters, during the confrontations. That week was a portent for much to come in twentieth-century political history. Saltley was a kind of harbinger for the far more violent confrontation, twelve years later, at Orgreave, Yorkshire, whose repercussions persist to this day.

But now, crossing Saltley Viaduct, which takes the road from Birmingham comfortably over railways and the River Rea and the Grand Union Canal, all of which helped bring industry here, we arrive at the scene of a later, more permanent, destination for new arrivals to Birmingham: Washwood Heath Road. And here I leave my bus to note down the names on the shopfronts, which tell you a lot. Ariana Fresh Naan. Whaheed's groceries. Bani's Pizza and Kebab House. Kami National Halal Meat and Poultry. Ali hairdresser. Taz's convenience store. Malik and Son's Cash and Carry (in a building that looks like a former cinema). A hair salon where braiding's a specialty. Fifty years ago, it was Exotique, ladies' hairdressers, the Fryery fish and chips, three Co-op shops – a grocer's, a butcher's and a 'self-service laundry'; Leslie Powles, fruiterer; J.G. Green, cooked meats; and a series of shops belonging to Thomas Herbert Young – men's and women's outfitting, hairdresser's, draper's. Then, beyond Aston Church Road, Henry Stokes, boot and shoe dealer; Archibald Hindle, hardware dealer; L. and G. Withers, confectioner; Mrs C. Withers, baby linen. The kind of trades and surnames Birmingham had always been used to. Not a lot here remember that Birmingham now; but some do, and no doubt rub their eyes at the one that's replaced it.

Washwood Heath Road is a protracted affair and doesn't give up till its numbers have topped 800. On the south side part way along is a gentle, restorative park with a lake, now busy with ducks, once a place to go boating, with a boathouse that's now abandoned. On this bleak November afternoon Wood End Park is almost deserted. Two studious middle-aged men walk with slow, conspicuous dignity along the lake, engrossed in conversation. Away from the road, the only sounds are the cries of birds. Across the road, on the corner of Drew's Lane, there's another sign of greatly changed Birmingham: a muddy, razed patch of land with a sign that still proclaims the home of LDV vans. Once Wolseley cars, which were better than most, were made here; then Morris cars, then Leyland DAF vans, and then from 1993 vans by LDV, a separate company which suggested continuity by retaining the same initials. But in 2009 LDV collapsed under the weight of debts totalling £75 million. This is one of the many graveyards across this city of its once predominant industry.

Washwood Heath Road at last expires at a crossroads called Fox and Goose, one of those places which takes its name from that of a pub. Here again there are names that echo the city's diversity, though this a different mix from the one at the other end: Stavros, gentleman's hairdresser; Kurdish Naan, Magdalena Restaurant, Romanian traditional; Banat Bucovina Oltenia Dobrogea Transylvania Moldova: Romanian and English meals to take away . . . More multicultural, this lot, with the flavour of migration from Eastern Europe, in territory that was once a quintessential twentieth-century English shopping parade. And there's a giant Tesco north of the Fox and Goose and an Aldi to the south of it, as if to remind you why the quintessentially twentieth-century shopping parades are no more.

*****

That so many names now suggest the subcontinent and especially Pakistan reflects an essential element of Birmingham's story. At the 1961 census, by far the largest contingent among Birmingham immigrants, still, were the Irish, accounting in round figures for 58,000 out of a total of 100,000. The Caribbean came next, at 16,000; then Pakistan and India, with 10,000; then people classed as 'European foreigners', 8,000. By 2011, the picture was greatly changed. The census returns for Birmingham then found that 53 per cent were classifiable as white English. The next largest group, by a substantial margin, was those listed as Asian or Asian-British Pakistanis, at 13.5 per cent (4 per cent across the West Midlands, 2 per cent for England), with Indians accounting for 6 per cent, black Caribbeans 4.4 and black Africans 2.8. Of the ten areas with the highest percentages of Muslim Asians picked out in the 2011 census, four – Saltley, Washwood Heath, Ward End and Fox and Goose – are on the route of the 94.

As with the Irish earlier, there have sometimes been flashpoints. In 1954, a majority of Birmingham bus drivers objected to 'coloured men', as they were classed, being employed on the service; as Anthony Sutcliffe and Roger Smith note in the official history of the city, a majority of these drivers were Irish. The city council's transport committee, which ran the service, ignored them. Five years on, a Liberal exponent of community politics, Wallace Lawler, fighting the Ladywood parliamentary seat in a by-election in 1959, alarmed some more conventional Liberals by his apparent readiness to exploit concerns about immigration. He won.

Tension reached a new pitch when in April 1968 the West Midlands Tory MP Enoch Powell, representative of Wolverhampton but Birmingham-born, delivered the inflammatory speech at the city's Midland Hotel on this issue which contained the sentence: 'As I look ahead, I am filled with foreboding; like the Roman, I seem to see the River Tiber foaming with much blood.' The Conservative leader, Edward Heath, removed Powell from his shadow cabinet after this speech, but elsewhere there was welcome and acclaim. There were further outbursts through the 1980s and after, several in Handsworth to the north-west of Birmingham's city centre. In 1985, echoing earlier riots in Brixton, London, Toxteth in Liverpool and Moss Side in Manchester, riots broke out in Handsworth after the arrest of a black taxi driver over a parking ticket, inflaming existing tensions between the black community and the police; two Asian men died when their post office was torched, and the cost of the consequent riot damage was put at £7.5 million. There were further eruptions in 1991 and again in 2005 after rumours spread of the rape of a fourteen-year-old Jamaican girl by three Pakistani men; and yet again in 2011, as rioting spread from Tottenham through London and then beyond after the shooting of Mark Duggan by the police.

Yet the rivers of Birmingham, the Rea and the Tame and the Cole – all crossed on my journey today – have declined to foam in fulfilment of the prophet's forecasts. And as time went on immigrants from the subcontinent have come to take an increasingly front line role in the city's life. In 2015, one in five of Birmingham's councillors was a Muslim, as were two of the city's eight Labour MPs. Senior appointments in many departments of local life were now being entrusted to Muslims.

Even so, in March 2014, when apprehension was spreading about the rise of militant Islam, there blew up in the city what became known as the Trojan Horse affair, after a document came to light which appeared to show Muslims plotting to introduce extremist Islamist standards into some of the city's schools, one of them in Saltley. Whether or not the letter was authentic was never finally settled, but soon that no longer mattered, since evidence began to accumulate that the methods complained of had certainly been used in some schools. Several investigations began. The stories they told had much in common: governors and heads were introducing practices, including the segregation of pupils by sex and the redrawing of the curriculum, in some cases to exclude the teaching of health and sex education and much of conventional science (some were teaching creationism) along with music and drama. In some schools the teaching of modern languages was restricted to Arabic and Urdu. A former head of counter-terrorism at Scotland Yard, Peter Clarke – his selection for the job was contentious, since it seemed to assume that the practices under scrutiny had a terrorist aspect to them – concluded that there had in some of these schools been 'an intolerant and politicised form of extreme social conservatism that claims to present and ultimately seeks to control all Muslims. In its separatist assertions and attempts to subvert normal processes it amounts to what is often described as Islamism.'

Some heads who opposed these practices, the evidence showed, had been forced out of office. In the subsequent inquests, governors were made to resign, schools were taken into special measures, and cries went up that a witch hunt was under way. But the Birmingham Muslim Labour MP Khalid Mahmood had no time for that. 'Over two hundred people complaining to the local authority about what's gone on and you can't really claim that it's a witch hunt,' he said. Mahmood was one of many who castigated the city council for its failure to act long before on evidence that had been supplied to it.

As with the Irish tensions before, the bridge-builders in the religious organizations and elsewhere went quickly to work, but a year after the story first broke, the trouble was still far from over. There have always been tensions in Britain over immigration: the Flemings felt them; the Huguenots; the Irish in this city and widely elsewhere; the arrivals from the Caribbean, from Africa, from the Indian subcontinent; and latterly, on a scale never even imagined before, from the European Union and from the wars and persecutions of the early twenty-first century. Few themes are more resonant for any account of how Britain has changed and is changing.

*****

And now the 94 bus leaves Birmingham as it is now defined. We are, the map informs me, in the borough of Solihull. So much for lines drawn on maps. Look out of the window: the rest of this route may not strictly speaking be Birmingham, but it has Birmingham stamped all over it.

The penultimate phase of the journey takes you through the largely indistinguishable districts of Fordbridge and, across the River Cole, Kingshurst, into Chelmsley Wood – celebrated Chelmsley Wood, winner of architectural awards for building and landscaping; notorious Chelmsley Wood, a place unsparingly dissected in a wonderful book, *Estates*, by a writer called Lynsey Hanley, who grew up there.

Having read her, I expected dejection. On the face of it, it is better than that. The names they chose for the roads of the estate streets illustrate the planners' intentions: Larch Croft. Hedgetree Croft. Beech Avenue. Clover Avenue. Perch Avenue. Grayling Walk. Woodbine Walk. Indeed the entire development took its name from a bluebell wood to which Birmingham had flocked on Sundays and at holiday times, arriving at Marston Green station and treating themselves to a vernal afternoon before concluding with tea. This was to be *rus in urbe*, that dream of the new towns movement. The houses too look decently built; the tower blocks are fairly few (there were once twenty-nine of them, but Birmingham has pulled most of them down).

The bus ends its run outside a shopping centre which the Queen came to open in April 1972; now it's fast foods and bargain shops, Poundland and 99p Stores, and Cash General ('the big buy, sell and loan store') and betting shops – but also Boots and the Halifax Building Society and Argos and Greggs, and even healthy old Holland and Barrett; and behind them all, a colossal, high roofed, mega-car-parked Asda. Lynsey Hanley, on supermarkets in the *Guardian*, April 2014: 'Take the Asda closest to my mother's house, outside Birmingham, whose opening in 2009 in effect closed down most of the local shops (including the butcher's and greengrocer's, where once she might have had genuine, perhaps even "engaged" conversations with fellow shoppers). This branch is the size of an aircraft hangar, with all the intimacy of one, and much of what it offers is distinguished by a "£1" sticker . . .' Notices on the wall of the centre talk of CCTV and Asbos. Obese mother to obese child outside one of the food shops: 'You've just *had* sausage rolls!' Obese child (whinily): But I'm not *full* yet!' In 2010 the Association of Public Health Observatories identified the West Midlands as the region with the highest proportion of obese adults in the UK.

Hanley's case is that Chelmsley Wood was wrong from the start. There had long been a wealth of evidence that people did not want to live in tower blocks. And though homes were built on time, those who lived in them were denied the social provision that goes to make a community. In the beginning, there wasn't even a pub. You had to go back to the city suburbs to find one. Later, the neighbourhood shopping centre could not survive the coming of the supermarket. As Asa Briggs, the great historian of Birmingham, had noted long before Hanley was born, 'tenants on the windswept roads and shopping centres compared their new home to Siberia.'

But worst of all, according to Hanley, was how this flavourless, featureless place – 'it was the anonymity and conformity of the estate as a whole that threatened to consume me' – crushed aspiration. People growing up in her predicament didn't expect to succeed. They were from the council estate, they were from the Wood: that labelled them. What held her back was 'the wall in my head': the crushing entrapment which as she grew up cut her off from any sense of what was there to be gained from and savoured in the world outside the estate. And what then appeared as agencies of escape and redemption? College in Birmingham, its friendships

as well as its teaching, discovering the *Guardian* – and the buses. Back in
the 1930s, investigating Bolton, Mass Observation had noted how the bus
appeared to be the connecting link between two worlds as typified by the
town and the outlying estate, and Hanley's experience was precisely that:
'So different were the lives lived at either end of my half-hour bus route
to college that I could feel a physical change taking place on the way from
one to the other. Four miles and a world, that's all.'

So why was it built? Essentially because Birmingham insisted it needed
it, and the brilliant, mercurial, unreliable Labour housing minister Richard
Crossman ordained it. Though she understands the pressures he was under,
Hanley is hard on Crossman: 'he never went quite as far as to say that the
green belt was a bourgeois luxury, but the eagerness with which he signed
off great tracts of virgin land to local authorities which, only a few years
earlier, had had their planning applications refused by the Conservative
government, suggested that he felt as much. His efforts are the reason
why most major towns and cities in Britain wear a ruff of identkit Woods,
peripheral council estates whose blank solid swathes, joining earlier
waves of outwards building from the Depression years and the late 1940s,
can be dated back to the period between 1964 and 1971.' And it's true
that, as he records in his diaries, Crossman did not regard green belts as
sacrosanct. 'I've decided', he says in his entry for 6 December 1964, 'that if
rigidly interpreted a green belt can be the strangulation of a city.' But the
problems were urgent. Birmingham had to house its otherwise homeless
somewhere, and a series of bids to build outside the city boundaries had
been turned down.

What strikes me as the saddest aspect of Chelmsley Wood is its lack
of any inspiriting history. It's a place plonked down, not a place that
evolved. A place with no sense of its history will always struggle to make
good sense. Maybe, I thought, as my bus set out back on the monotonous
journey back to Washwood Heath Road, the Wood will in time acquire
a sense of history. But here's a thought to cheer up Lynsey Hanley. Sure,
there's certainly a dissatisfaction, a disillusion here, but maybe it's taking
a new direction. Once there was a BNP surge in local government voting in
Chelmsley Wood. That faded away. More recently a further surge occurred,
but this time it went to the Greens.

*****

And so back to Birmingham, with a sense that begins to mount from
Washwood Heath onward, of sights to see, of something happening.
There's a liveliness in quite modest main streets in the city of which

there is scarcely a trace in Chelmsley Wood, and the nearer you get to the centre the more you can feel it. It's twilight now, and the broken factory near the Aston triangle that I saw looking so mournful this morning has assumed a certain melancholy majesty. We preserve shattered monasteries as testimony to an age that flourished and died. Perhaps on the same basis shattered factories deserve that too.

And now as the bus returns to Priory Queensway one catches the excitement of the big city. Large crowds out to enjoy themselves, shops brilliantly lit and still open, pubs and bars and coffee houses and night clubs, and restaurants, expensive and less expensive, and beyond in Chamberlain Square and through Paradise Forum, the dashing, glitzy new library, superseding the one that Prince Charles condemned, and Symphony Hall, no longer the home of Simon Rattle but still home to the classy orchestra he helped to create. And radical amendment, change through deliberate choice rather than force of circumstance, is everywhere under way. New Street station has been transformed and is due to reopen soon with a shopping centre including a John Lewis store, which Birmingham lacked till now. Close to Priory Queensway there's a tramway under construction, which, it is promised, will revolutionize the way people travel to and around the city. Never in its long history can the place have had such a buzz. You know nowadays, as you didn't for most of the previous century, that you're in a fine international city.

I remember particularly now at the end of the day a conversation I had with a man met a bus stop on my way to Chelmsley Wood. He was, he told me, seventy-five. His family had come from Scotland in search of work and settled in one of the poorest districts in Birmingham, where they lived in a back-to-back house in a murky street. And where did he live today? We're about to pass it, he says. Look! And there is a house much like all the others, with a car much like all the others parked in front. And the man who had grown up in a back-to-back was quietly but glowingly proud of it. 'Our grandparents – even our parents –' Lynsey Hanley says in her book, 'do not forget how good it feels to have your own bath and an inside toilet, but neither do they forget what it's like to live in a place that feels knitted into the fabric of the town or city it forms part of.'

5

DAVID AND WILLIAM AND GAVIN AND STACEY

94 Cardiff–Penarth–Sully–Barry

EVERY AGE ENSHRINES – or invents – its own heroes. One offers a kind of public obeisance to aristocrats a portion of whose almost impossible wealth has gone to enrich their community; another, nine miles, 130 years, and a whole reshaped culture away, lavishes an echoing adulation on a working-class couple who do not even exist.

On the last day of January 1883, in the forty-fifth year of the reign of Victoria, a glittering array of those considered (at least by themselves) Cardiff's brightest and best assembled at Cardiff Castle, the magnificent home of John Patrick Crichton-Stuart, 3rd Marquess of Bute. They were there to celebrate the opening, nearly fifty years after his father had initiated the first one, of Cardiff's new dock, for which the marquess had obtained parliamentary sanction. No women are recorded as having been present. It was the general custom on such stately occasions that men alone made the speeches, proposed the toasts and responded to them; the only women present would be those there to serve, or sometimes to sing, though tonight even the harpist was male. This was the formal close to a day of high festivities – the mayor had ordered it be observed as a public holiday – beginning in the way of these things with a Grand Procession: at its head, the constabulary and the firemen and the county artillery volunteers, drummed along by their band. Behind them marched the mayor and the Corporation, the Corporation officials, the magistracy, the clergy, a contingent of solicitors and a little posse of medical men, followed by representatives of trade and industry, some accompanied by wagons equipped with emblems of the town's working life, such as anvils and lathes. Next came engine drivers, more firemen, bricklayers and carpenters and shopkeeper marchers – the bakers with a succession of wagons emblazoned with appropriate slogans. Last of all came the town's societies – Oddfellows, Foresters, Freemasons and the like.

At the dockside, they were joined by additional dignitaries who had not managed the march. Having been lavishly thanked for his presence, the marquess drew a sword manufactured for the occasion by local craftsmen emblazoned with the family coronet, and set Cardiff's future in motion.

In return for what was described as a sincere expression of the town's good wishes to his lordship and his family, the marquess expressed his deep gratitude and his hope that this day's new enterprise would enrich not just his family trust, which owned and managed the docks, but the whole community, from its wealthiest to its humblest. The pilots of the port then presented him with an Address, and Mr Freke, photographer, recorded this historic moment for posterity.

Meanwhile, a townspeople's dinner was under way in the less exalted circumstances of the Royal Hotel, while dockland officials were gathered at an even less grand one. The chairman at the townspeople's dinner had claimed that such adulation was in no way founded on sycophancy; yet today it seems that the whole of the day's proceedings were drenched in obsequiousness, reported with matching obsequiousness by the town's daily newspaper, the *Western Mail* (and guess who had founded that). Yet all this, in the context of the institutions of the day, was wholly predictable. In the hierarchy of Britain, John Crichton-Stuart, 2nd Marquess of Bute, and the present marquess, his son, might have ranked no higher than marquess, but in Cardiff they had something of the status of kings. True, their deepest loyalty was always to Scotland, from where the family came, and of which they owned vast tracts. But fate, and a chain of inheritances, had brought them to Wales, where they owned much of the land in and around Cardiff. They had renovated the medieval castle and created the park that belongs to the people today. And no doubt the present object of reverence, the 3rd Marquess, a scholarly figure, a traveller and translator, a patron of art and particularly of architecture, a deeply religious man who later turned to spiritualism, meant what he said when he claimed that the family's mighty enterprise was devoted to the public's good as well as its own. Yet under this marquess, as under his father, the name that emerged for the district south of the centre and running down to the docks might have seemed appropriate for the whole of the place. That name was, and is, Bute Town.

Today's journey, however, will take us to another community which in a totally different way was a Bute creation too. But for the arrogance of Cardiff's great family and its chosen agents, the town and port of Barry, nine miles or so south and west down the Glamorgan coast, which was to become their most formidable rival, might not have come into being.

Before long, my 94 bus has broken free of the Butes. It is heading now, more or less directly, for Barry, down the Penarth Road, home to a striking succession of showrooms for cars old and new. Soon we are out of the city of Cardiff and into Glamorgan, where in a moment or two the bus will set me down in Penarth.

Penarth, to be sure, has its hints of Bute, but here another great family name is dominant. This one is Windsor, a lesser force in this region's history, perhaps, but one which in time would spell trouble for Cardiff. At present, though, the place is reassuringly peaceful, and if having got off the bus in Windsor Road, you shun the shopping street where the bus swings away and go straight ahead, you're in Windsor Terrace, which by the time it has changed to Beach Road has begun to demonstrate why Penarth chose to style itself, as it still does, 'the garden by the sea'. There are lofty, lordly houses along the way, and across the road an inviting glimpse of green parkland. And below, as you round a curve, there is the sea or, to be strictly and boringly accurate, the Bristol Channel. Here the road becomes The Esplanade, opened in 1884.

It is not, this morning, quite as Victorian holidaymakers would have seen it. You're no longer able to stay at the Esplanade Hotel, since that burned down in 1977. But some of the galleried terraces still survive – one houses a boathouse – with a big brick block of flats, slightly too domineering to suit the scene. And there, though no longer baths, are the Baths, also of 1884, a building bursting with Victorian confidence. Best of all, Penarth has a pier, one of only two in South Wales, created in 1895 as part of the town's claim to be recognized as a high-class Victorian resort, with a pavilion, added in 1930 as if to catch the kind of architectural mood that five years later inspired, at much greater expense and on a more extravagant scale, the celebrated De La Warr Pavilion at Bexhill.

From here you could take a paddle steamer across the water to the Somerset coast. On the opening day, two such steamers, the Bonnie Doon and the later famous Waverley, called at the pier to inaugurate their regular service. People warmed to their pier, encouraging the addition of a bijou pavilion at the sea end for concerts and similar entertainments. That too was burned down, in 1931, but with the new pavilion established they saw no need to replace it. Even on this unenticing morning the café in the pavilion is busy, while beyond, half a dozen people are solemnly fishing.

Like so many Victorian resorts, Penarth is not what it was, but it's more what it was than most others. The whole place has a sense of the right and proper that the 1880s would surely have savoured. That is also to some extent true of the centre of town, where the library of 1905 catches something of the original flavour. Across the road, again with a whiff of art deco, is a complex called the Washington, which began as two houses knocked together to create the Washington Hotel, its name chosen in the hope of luring Americans.

Beyond Penarth is Sully – its name translated into Welsh as Sili, which caused some consternation at the time. This might be considered an unremarkable place. And yet it's the chosen headquarters of an international organization. There are other organizations concerned with the care and welfare and study of tortoises, some of which, rather than using the designation tortoise, prefer the word Chelonian, this being the order to which your turtle and tortoise belong. The World Chelonian Trust has its office, I see, in a city called Vacuville, California, part way between Sacramento and San Francisco. The International Tortoise Association is stationed in Sully because this is the home of Ann Ovenstone, co-founder with her late husband Jack, who grew up with family tortoises, perpetuated that with their own children, and accumulated a stock of questions and answers which she suspected others might wish to share. Her own collection of tortoises was augmented by others that came to her, some from the RSPCA, rounding up strays, others from airports, where they had been detected as illegal immigrants. Ann's operation has now grown to a point where some 400 tortoises are being fed and nurtured. Since I am there in November, many have shut down for winter. But not by any means all. Some of her younger constituents are merely sleeping off lunch; others are wide awake, and some are actually lively. This was especially true of those aged around three or four. 'They're teenagers,' she tells me. Even while we are talking, two teenager tortoises have come face to face, even mouth to mouth, when another, approaching at right angles with some definite destination in mind, simply climbs right over them. That's what tortoises do, Mrs Ovenstone says. They don't like to go round: they go straight.

*****

If only my onward bus – a full twenty minutes late at Sully – could follow the same simple principle. The first stretch is agreeably straight and purposeful. But beyond that comes Cadoxton, and here the bus seems to lose its sense of direction and begins to snuffle around like some disoriented mole though Cadoxton's glum streets. The relationship between this place and Barry has shifted. At the 1851 census, Cadoxton boasted 293 inhabitants, where the tiny hamlet on Barry Island could only muster a mere 63. Cadoxton grew with Barry, but Barry grew much faster, leaving Cadoxton as the junior partner. And that's very much the case now. Barry, when the bus finally delivers us there, has an imposing town hall, looking on to King Square, and a stately dock office still evoking its greatest days, with before it a statue of the man who, feeding on Bute intransigence, above all made Barry: David Davies, habitually known, since Wales sports so many David Davieses, as David Davies, Llandinam.

The story of modern Barry starts here. Davies was born in December 1818 in a village in Montgomeryshire, a hundred miles or so from where his statue now stands. His father, a farmer who was also a sawyer, was able to keep his son at school till the age of eleven, which is more than most children in such a place could expect. When he was twenty, his father died, and the young man took over his businesses. Soon he was building roads and bridges, and as the railway age developed he moved on to the building of lines through Mid and South Wales. Even that was overtaken by a new priority: coal, an industry burgeoning so dramatically in the north of Glamorgan that the Rhondda Valley began to be called the California of South Wales.

The reach of its export trade seemed boundless, so much so that the coal owners began to complain that the Bute docks at Cardiff were inadequate to cope with the volume of trade they hoped to push through them; and that this would not improve while the Bute interest, allied with the reliably obedient Taff Valley railway, continued to run them. So, backed by local landowners and influential shipowners, they resolved to set up their own Barry Dock and Railway Company. The chairman of the venture had, of course, to be an aristocrat: in this case, Robert George Windsor-Clive (Eton and Oxford), from 1869 4th Baron Windsor, though in time he would be elevated to even greater heights as the 1st Earl of Plymouth. Windsor owned large parts of Glamorgan, as also of English border counties: Barry Island was a neglected but promising tract of land that he'd bought for a mere £8,000 from a local pharmacist.

The rank of baron fell short of that of marquess. The Windsors were hardly a match for the Butes in influence and connections, and this Windsor may no doubt have reflected from time to time on the ironic circumstance that the Butes' fabled fortune was in large part derived from the marriage of one of that breed to a Windsor. But while Windsor was a smart businessman, it was his vice-chairman Davies who most of all shaped the enterprise and became the heart of the company. Later in life he recalled the moment that had inspired his great adventure. 'I had no wish to go to Barry', he said, 'or elsewhere, but when I was told, while attempting to negotiate with Cardiff, to go and build a dock of my own, I felt the sting, and determined from that moment it should be done.'

Who it was who spoke those fateful words in Cardiff is not recorded, but there is one overwhelmingly obvious candidate. What was so often attributed to grand aristocrats was often the work of humbly born agents, and unlike his proactive father, the 3rd Marquess did not engage in this kind of negotiation; he left that to trusted henchmen, of whom the most trusted was William Thomas Lewis. By 1864, when he was twenty-seven, he'd become the 3rd Marquess's chief engineer and by 1880 had control of all the Bute estates in Wales.

Lewis had much more in common with Davies, with whom he had to do battle, than he had with the Scottish aristocrat who employed him. He had left school at thirteen, and begun to work with his engineer father as an apprentice. But where Davies made his fortune entirely though his own imagination and effort, Lewis built his on his Bute connections. He saw as his mission the safeguarding of the monopoly rights the Butes had established in conjunction with the compliant Taff Valley railway, and he fought his corner with a steady intransigence, which as Barry began to thrive would damage his master's interests..

In contrast with many Welsh colliery owners, Davies of Llandinam was revered, even loved, by those who worked for him, whereas Lewis, when he turned from the service of the Butes to a role as a colliery magnate, became feared and loathed for his harshness and belligerence. What was long remembered against him was the disaster that struck his Universal Colliery at Senghenydd where in 1901 'a mighty explosion' occurred. Eighty men died. Sir William, on holiday in France, declined to come home. And in 1913, two years after his ennoblement, an even greater tragedy devastated the village. This time 440 men died – and died, an inquiry found, because the faults that had been found to blame for the 1901 explosion had never been remedied. Again his lordship was on holiday, this time in Scotland; this time he turned up, though only after reports that the King would be coming.

*****

The Barry project had caused deep consternation in Cardiff. In January 1883 the town's MP, Sir Edward Reed, wrote to Bute's agent Lewis pointing out that if no way was found to stop it, was likely to 'put a check, and possibly, a permanent and final check, upon the progress of Cardiff'. The *Western Mail*, that unswerving champion of Cardiff and champion of the family to whom it owed its existence, warned against the Barry venture in terms which spilled beyond criticism into malevolence.

The Barry scheme had to be approved by Parliament, and here, especially in the Lords, the Bute interest had powerful connections. A Commons select committee had been impressed, not least when Davies, asked what would happen if the company could not raise the funds it needed, replied that he would pay for the project himself. The Lords, even so, threw the bill out. Yet even the forces of Bute were unable to halt it when it came back the following year. By the summer of 1889 the docks were ready to open. The newly established *Barry Dock News* was ecstatic. The opening of this formidable and unrivalled concern, it trilled, had been a brilliant success. And, of course, this being Victorian Britain, there was a luncheon, given by the directors for 2,000 guests, many brought by train from London.

And yet curiously both barrels of the *Mail*'s assault on the Barry project would in some ways prove to have been well targeted. Barry did indeed take trade that might otherwise have been Cardiff's, so much so that it grew by 1913 to be bigger than Cardiff. But beyond that the dock went into decline. The coal industry, and the export trade with it, were dwindling by the 1920s and, compared with Barry's heyday in the opening years of the century, seemed vestigial by the thirties. During the Second World War the docks were busy and useful, but thereafter the prospects looked bleak. From 1959 onwards, they were largely sustained by the arrival of Geest, importers of Caribbean bananas, but in 1993 the company shifted to Southampton. The dock that had come to life in 1889 now closed; a second, opened in 1893 to the east of it, continued to operate, but the best days of David Davies's brave venture were done.

Some of the vacuum which this left behind was filled by a second industry. Until 1893, Barry Island was accessible only by foot across the sands at low tide, or by paddle steamer. Then a causeway was built, and three years after the causeway, a railway. From Cardiff and well beyond, the customers poured in, with packed, excited trainloads arriving in summer every ten minutes. After that came a fairground and an adventure railway, replaced in time by a roller coaster. On one bank holiday, it was estimated, around 150,000 people had swarmed into and over the island. And that was just the beginning. What began on the beach was transferred as custom expanded to a dedicated amusement park. Over the August Bank Holiday weekend of 1934, the visitor traffic was logged at over a thousand coaches and charabancs, 8,000 motor cars, 3,000 motor cycles and 10,000 bicycles, quite apart from the legions that came by rail or service bus. On the Monday, an estimated 250,000 people were clamouring for space, more than the island could take; some had to be turned away. Four years later, a further surefire attraction was added: a scenic railway, claimed to be the biggest in Britain.

But the following year was blighted by the prospect of war. The island's momentum flagged and would never fully recover. The big post-war boost was the creation in 1966 of a Butlin's holiday camp. But by now Britain discovered Abroad. Package holidays leeched away a trade that once had happily settled for Barry, and the island, like the docks before it, went into an irreversible decline. In 1987 Butlin's decamped. The money-spinning throngs of the 1930s would never return, and soon the pleasure park was in trouble. Bids to revive it were floated but not pursued. On my visit, in November 2014, the local paper, the *Barry and District News,* is featuring yet another attempt to breathe life back into it. Previous bids had foundered, but this time what Barry had hoped for was about to occur: the refurbished pleasuredrome would reopen the following spring. (And it did, in time for the Easter holidays.)

Yet already sustenance for the town's tourist trade had appeared from an unlikely source. In 2007, the BBC began running a series called *Gavin and Stacey*, built around four main characters. Gavin (Matthew Horne) from Essex (specifically Billericay), Stacey (Joanna Poole) from the very different culture of Barry, and their respective best friends Smithy (James Corden) and Nessa (Ruth Jones) – the last two played by the writers. More familiar TV faces appeared among the supporting cast, including Rob Brydon and Alison Steadman. It ran for only twenty episodes, but picked up a string of awards, was promoted from BBC3 to BBC2 and ultimately – the final accolade – to BBC1.

By then it had mustered a faithful following whose initial enthusiasm swelled to devotion. From time to time rumours appeared of another series, but the team that had made it work were reluctant. Yet the number of devotees continued to burgeon, and before long Barry found itself blessed with a brand new tourist attraction. The centre of town today is King Square, out of which runs the main shopping street, Holton Road. South-west from there, as the shops diminish, are Broad Street and behind it, High Street – names that suggest this sector was once the core of the town. And north off Broad Street, up a breathtaking hill, is Trinity Street; and here, near the top of Trinity Street, is number 47: the home in *Gavin and Stacey* of Stacey's widowed mum, Gwen, where Stacey tends to be found a lot of the time. It wasn't the case in November, but people I met in the street said in summer Trinity Street has become an unlikely Mecca for tourist coaches, stopping near number 47 as part of the town's now flourishing Gavin and Stacey tours.

You can get a taste of what is on offer from the website of what is described as the Official Gavin and Stacey Tour. 'A tour like no other', it says, in the tone of people confident that they're offering the irresistible, and 'a tidy choice for fans of the show'. 'Tour the locations from the TV show in the original Dave's Coach from the show and visit the street that Stacey lives in, the arcade where Nessa works and the church where she nearly gets married to Dave' [a coach operator based in Sully] 'and much more . . . You'll have opportunities to stop, take pictures, and see the locations up close. As tour guests you will have an exclusive opportunity to sit in Nessa's chair in the amusement arcade when making a purchase and get discounts at some of the vendors on the sea front. See Gwen and Stacey's home (*exterior only*). Get inside the church where Neil is christened and where Vanessa "Shanessa" Jenkins nearly gets married to Dave Coaches. See where Nessa works as a mime artist. Stop off at the caravan where Nessa and Dave live with baby Neil. Tour the locations in the original Dave's Coach from the TV show.' The cost for an adult: £26. Under 15: £19. Group tickets (ten or more persons): £22. Tour and 3-star hotel package: £180 for two people sharing.

As a boost for the future of Barry this is hardly in the David Davies league. Even so, it's a bonus at a tough time. David Davies has his statue in front of the old Dock Office. At present Gavin and Stacey have to make do with a series of cardboard cut-outs near Marco's Café, another object of pilgrimage for true fans. It can't be long before someone decides that they deserve a more substantial and durable honour. Perhaps the tourist office should have a word with Sir Antony Gormley.

6

LEST OLD ALLEGIANCE BE FORGOT

94 Newcastle-under-Lyme–Tunstall–Biddulph

NEWCASTLE-UNDER-LYME, STAFFORDSHIRE: 'not to be confused', we are warned, 'with Newcastle upon Tyne.' I wouldn't have thought there was much danger of that. If you're in a fine city with a cascade of great bridges over a mighty river, with the many handsome streets created by Grainger and Dobson, and the Eldon memorial, and constant dazzling, dizzying changes of level that make for as thrilling a townscape as you'll find in these islands, you are probably on the Tyne. If not, you're more likely to be in north Staffordshire.

Another potential confusion has, however, troubled this Newcastle rather more. For years it had to fight off the popular illusion that it was part of the Potteries, one of the towns which formed the federation known as Stoke-on-Trent. Six towns came together to create what is now the city of Stoke. Some people think there were only five, but that's because the real-life Potteries have a kind of alternative existence in the novels of Arnold Bennett: Bennett thought the word 'five', with its open vowel, had a more euphonious ring than the authentic 'six'.

The Potteries towns began pondering unification as far back as 1817, and that took on a new impetus when the 1832 Reform Act established them as a single parliamentary borough. Why have six separate authorities, it was increasingly asked, when a federation would be much more efficient – and cheaper? For much of the nineteenth century, attempts foundered on the resentments and envies of one or two towns against the rest. The hardest case to resolve was Burslem's, since that town had always regarded itself as the mother of the Potteries and did not wish to surrender that honour – especially when the likely beneficiary would be upstart Hanley.

Bennett's novel *The Old Wives' Tale* reflects the often bitter emotions which the prospect of federation fed. Indeed, the determination of one of the two Burslem sisters around whom the story is built – Constance Baines, after her marriage Constance Povey, daughter of the town's most successful draper – to go out, ill as she is, and vote against federation leads to her death. In the final stages of the push for federation, Burslem voted against it by a margin of three to two. But a public inquiry found for it, the responsible minister was fiercely in favour, and in 1908 the legislation went through. And before very long, Stoke was setting its lascivious eyes on candidates for further absorption. One was Wolstanton, a mining village to the west of it; the other, far bigger prize was Newcastle.

To Newcastle, what Stoke demanded was not merely undesirable: it was insulting. Here was a town, in the shadow of the Lyme Forest, chartered as a borough in the twelfth century, its fortunes built in the Middle Ages on iron and thereafter on hatmaking, brewing, and agriculture, with nothing much in the way of pottery apart from a modest trade in fine earthenware. It had watched the eruption down in the valley of an industrial conglomeration with which it had nothing to do, and yet which now aspired to reduce it, as local patriots thought, to vassal status.

For a while the issue simmered. But through the 1920s, when many cities were constantly asking for more (Sheffield was after Rotherham, Liverpool after Bootle, Manchester after Salford), Stoke came up with a series of predatory propositions to annexe Newcastle, Wolstanton and a sizeable chunk around it. Newcastle and Wolstanton rejected these schemes by overwhelming majorities in a postcard poll. Yet after three weeks of solemn consideration, a Commons select committee agreed – unanimously – to let them proceed. Independent Newcastle had begun to look doomed. But saviours appeared in the form of the House of Lords, pursuing that traditional role as a bulwark against change. They quashed it. In Newcastle, the *Manchester Guardian* reported, the mayor, returning from London, was carried shoulder high from Stoke station to his official car, while the church bells 'rang merry peals for several hours'. And when Stoke came back with the same agenda, the Lords thwarted it by an even more crushing margin. Thus the federal city failed to capture Newcastle: and nearly a hundred years later, Newcastle remains a separate borough within the county of Staffordshire.

And indeed the claim advanced by Mr Tyldesley Jones MP, counsel for Stoke, that there was nowadays little detectable difference between Newcastle and the city of Stoke, was pure fantasy. Even on this bleak day, with a cutting wind and a light but spiteful rain, the town has a cheerful Saturday morning feel about it; for all the change it has undergone, it still has the look and sense of an old English market town, with a broad, curving shopping street climbing the hill, presided over by the sombre 1713 Guildhall, and a good representation of local names displayed on shop fronts.

This was a favoured stopping-off point on the main route from London to Carlisle. Some pleasing Georgian building survives; one can almost sense the spirit of Newcastle saying: you'll not find much to match this in Hanley. As to what precisely it was that made Newcastle so determined to stay separate, there were factors other than pride in its history. Newcastle was well-to-do, a tidy and regular place, not to mention middle-class territory. The Potteries were ugly and working class. The writer Paul Johnson, once a left-wing firebrand, later a stalwart champion of Margaret Thatcher, grew up in Tunstall, one of the Potteries towns. The family had moved there from Manchester, and his mother never adapted to what she saw as a 'catastrophic descent'. 'No one', she said, 'goes to Burslem unless they have to.' But his father saw the Potteries differently. Change always brought losses, he said, and he understood why perhaps the pottery towns were thought of as hideous, dirty, wasteful and perhaps inefficient. 'But it's beautiful. Your mother doesn't see it. Nor do most people.'

Bennett knew Newcastle well. He went to school in the town for a time. People in the Potteries tended to look on Newcastle as condescending and snooty, a sentiment with which Bennett seems often to sympathize. He calls it Oldcastle in the novels. *Clayhanger* begins with an instance of that:

> Beyond the ridge, and partly protected by it from the driving smoke of the Five Towns, lay the fine and ancient Tory borough of Oldcastle, from whose historic Middle School Edwin Clayhanger was

now walking home. The fine and ancient Tory borough provided education for the whole of the Five Towns, but the relentless ignorance of its prejudices had blighted the district. A hundred years earlier the canal had only been obtained after a vicious Parliamentary fight between industry and the fine ancient borough, which saw in canals a menace to its importance as a centre of traffic. Fifty years earlier the fine and ancient borough had succeeded in forcing the greatest railway line in England to run through unpopulated country five miles off instead of through the Five Towns, because it loathed the mere conception of a railway . . . Oldcastle guessed not the vast influences of its sublime stupidity.

*****

As befits a bus that emanates from Newcastle, the 94 Bakerbus (Baker's have since been taken over by D&G Bus of Crewe), clad in a raucous yellow tinctured with orange, begins its journey by steering well clear of the Potteries. Signs pointing to Burslem are rigorously ignored. We are coming instead to Wolstanton, once a mining village which claimed to have the deepest mineshaft in Western Europe – a reminder, that Staffordshire, though famous for potteries, was built on coal, which, like Staffordshire clay, the pottery industry required to sustain it. The pit was badly affected by the miners' dispute of 1984 and folded a year or so later. The community is a mixture now of ancient and modern: the church of St Margaret, red sandstone, an Asda (where the pit used to be), a Methodist church, a working men's club, the Village Tavern across from Kebabland.

We are high at this point above the city of Stoke, whose six component communities trail deep through the valley, and firmer hints of the world that grew up in that valley have begun to creep in. One can now and then see surviving examples of the once iconic constructions so characteristic of this landscape: the bottle-shaped pottery kilns of which at the end of the Second World War there were thousands, a population now gravely reduced but happily not yet extinct. And it's soon apparent that the 94 has succumbed: the territory here is pure Potteries. At Longport, where the road crosses the Trent and Mersey Canal, there's an eye-catching factory, Grade II* listed, with a courtyard containing what the official categorization describes as a large bottle kiln with a wide circular hovel – a hovel in this case meaning a conical building enclosing a cone.

As we close in on Tunstall, the most northerly of Stoke's six towns, there are large tracts of cleared land that seem to cry out for development.

This is a world away from spruce and ordered Newcastle. There's a long wandering main street with a square on the western side at the head of which is a clock tower, with a clock which actually works. Here too are the Sneyd Arms pub, the Crown and Anchor and the Oddfellows Arms, despite the vaguely menacing presence of a shop called Bargain Booze – though ominously the Crown and Anchor is up for sale. But the old town hall, whose presence would once have proudly proclaimed: We Are Tunstall, is now dishevelled and drab and reduced to the status of mere local office of Stoke, which even then occupies only a part of it. The top of the high street too has a look of hard times: Posh, Shoe Zone, Talk of the Town have gone, though Subway survives, alongside the Salvation Army.

I had hoped to find Tunstall *en fête*, perhaps with glowing accounts in the local newspaper of a proud parade of its local heroes through the streets on an open-top bus, since the town's football club had in the past few days notched up a historic achievement. But Saturday afternoons are the time to think about football, so I'll need to come back and catch up with that later. And meanwhile, the 94 has begun the last stage of its journey to Biddulph.

Now the setting is changing again. Further episodes of the city of Stoke succeed each other so fast that they're difficult to disentangle. Down a dark narrow street there's a church which has converted from Methodist to spiritualist. What would Wesley have said? It comes as a somewhat irrational culture shock in an area so interwoven with Nonconformity, though no doubt more godless now than it was. Margaret Drabble, Arnold Bennett's biographer, says that by 1851 there were forty-six Methodist chapels in the Potteries and only seventeen churches. And then, past a preserved pit head, we're out into open moorland, close to the Staffordshire–Cheshire borders: no longer in the city of Stoke but encased in the district of Staffordshire Moorlands. The map makes Knypersley sound alluring: there's a generous reservoir, prized by anglers. But the bit we see from the bus is dominated by a parade of militant industrial buildings, flaunting such occupational terms as 'logistics'; a word which, as people who travel the motorways know, is rapidly taking over the world.

Though signposts point boldly to Biddulph, the bus seems unpersuaded, and shuffles away down a side road as if not ready to grapple with Biddulph until we've been given a chance to inspect what might be called Outer Biddulph. It isn't exciting; but then neither is Biddulph. Its one magnetic attraction seems to be a monster Sainsbury's, close to such other prominent landmarks as Biddulph Town Hall and the Biddulph Conservative and Unionist Club, but comfortably eclipsing both. Down side streets there are nailbars and tanning salons and a butcher's, though today at noon there is not a sausage in sight, and an outfit that trumpets Povey's Oat Cakes – 'Biddulph's biggest export'.

I had never before encountered north Staffordshire's obsession with oatcakes, but I'd started to scent it in Tunstall, and this week's local newspaper is leading with an oatcakes exclusive. Under the legend: '84-year-old victim angry at doorstep oatcake con', it tells the distressing tale of a 'mystery woman' going from door to door through Smallthorne, Norton, Fegg Hayes, Burslem and Chell flogging oatcakes from door to door at prices well above those that people normally pay. The victims are predominantly elderly. 'I'm disgusted,' one tells the paper. 'If I saw her again I would punch her in the face.' A woman who spotted the trickster in Smallthorne describes her as 'pretty normal. Middle-aged with mousey hair.' It seems the mousey-haired miscreant has been raiding bins and retrieving discarded delicacies. High Lane Oatcakes baker Nick Copeland tells the paper he's now cutting up surplus oatcakes before he throws them away.

I've started to think that maybe the 94 bus was moved by a laudable instinct when it turned down the side road instead of pressing on to the town. This manoeuvre occurred at a crossroads where the road we took, signposted to Biddulph Moor, ran east while another, signalling the nearby presence of a place called Mow Cop, headed west. Each sounded in some way promising. Dedicated explorers taking the road to the moor have some chance of tracing the source of the Trent, the river which has traditionally, if somewhat eccentrically, been used as a kind of dividing line separating the north from the south. Tom Fort, who wrote a book called *Downstream* based on travels sometimes by bike, sometimes on foot, but mainly in command of a plywood punt, went to look for it. He had to make a second attempt to locate it. 'I thought', he says, 'of Speke and the Nile and Lake Victoria.' Except that in this case the cherished spot consisted of 'a chipped concrete pipe, a weed-choked hole in the ground, a muddy dip in a sheep field. There was little here of the pure and the sacred.'

Ah, well: perhaps those in search of the pure and sacred would be better advised to take the alternative road westwards to Mow Cop. It's a low hill crowned by what looks like a ruined castle, though in fact it was built as such by a local landowner called Randle Wilbraham to create a romantic scene for himself and his friends to gaze on from his home across the border in Cheshire. In time it was bought for use as a quarry, which led to demonstrations and obstructions, but in 1925 the National Trust took it over and quarrying stopped. The ruin remains, but that's only the lesser part of Mow Cop's history. It was here in 1807 that Hugh Bourne, a

carpenter from Stoke, and William Clowes, a potter from Burslem, staged
the first of what became known as camp meetings, inspired by accounts
from a man called Lorenzo Dow of similar impassioned gatherings in
America. Both were Methodists; but when the Methodist conference
heard of these meetings, it became alarmed, and ordered that they be
stopped. Bourne and Clowes defied them, and found themselves expelled
from the Methodist Church. So they formed their own organization,
which came to be known as Primitive Methodism. What's not in doubt
is the place's pronunciation: the word Mow, I was warned, rhymes with
cow, not Coe.

There's a third attraction worth seeking out, though again it's not really
in Biddulph. A family called Bateman lived in some style at Knypersley
Hall on money made out of coal and steel. A son of the house, James
Bateman, drew on these resources while still an Oxford undergraduate to
begin a collection of plants. His particular passion was orchids, and he
used agents abroad to find them. Around 1840, he left Knypersley Hall and
bought Biddulph Grange, north of the town, where he and his wife, Maria,
began to create a kind of international fantasy garden, with selections
representing the Himalayas, Egypt (the entrance to their Egyptian gardens
was guarded by sphinxes) and, most of all, China. It is said that 2,000
men worked for eight months to fulfil his vision, and that the exercise left
him with crippling debts. What he created reflects his obsessions, initially
with orchids, and later with the roots of trees, which he liked to expose.
In 1861 the Batemans left for Kensington, London. By 1988 the gardens
had long deteriorated, but now the National Trust came to the rescue, as
it had with Mow Cop. Apart from the Bateman collection, restored to its
earlier glory, azaleas and rhododendrons pull in the crowds from across
the Midlands and the North West.

And might in other circumstances have pulled me in too, but now
Tunstall is calling me back. The team which has recently cemented its
place in the record books is shortly due to kick off. Tunstall Town of the
Staffordshire County League second division are fresh from conquering
Betley Reserves by three goals to two, thus ending a run of 171 matches
without a victory. Their only previous point in recent years had been
achieved in January 2013 when they drew 1–1 against Whittington, after
losing 143 games in a row. In 2008–9 they played twenty-two games,
losing the lot with seven goals scored but 166 conceded. The following
season they did better at one end of the pitch – sixteen goals scored – but
worse at the other, with 208 let in. The 2011–12 season was less successful,
with ten goals achieved but 228 conceded.

Despite their recent national – and as I'm about to learn, even international – fame, making your way to a Tunstall match isn't much like going to Wembley. The ground takes some finding – it's in Sandyford rather than Tunstall proper – and even when found takes some squelching across. The Tunstall Town manager is wearing wellington boots, something you never see from José Mourinho. And now the Town's heroes are splashing across the terrain to line up against Whittington Reserves. Today's crowd (which numbers half a dozen or so) seems excited, as do the portly manager and his portly comrade, no doubt the coach – less so, perhaps, by the expectation of another victory than by the kudos which came from the first one. Sky Sports has saluted their triumph, as has BBC Radio 5 Live. On the touchline today is a man from Czech Radio, ready to furnish the expectant people of Prague with news of this record achievement.

That they no longer lose every match, often with scores against them of 15 or more, is attributable, it appears, to their adoption of a youth policy. At the height of their tribulations they regularly fielded players well past sixty or even seventy. In one match the total age of their goalkeeper and their four back line defenders was said to exceed 300. Today there are only two or three on the pitch of whom it might be remarked that, as W.S. Gilbert says of the rich attorney's elderly ugly daughter in *Trial by Jury*, they might very well pass for forty-three in the dusk with the light behind them. Whittington, I also note, play in red, which sports psychologists say gives teams an inbuilt advantage, while Tunstall turn out in blue, with their sponsors' names on their shirts. Their sponsors are a local stairlift company.

At last the whistle blows and we're off, and Tunstall, no doubt fired by their recent acclaim, are attacking with spirit, if not yet with inspiration. Town's goalkeeper, by the look of him one of the older inhabitants, summons a splendid leap to tip a threatening shot over the crossbar, and at one point Town win four corners in quick succession. Their number 11 is impressively quick, too quick for most of his colleagues to keep up with, and one of Town's younger players achieves a pretty effective bicycle kick, only for a cry to come from the stands: 'Don't be cocky!' (It isn't really a stand of course, simply two dugouts and a pitchside railing.) But suddenly it's one–nil to Whittington, and soon after, two–nil. Before long, a third goes in, and the manager and his accomplice are getting despondent. 'The problem is', says the manager, 'our lack of pace at the back.' True, though it isn't the only one. At half-time I have to set off back to Newcastle. The final score turns out to be 6–1 to Whittington – disappointing but not that bad, given this outfit's history.

It has to be said that since then Tunstall Town have developed a habit of winning, or at least of not losing, or not losing by quite so much. They didn't even finish bottom in the 2014–15 season. Clearly with today's new selection policy Methuselah would have little chance of getting on to the team sheet. On the other hand, I wouldn't rate their chance of catching the eye of Sky or BBC 5 Live again very often in future. Or, in the case of Czech radio, ever.

7
THUMB-SNECK STREETS, BRASS-RAPPER AVENUES

394 Huddersfield–Milnsbridge–Slaithwaite

A COLD BRIGHT MORNING IN HUDDERSFIELD in what used to be the West Riding of Yorkshire. I'm on my way to a place I cannot name. I know how to spell it, and by the end of the day I will grow very fond of it. But how should one pronounce it without falling foul of the locals?

It may be less swift and less convenient, but aesthetically the best way to come to Huddersfield is by bus rather than by train. It's then an ascending progress through to the station, which is the great architectural treat of the place. It was built in the classical style after the railway arrived here in 1847 by an architect from York, James Pigott Pritchett. John Betjeman rated its façade second only to St Pancras in the pantheon of British railway stations, while Ian Nairn described it as 'a sort of stately home with trains in', which catches it to perfection. The site chosen for Huddersfield station was a little way out of the centre, and to link the two the town established a square in front and surrounded it with buildings, mostly by Pritchett, not far short of its quality. On one side is the George Hotel (not by Pritchett), perhaps most famous subsequently as the birthplace, in 1895, of rugby league football. Opposite the hotel is Britannia Buildings, created for Joseph Crosland, a successful local manufacturer, which after his death became the headquarters of the Huddersfield Building Society. And facing the station there's the Lion Building, with an arched arcade and the eponymous beast strutting its stuff on top. It's a solid, substantial place that proclaims the town's importance, as a good square should.

Huddersfield owes this splendid introduction to the Ramsdens, the family who became lords of the manor of Huddersfield in 1599. The name is written all over the town – literally so, for several important streets were named (by them or their loyal agents) in their honour. They continued to hold their traditional sway for over 300 years. Then, in 1920, the town was ready at last to stiffen its sinews, summon up its blood and, as it were, purchase itself. From now on this would no longer be Ramsdenville, but Huddersfield's Huddersfield.

Yet leave St George's Square, its station, its hotel, its stately buildings and walk through the principal streets, and the pleasure of the place begins to ebb. The town hall, built in stages between 1875 and 1881, seems surprisingly modest and uneventful for a town that can boast such a square. Halifax, some nine miles from here, entrusted the building of its town hall to Sir Charles Barry, architect of the Houses of Parliament, though it fell to his son, Edward Middleton Barry, to complete it. Huddersfield used its own borough surveyor. The public library of 1937, opened, as it proclaims on the front, by Councillor Thomas Smailes, chairman of the library and art gallery committee, has a suitable swagger about it, with a plaque to memorialize Harold Wilson, the locally born Labour prime minister, and another for the 'internationally renowned film star' James Mason. Mason, whose father was a prosperous manufacturer, was born at the more expensive end of a suburb called Marsh, on the edge of posh-mansioned Edgerton. But the 1960s shopping centre across the road from the library lacks any such presence. And the main shopping street, most of which is called New Street, having pushed on efficiently but hardly memorably as far as Primark, suddenly stops, as if to say, as in the old Tom n' Jerry cartoons: That's all, folks.

Of course, there's much more to Huddersfield than one sees on such a modest excursion. There's plenty of proud Huddersfield history to appeal to the ears as well as the eyes. This is the home of the Huddersfield Choral Society, many of whose performances, including Handel's *Messiah* before Christmas each year, are staged in the concert hall within the town hall, an altogether grander experience than its exterior suggests. There's an annual Contemporary Music Festival, with works by composers you may not have heard of yet but, in some cases, will. Brass bands flourish still, as they always have in this part of England. There's also a proud radical strand to this town, embracing a Tory reformer like Richard Oastler, campaigner against the exploitation of labour and an amended Poor Law certain to do the vulnerable down, as well as Luddites, Chartists and other working-class heroes who frequent the pages of E.P. Thompson.

Huddersfield is celebrated too for having given the world such great cricketers as George Hirst and Wilfred Rhodes of Yorkshire and England, and Percy Holmes, senior partner in the famous Yorkshire opening partnership of Holmes and Sutcliffe, who one memorable day took 555 runs off Essex at Leyton. Yet Huddersfield's right to crow has to be tempered: Hirst and Rhodes were both on any definition born in Kirkheaton, east of the town, rather than in Huddersfield proper. Leeds Road (a ground now replaced, like so many, by something more grandly ambitious), which is uncontestably Huddersfield, was home to one of the greatest football clubs in the land in the 1920s, when they won the FA cup in 1922 and topped the old first division three times in a row. Outside the centre too there are sights to be seen: perhaps above all the countryside that surrounds it, but also some fine Victorian mansions on the road north-west towards Halifax, especially in the area that, taking its name from a single great Georgian house, became known as Edgerton. This is where prosperous Huddersfield lived, and prosperous Huddersfield was immensely prosperous. It was sometimes said to be home to more Rolls Royces than any town of its size in Britain.

*****

And so to the bus station, where a host of possible destinations are on display. You may ride from here to Skircoat or Salterhebble, Scissett, Skelmanthorpe, Golcar, Thongsbridge and Netherthong, Marsden Dirker (what is a dirker, exactly? I can find no reliable explanation), Houses Hill; Quarmby, ominous Scapegoat Hill, and close to it, the one which is my destination today and which I still haven't learned to pronounce. This bus is run by E. Stott & Sons ('taking people to places'). It's a 394 intertwined with another using the same local prefix, the 395 taking a slightly modified route to the same terminus. But first we are destined to visit Milnsbridge, which, whatever Huddersfield says, has a rather superior claim, I have come to think, to be the birthplace of the forty-sixth British prime minister.

As the bus takes us west along the valley – the valley of the River Colne, whose presence both animates and partially explains the whole of this area; the textile industry needed water and particularly this kind of water – the weather darkens, and by the time the bus reaches the village, a kind of surly drizzle is setting in. Poor Milnsbridge: even the weather's against it today. As are so many other more permanent circumstances. This is a spot where three crucial lines of communication run east–west, Yorkshire towards Lancashire: at the south of the town the Huddersfield Narrow

Canal; above it, the River Colne (Yorkshire only); and beyond that, the railway. Milnsbridge is doing its best with what it has got, but it's clearly a struggle. There's drama in its geography: the viaduct across the north of the town, with a mill (long out of use, now divided into apartments) towering up beside it; the views across the valley from Manchester Road to the south, with the terraced houses stacked up on the hills row upon row, have a real industrial majesty. But this is a village – or rather a township, a term which I use to designate places that used to be classed as towns and remain something more than villages – that grew out of textiles and little else, and it now has the air of a place robbed of its purpose.

If I were Milnsbridge, I'd be spitting with envy of the village for which I am bound. The viaduct encapsulates the gap in fortune between them. People in Milnsbridge constantly see the trains that speed across and above it on their cross-Pennine journeys, but they cannot get at them. Their station (Longwood and Milnsbridge) was closed in 1968, and though there's now a campaign to get it back, they have little chance of success. It's a very rare place that having lost its station is given it back. Only a very rare place; and yet it hardly needs saying now, Slaithwaite, today's destination, is one.

Milnsbridge has a riverside walk but it has to be said that it isn't much of a riverside walk. You get to it through the Aldi car park. Walk back towards Huddersfield, and you find a millennium seat. Walk west towards Marsden, where the Colne rises, and you come in time to a weir. Unhappily, on the other side of the river, there's a promenade of industrial buildings that could raise the spirits only of someone enraptured by the sight of corrugated iron. On the eastern side of the bridge in the village centre there's a side street down which a sign points towards Milnsbridge House, once considered the best in the area. Nineteenth-century pictures make it look grand and romantic. Today a disconsolate tramp down George Street fails to disclose anything answering to such a description. But, yes, it's still there. Only on the way back do I spot the shabby debilitated-looking building on the corner with Dowker Street, now home to the Peter Preston Engineering Company. It awaits a long-promised refurbishment which, if and when it comes should enhance the village.

Yet this is a house with mixed implications for a working-class township like Milnsbridge. In the early years of the century it was home to Joseph Radcliffe, a Huddersfield magistrate who established himself as the scourge of the Luddites, and was instrumental in getting some of them hanged. A manufacturer called William Horsfall, who owned a mill at Marsden, further west up the valley, had vowed to ride up to his saddle girth in

Luddite blood. This did not go down well with Luddites. In April 1812, he was waylaid at a place called Crosland Moor by a twenty-two-year-old man called George Mellor and three associates, Thomas Smith, Ben Walker and William Thorpe, who shot at him and left him fatally wounded.

Radcliffe, who ran a network of spies and informers, identified them and had them brought to trial. The evidence against them was thin, until Walker turned King's Evidence and testified against his comrades. Mellor, Thorpe and Smith were tried at York Assizes and hanged on 8 April 1813. A few days later the trial took place of seven more Luddites who had taken part in an earlier attack, inspired by Mellor, on a mill near Brighouse. Five of these, too, were hanged. Threats were repeatedly made to kill the magistrate Radcliffe, and on the day of Mellor's execution at York, shots were fired at his house. In the following year, Radcliffe was made a baronet, in recognition of his fervour in combatting Luddism.

As for Wilson's birthplace, to find that, you have to walk south across the canal, climb a steep hill, cross the Manchester Road and search out the modest terraced house which the Wilsons rented in Warneford Road until, soon after Harold was born, they found they could afford to buy a better one in nearby Western Road. So Harold, though commemorated in the square outside Huddersfield station in a statue by the sculptor Ian Walters which catches him as if hurrying towards Westminster, was really a Milnsbridge rather than a Hudddersfield man. Except that this district is identified on the map as Cowlersley, and Ben Pimlott, Wilson's biographer, places him very precisely in Cowlersley. This may all seem like a bit of a quibble, but it's more than that. It tells us something essential about the place we call Huddersfield: that it is really the core of an agglomeration of villages most of which had, and like Milnsbridge still have, their own separate identity.

*****

The bus journey out of Milnsbridge through Wellbridge is a kind of switchback affair, sometimes running high on the hill, sometimes dipping down to the valley. It's these changes of level that makes this terrain so dramatic. At one point we pass a high mill whose top floor is only just above the level of the road the bus is pursuing; at another, a woman leaving the bus sets off down what looks like an endless stairway to reach her front door. And now that we're clear of Milnsbridge, the sun has come out again. By the time we reach Slaithwaite, we can even luxuriate in it.

But I still don't know how to pronounce it. Before I left London, well-wishers who knew this territory solemnly warned me not to say Slay-thwaite. If I did, they advised, I'd be marked down straightaway as an ignorant and probably arrogant Londoner. But if not Slay-thwaite, then what? An elderly couple, back from a morning's shopping, are sitting in front of me on the bus. So I ask their advice. 'It's Slar-wit,' the wife says. 'It's Slough-wit,' her husband tells me. 'Sl—ou—it,' he repeats, lovingly drawing it out. 'Mind you,' he adds gathering up his bags, 'I always say Slay-thwaite myself.'

Whichever way you say it, the place is a treat. The bus puts us down close to the point where river and canal come together and run side by side through the village, presided over by a mighty monument to the worsted industry called Globe Mill. Across the road from the canal that runs alongside it, there's a fine and diverse line of shops of the kind that Milnsbridge could never hope to muster: grocers, greengrocers, butchers (and 'award-winning' pie-makers), a post office, opticians, men's outfitters, Slawit and Golcar Cars, interspersed with some of its pubs. Nearby are boutiques and galleries and a fish and chip shop called Little Compo's, after one of the characters on the long running TV series *The Last of the Summer Wine*, though that really belongs to Holmfirth, where it was mostly set. Slaithwaite too was the scene for a series, *Where the Heart Is*, but that never took quite such a hold on the viewing public's affections. There's even a Conservative Club. The canal, which contributes so much to the scene, was only rescued from long disuse in 2001. Locks were resurrected and new ones added, including one which looks like a guillotine: lock users hate it. The reopening of the canal, like the restoration of the station, has been hugely beneficial for the place, bringing in visitors who otherwise might well have missed it.

All of this, and more like it, add up to a sense that Slaithwaite, having largely lost its essential engendering industry, has found a new relevance. Unlike Milnsbridge, it is once again pretty sure what it's there for. Indeed there are murmurings about this process being taken too far, apprehensions that the place might be 'Hebdenized', like once grim and gritty but now dauntingly trendy and even verging-on-twee, Hebden Bridge, beyond Halifax. But then, Slaithwaite has always been by the standards of this part of Yorkshire a bit on the smart side. Lewisham Street, smart enough to be named after the aristocratic family who owned a lot of it, was commonly tagged Brass Handle Street. This use of front doors as a social indicator was not unique in these parts. The Revd Alfred Easther's *A Glossary of Dialect of Almondbury and Huddersfield*, published in 1883, records that when the vicar of Huddersfield was about to make an appointment, a Slaithwaite parishioner told him: 'Yo' mun ha' one 'at'll go to' t'thumb-sneck as well as to t'brass rapper.'

This was even a spa town, once described, perhaps rather fancifully, as the Harrogate of the area. You can find the site of the spa by searching out another fine old mill, Spa Mill, still true to its textile history as home to Spectrum Yarns, Stylecraft Yarns and Glenbrae Knitwear, crossing the river and following a riverside walk which really feels like a riverside walk and leads into playing fields. It's mid-afternoon, and a group of mothers, children and playful dogs are arrayed on the bridge across the canal enjoying Slaithwaite's spring sunshine. We come here a lot, one of the mothers tells me. We're hoping to see the heron. We quite often do.

*****

Though today as we'll see is a special day, perhaps the most special in Slawit's calendar, there's a cheering sense that this is a place where things happen on most days. By design, as with the festivities due to take place tonight, but possibly by accident too. It had not, for instance, been part of my plan to take lunch with UKIP's candidate for the Colne Valley constituency in the general election now only three months away. But this being Slaithwate/Slawit, it happens. We have both picked out the same café; there is only one table left, so we share it. That enables Mel Roberts to explain to me how a previously non-party-political person – born in the East End of London, mother of eight, divorced, smallholder, until quite recently the proprietor of a local bookshop (it has now gone online) – came to be standing here. (She'd already been UKIP's candidate in 2010 before the party took off, finishing fifth with 2 per cent of the vote; the British National Party was fourth.)

This encounter also sets off a conversation about the Colne Valley constituency's unusually vivid political history: an MP who disappeared without trace, perhaps even murdered; another, his successor, the only modern MP ever removed from the Commons by reason of lunacy. The first was Victor Grayson, chosen by local members of the Independent Labour Party to fight a by-election in 1907, though the national party had enough doubts about him to refuse to endorse him. He had once intended to become a Unitarian minister, but had taken to preaching socialism with evangelical fervour. On Friday 19 July the result was announced at Slaithwaite Town Hall. Grayson, fighting, as he told cheering crowds outside the Dartmouth Arms, on an unequivocally socialist programme, had beaten both the Liberal and the Tory. But his time at Westminster would damage him. He was rarely there, preferring to make campaigning speeches around the country. He rarely spoke in the Commons. He consistently alienated potential allies. He had to be suspended from Parliament after disrupting a debate on the licensing laws by making a speech about unemployment: a far more important issue, he insisted, than licensing. Maybe, but this intervention, it was generally judged, even by former sympathizers, owed less to some overpowering political conviction than to too much booze.

At the general election of January 1910 the charismatic Grayson lost the seat to a markedly uncharismatic Liberal, the Reverend Dr Charles Leach. Even then, local supporters pressed him to stand again at the next election, but he pleaded ill-health. Instead he put up in London and was heavily beaten. There was talk after that of a political comeback in Yorkshire, but a speech he was due to make in Huddersfield had to be cancelled: he was too drunk to speak.

And then he disappeared. Sightings were claimed all over the world, but none was confirmed. Lurid theories circulated. He had run away from his creditors. He had fled from some enraged husband (Grayson was as famously addicted to women, who often pursued him, as he was to drink). He'd been murdered by Maundy Gregory, pedlar of political honours under Lloyd George, whom he'd tried to expose. None of the trails led anywhere.

His successor, Leach, himself an old ILP man, was sixty-three when elected and when war broke out in 1914 he enlisted as an army chaplain, working in London hospitals. His behaviour in the Commons became more and more bizarre, to a point where the Speaker was persuaded to tell the House that the member for Colne Valley was suffering from unsound mind, brain deterioration and loss of memory, and the Lunacy (Vacating of Seats) Act of 1886 would be used to remove him. Nowadays his condition would no doubt have been diagnosed as dementia.

Tonight is the final night of Slaithwaite's Moonraking Festival, which happens only in odd numbered years. It commemorates an alleged occasion when excise men came on smugglers trying to recover goods they had hidden in some kind of waterway: what kind of water depends on where the story is propagated. It is famously told in the Wiltshire town of Devizes, where it features a pond called the Crammer. I had never till now known that such things had also been said to have happened in Slaithwaite. They are always portrayed as having been events on a moonlit night, enabling the smugglers to claim they were trying to fish out the moon. There are various versions of how Slaithwaite came by its festival, but it seems to have been the product of a conversation between two people who lived in the town and wanted to think up some occasion which might lift its spirits at the end of a Yorkshire winter, and someone who lived outside it but knew the moonraking tale and thought that might serve the purpose. Whomever and however it came about, it's turned out to be inspired. At least a thousand people, perhaps substantially more, young and old, Slawitian or visiting for the occasion, are assembled tonight below the Globe Mill. Many have brought with them the fruit of a week's endeavour in classes held in the village devoted to the making of paper lanterns – a tradition which also helps solve the problem of how to entertain the kids at half-term.

At around half past six an imperious amplified voice commands the crowds to Make Way for the Moon! And here indeed is the huge paper moon, lofted along by a team of villainous-looking men with heavy black beards and cloth caps, representing the smugglers. Behind comes a second contingent, assembled this year because this is the thirtieth anniversary of the festival, dressed as pastrycooks and escorting a lantern-cake. They are followed by a motley collection of lantern-bearers whose paper concoctions honour this year's theme – famous landmarks, at home and abroad. Here, lovingly formed out of paper, and clutched sometimes by small pink hands, sometimes by elderly gnarled ones, are Big Ben and Tower Bridge and the Millennium Dome, the Angel of the North, as well as many I did not see but others did and enthused about: Sydney Opera House, possibly Leeds Town Hall, and certainly Huddersfield railway station, along with strange beasts the like of which were never seen on sea or land. And mixed up among the marchers, the music. I thought I could hear a bagpiper while we waited below Globe Mill, but here now, loud and unmistakable, are a brass band, of course, and some way behind, a percussion band, beating out dancing rhythms.

A great tide of joy and excitement flows past the shops, past Slawit and Golcar Cars, past Chopsticks, the Chinese restaurant, past the Commercial, past the Shoulder of Mutton, which looks to be making a fortune tonight, and on to the locks which punctuate the canal, where the moon is treated to a waterborne ride. The procession will culminate with the release of the moon into the night-time sky. The sky this evening is wonderfully clear, so you can see the real moon looking down coolly upon these proceedings, no doubt mystified as to what, if anything, they might portend.

There are other festivals, in other places, which no doubt match this one. Marsden, just down the road, has an annual Imbolc Festival, marking the end of winter, where the Green Man (Spring) takes on and vanquishes Jack Frost (Winter). And when I get back to London, my granddaughter describes the New Year celebrations in the Chinatown district of London, again all high spirits and music and lanterns – though where Slaithwaite was blessed with a crisp clear evening, the people who came to that one got drenched. But Slaithwaite comes away boisterously happy, and buoyed by the sense of impending spring and summer. It is all, of course, quite ridiculous. But it's also entirely wonderful.

8

BONGS AND BENT AND ATICO'S HAIR AND BEAUTY

694 Leigh–Tyldesley–Atherton–Leigh

A SUNNY AFTERNOON IN JULY, and at least 3,000 people are complying readily, joyfully, even at moments ecstatically, with an injunction posted around their town by its governing authority. And this, not in North Korea, but in the metropolitan borough of Wigan, which has put up posters and banners all through the town instructing its people: 'Believe in Leigh'. Yet believing in Leigh can't always have been easy. To begin with, there wasn't a lot of Leigh to believe in. This was a parish made up of six communities, most dominated by an appropriate family: Pennington, just south of today's town centre, with its de Penningtons; Westleigh, to the west, with its de Westleighs; Astley (or East Leigh), with its de Astleys to the east and Bedford with its de Bedfords to the south-east; together with, a little more distant, Tyldesley-with-Shakerley with its de Tyldesleys and its de Shakerleys, and Atherton with its de Athertons. Leigh was a mere cluster of houses then, along the packhorse road from Bolton to Saint Helens.

Yet when the main components came together to form a single community it was humble Leigh that was given the name that now covers them all. The sense of Leigh as a place to believe in is clear enough when you come to what was once the market place and the home of its councils, Town Hall Square. On the northern side is the church of St Mary by the celebrated Lancashire architects Paley and Austin, completed in 1873 and replacing a medieval building deemed no longer safe. Across the square on the southern side is Leigh Town Hall, built in the first decade of the nineteenth century by an even more local architect, James Caldwell Prestwich, a building that modestly but firmly expressed the local conviction that this Leigh was an independent town that would shape its own fortunes.

Yet here, as in Milnsbridge across the Pennines, one gets the sense of a town that as time went on had its essential purpose wrenched out of it. This is a mining town where coal is no longer dug, a mill town where long ago the machines fell silent. They will tell you in Leigh that the spinning jenny was invented not by Richard Arkwright, the Preston barber who is usually given the credit, but by a son of Leigh called Thomas Highs.

He thought it up, where Arkwright merely exploited it. As the market changed, Leigh moved from the manufacture of fustian to silk, and when that was overtaken, to cotton. Later came new manufacturing industries, some of which survive.

As you walk from Town Hall Square to the main shopping centre there are signs of a dedicated and no doubt expensive effort to recreate Leigh for the late twentieth century and beyond. That process is far from complete. The bus station, so notices at its entrance proclaim, is getting a facelift: 'work has started to deliver a better passenger experience.' Bradshawgate remains the main shopping experience, bright and busy and cheerful on a sunny Saturday morning, though hardly exuding affluence. Poundland looks full to bursting. The Spinning Gate Centre, which turns off the street, helps to confirm Leigh's shopping status. It is one of those half-way towns which doesn't run to a Debenhams or a House of Fraser but contents itself with a Peacocks.

Beyond the precinct, cheeringly, is a proper Lancashire market. You walk through an open-air version into a covered one, where encouraging queues have formed at Arthur's Best Value Cakes and Biscuits, sandwiched between the well-stacked stalls of Matthews' cooked meats and Des West and Sons, fresh fruit and veg, with Hotchix, which goes in for eggs and pies and cooked meats and near eponymous hot chicken, a bun's throw away. Press on, and you come to a sizeable Tesco. There's a Lidl stationed at a challenging distance nearby, and a Cineworld, and across the great open space beyond, a ghost of old Leigh, a solemn reminder of why the town came into being, in the distinctive shape of a former mill.

For the young, the most potent lure, to judge by the twittering crowds swinging their acquisitive handbags at the relevant stand at the Saturday morning bus station, is the Trafford Centre, in the district of Dumplington west of Manchester, taken over in 2011 by a group called Intu Properties, owners also of such out of town giants as Merry Hill in the West Midlands, the Metro Centre on Tyneside and Cribbs Causeway near Bristol, whose buying price of £1.65 billion for Trafford made this the biggest single property acquisition ever recorded in Britain. A 126 bus can sweep you there in just in half an hour. But here I must pause my surveillance of Leigh, as it's time to begin today's journey.

*****

Ian Nairn complained that the outskirts of every town were increasingly beginning to look like the outskirts of everywhere else, but in Leigh you notice a difference in the prevalent building material, red brick. Even strong men might flinch from the rampant redbrickness of the church of St Thomas in Chapel Street. Towards Astley, the town begins to abate. And here there is a reminder of what this tract of England was once about: a pit head wheel, gaunt and severe, silhouetted against the grey sky. It's twenty minutes or so from Leigh to the centre of the township of Tyldesley, where the bus puts me down at a strikingly unprepossessing spot. Here, close to the Mort Arms and the Black Horse pub, is the old town hall, now shabby and looking unloved in its role as an office of Wigan children's services. Much around it is drab. Half past three on a Saturday afternoon, and where are the people of Tyldesley? A ceaseless procession of vehicles crawls westward along Elliott Street, the main street, built on the height of the ridge where the present township began.

The orginal Tyldesley was only vestigially the Tyldesley now served by the 694 bus. Today's version is largely the legacy of a later lord of the manor called Johnson, from Bolton, who perhaps set on softening the place's old reputation, gave it a name that by Lancashire standards might seem to verge on the twee: Tildsley Banks. This swiftly became in local parlance Tildsley Bongs, and even today the place is often talked of simply as 'Bongs'.

As the disconsolate town hall suggests, it isn't today the kind of place that Johnson must have envisaged. Many of the shops on Elliott Street are shuttered. Where they're open, they mostly offer one of just three allurements: bargains, betting or booze. There is work under way to refurbish the old market square in front of Tyldesley Top Chapel, once the treasured property of the Methodist sect known as the Countess of Huntingdon's Connexion, but even this is unlikely to give the place any real sense of occasion. The spruced-up drinking fountain presented to the town by John Buckley helps, though it would not give me a drink, but too many of the buildings on the square are mean and flavourless.

Turn northwards down the hill into parallel Shuttle Street, a kind of other half to Elliott Street on the town's one-way system, and you may think you've found the principal sucker. Here is Morrisons, its car park well attended, with posters above the pavement signalling the presence of Dr Oetker's pizzas, half-price, and litres of Pimm's at a mere £12 each. Then turn south down the matching hill from Elliott Street and you come to a site which its progenitors hope may help resurrect Tyldesley.

Along what was once the line of the Wigan–Manchester railway, constructed, because the collieries clamoured for it, in the 1860s, but closed as the collieries packed up a century later, they are building a guided busway designed to link the township directly with Leigh and by extension south-east to Salford and Manchester. I stop for a drink at the

nearby Railway Inn and ask what local people make of it. The landlady
replies guardedly that there are rather mixed feelings. A man with a pint
of lager says much more forcibly that he, and others he's talked to, think it
was probably a complete waste of public money, to be honest.

The guided buses will take their passengers close to one of Tyldesley's
undoubted assets: Astley Street park. 'Be alive!' Wigan Council, that great
deviser of inspirational exhortations, proclaims at the gate, alongside
another notice that says: 'this area is being monitored for antisocial
behaviour.' A further notice beyond the gates calls it a traditional Victorian
park, though as yet another notice has to confess it's less traditional now.
The bandstand, where once brass bands would have entertained somnolent
middle-aged couples in deckchairs after their Sunday dinners, has gone; the
bowling green too, where once men in caps would have been demonstrating
skills superior to those of their counterparts down south by playing crown
bowls rather than the flat surface kind, has had to make way for a football
kickabout space, while the smack of ball on racquet no longer sounds on the
tennis courts, now superseded by a 'multi-purpose games area'.

For rainier days, the park has been equipped with seats under metal
covers, but persons unknown have decorated them with scrawls and
squiggles and items of information for the visiting public: 'Ethan', one
asserts, 'is a bald bastard'; read on, and you'll find that isn't the only thing
Ethan is, allegedly.

At the top of the hill you reach the final segment of Elliott Street where
you come at last to the church of St George by Sir Robert Smirke, 1821–4.
Here, across a side street from a pleasingly handsome church school, one
may read the gravestones of some old Tyldesley families, and fall, in my
case, to musing what they'd have made of the township as it is now. Joseph
Quin, for instance, and Elizabeth, his wife; Thomas (a cotton spinner, I see
from the census returns, who later became a grocer) and Alice Smith; Peter
and Elizabeth Smith; Jacob (who moved from the cotton industry to be a
council labourer) and Esther Horridge; William and Jane Brobbin. Surely
they would mourn the loss of its former self-contained dignity?

The census material of 1881 and 1891 gives some flavour of the place
they knew. People wanted to come to Tyldesley, because Tyldesley offered
work. Some 9 per cent of residents in its core districts were Irish born; add
in the notably numerous children born in the township to Irish parents,
particularly in Clegg Street, James Street and Charles Street, and you get
the sense of a Little Ireland. Next to the Irish in numbers came the Welsh,
though the biggest contributors to the influx between the two census
stocktakes were Cheshire and Staffordshire. Some had come to work in the

cotton trade, but far more were employed in the pits. The result was a rise of almost 30 per cent in the population in the space of a decade.

Yet it's easy to romanticize the conditions of life in a place like this as they were, as against the way they are now. The *Victoria County History* of 1907 was unimpressed: 'the aspect of the township is eminently characteristic of an industrial district whose natural features have been almost entirely swept away to give place to factories, iron foundries, and collieries. Except from an industrial point of view this treeless district presents a most uninteresting landscape to the traveller.' And these gravestones tell a significant story. Thomas and Alice Smith lost a daughter, Mary, at seven months. 'We cannot, Lord, thy purpose see,' they reflected, 'But all is well that's done by Thee.' Peter Smith, having wed Elizabeth, died at twenty-three; his sorrowing widow died nine years later at thirty. The Horridges lived into their seventies, but lost sons at four and eleven months; the Brobbins had three sons who failed to reach their first birthdays. William himself was dead at twenty-seven in 1880. It isn't clear what happened to Jane. Deeper into the churchyard, too, there are graves of some of the twenty-five men and boys (the youngest eleven) who died two weeks before Christmas in 1858 when firedamp set off an explosion at Tyldesley Yew Tree Colliery.

*****

From here the 694 bus heads for Atherton, though first it's required to make a brief excursion to Tyldesley's old partner, the mining and nail-making village of Shakerley. Where Tyldesley is familiarly 'Bongs'. Atherton, north-westwards up a steep hill, is still sometimes 'Bent': short for Chowbent, which was once the established name for a chunk of what is now commonly known as Atherton.

It's clear as the 694 bus pulls into the centre that Atherton is less disconsolate than its neighbour. The main street has a few names most of the land is used to – Greggs and Boots are here, along with Bargain Booze and Pound Bargains – but shutters proliferate. No doubt its shopping street has surrendered its former shoppers to Tesco as Tyldesley's has to Morrisons. Yet the entry into this township gives you that sense of having arrived that Tyldesley's lacks. This has something to do with a succession of churches: on the way up the hill, the Catholic church of the Sacred Heart; Anglican St Anne's, like Leigh parish church, by Paley and Austin; the Church of the Nazarene; and at what constitutes a kind of gateway to Atherton proper, a 1980s Baptist church which serves to prepare the way for the best of the lot: the church of St John the Baptist by Paley and Austin, 1879. They had to shoehorn it into a limited site where lesser churches had stood before, yet these architects created the powerful, though delusional, aura of a church that was once the ancient heart of the town. It seems to be saying not just, as all churches want to do, God matters, but also, just one breath behind: Atherton matters.

Even so, the churches here are outnumbered by the pubs. I note, no great distance away from St John the Baptist, the Last Orders; the Jolly Nailor (not Sailor: this was a nail-making town); the Red Lion; the Atherton Arms; the Pendle Witch; the Punchbowl; the Mountain Dew; the Conservative Club – like so many Conservative clubs, you don't need to be a Tory to drink here; Old Isaac's, which proclaims itself a 'pound pub'; and at the further end of the main street, Market Street, the Letters End, capping the street. Some at least must be survivors of Chowbent days.

You wouldn't run coach trips to twenty-first-century Atherton. Yet again, I mustn't romanticize. Was life better, richer, more rounded when the people of Atherton walked early each morning – this being Lancashire, perhaps in their clogs – to their often insalubrious, sometimes dangerous workplaces? Such industrial sights as remain give the place atmosphere. Ena Mill, from 1908, has been saved and now houses a shopping outlet. But in 1907, the *Victoria County History* was no more impressed with Atherton than it was with Tyldesley: 'the centre', it said, 'of a district of collieries, cotton-mills, and iron-works, which cover the surface of the country with their inartistic buildings and surroundings, and are linked together by the equally unlovely dwellings of the people.' And the *Victoria History* didn't involve itself with figures for life expectancy.

*****

South of the Spinning Gate Centre in Leigh, and the Spinning Jenny at the edge of the bus station, and a modern town centre relief road called Spinning Jenny Way, there's a bridge that crosses the Leeds–Liverpool Canal, one of the keys to the town's former industrial success, especially when the link was cut to the Bridgewater Canal, which came here in 1795. Here you immediately get the sense of a seminal shift in the town's priorities. Once this place was all about work: it had to be, not only because work made its money but also in the sense that its labour force (predominantly men though women too in the mills) was at work for so much of the time. Until the 1850s even Saturday afternoons had to be worked; apart from four annual day holidays, the one leisure day was Sunday. Once the traffic on the canal belonged to the world of work. Today it belongs to the world of leisure.

It's Sunday morning. Fishermen, heads bowed over the water, line the banks by the bridge. The *Rum and Sass* from Lymm and *The Great*

Escape from Slimbridge glide slowly past; joggers and the odd unashamed shambler share the towpath with walkers plus or minus dogs, frequently interrupted by cyclists ringing their bells. There are still here and there industrial buildings proclaiming a continuing manufacturing life, and one warehouse by the canal has been successfully reborn as a pub called the Waterside. There is a country park nearby called Pennington Flash, with a lake round which you can sit watching the waterbirds, a fortuitous consequence of the subsidence which the mines created.

But the crowds this afternoon aren't heading for Pennington Flash. They're making for the ground of town's rugby league club, Leigh Centurions. Rugby league was born out of a clash of classes and cultures. Leigh, along with Tyldesley, had been members of the Rugby Football Union which came into being in 1871. But the game in the North always differed a lot from the game in the South. As its name implied, rugby had begun at a public school. In the South, it was largely a middle-class game, and that rankled in the North, where it belonged to the working classes.

To an extent that is hard to understand now, there were similar cleavages in two other great popular sports. In cricket, the amateurs, known as 'gentlemen', belonged to a different breed from the 'players', who took money for what they did, and the game was always insistent that this be remembered. On some grounds they had separate dressing rooms and entered the field through separate gates. At one time the gentlemen's names on the scorecard were prefaced by Mister or suffixed by Esquire; thereafter, the amateurs were given initials, with the players restricted to surnames. In one of the first matches that the England off-spinner Fred Titmus played for traditionalist Middlesex, it was thought necessary to broadcast over the loudspeakers a correction to the printed scorecard: 'FJ Titmus should read, Titmus, FJ'.

The Association game too was initially run by a Football Association dominated by the South and by the boss class, with cup finals normally won by southern teams, often products of public schools such as Eton and Charterhouse. The North, and particularly Lancashire, home of the working-class game, augmented by the Midlands, became sick of the Association's dominance and its haughty refusal, until 1885, to countenance the paying of players. In 1888 they seceded to form a football league, made up of twelve clubs wedded to professionalism, six each from the North and the Midlands, none from the South.

Rugby league began the same way. A meeting at the George Hotel in Huddersfield in August 1895 launched the Northern Rugby Football Union, which later became the Northern Rugby League. The union recoiled from the league almost as if it were an infectious disease. Anyone taking money was banned from the union game. Increasingly the league game took a different form from the union's. They sought to speed it up, make it more adventurous and so more likely to bring in (paying) spectators. They played thirteen a side – same number of backs, two fewer forwards. Above all, they got rid of the protracted rucks and mauls that in union followed a tackle by instituting a system called play-the-ball, where the tackled player simply heeled the ball back to a teammate. For true union addicts these rough scrummages are the joy of the game; they stir the crowd's emotions in much the same way as the crowd's emotions are stirred in boxing or wrestling. Non-believers tend to find them tedious. And there's clearly a draw for spectators in a game where on one estimate the ball is in play for fifty minutes out of the regulation eighty rather than thirty-five as in union. It's this game they are playing this afternoon at the home of Leigh Centurions, Leigh Sports Village.

At this point Leigh are enjoying their best season in their 120-year history. To date, they have only lost once, and have even vanquished two Super League sides in the challenge cup competition. They're in the top spot in the game's second division, the Kingstone Press Championship. They also achieved that last season. But that didn't then get them promotion to play alongside such great names as Wigan, St Helens, Leeds and Warrington in the Super League. That's because after the 2006–7 season the league authorities had abandoned the standard old-fashioned regime of promotion and relegation in favour of a licensing system, which also took into account the crowds clubs attracted and the size and condition of their stadiums. In other words, you needed to be well off to go up.

The chief victims of this change were this afternoon's visitors, Featherstone Rovers, from a mining town near Wakefield in Yorkshire that has never had much and has now lost its mines. Despite that, their club was capable in the past of humbling the greatest teams in the game and three times winning the Challenge Cup. Though they repeatedly topped the lower division, they remained there because of licensing. But now the system has changed and the top four clubs in the championship can contend for promotion. Leigh this afternoon are already assured of getting a place. What they now want to do is to finish way ahead of all other contenders.

Rugby league, once shunned by union for paying its players, has become union's poor relation. In 1995 the union lifted its ban on payment and went on to become big business. The league game, which had once been able to lure star players from union, now found the traffic running the other way. Soon England's international ranks were swelled by converts from league. League had always been heavily based in areas, such as Featherstone, where money was scarce, and it seemed at one time as though the game might be doomed. But a saviour appeared in the form of the media tycoon Rupert Murdoch. His people thought the game looked so great on television that they could make something out of it.

But Murdoch money comes at a price. The game was required to reshape itself. Till now a game for a winter Saturday afternoon, it would have to shift to the summer. Clubs like Leeds and Wigan would have to adopt American-style names: Leeds became Leeds Rhinos; Wigan became the Warriors; Leigh, the Centurions.

It's a sign of how precarious the finances of rugby league clubs remain that when the team scores today, an announcer reads out not just the name of the scorer but his sponsor's name too. This happens after seven minutes as Leigh move into the lead with a try from a conspicuous local hero: a substantial prop forward from Tonga, seventeen stone of mighty muscle and bulk under a supercharged hayrick of hair, called Fuifui Moimoi. This is duly announced as a try by 'Fuifui Moimoi, sponsored by Atico's Hair and Beauty', converted by 'Martin Ridyard, sponsored by Integrated Control Systems Ltd'. (The shirts of the referee and his touch judges, as if to confirm everything that crowds have ever suspected about match officials, carry the legend Specsavers.)

The celebrations have hardly died when the game turns against them and Featherstone storm, deservedly, into the lead. But the crowd seem unconcerned. They know that their side is too good to lose. And sure enough, their scrum half, Ryan-Brierley-sponsored-by-R.-Logistics-Services-Ltd, has very soon taken two more tries off Featherstone and put them into a half-time lead of 22 points to 12.

Rugby league teams give intermissions to some of their older players and bring them back after a rest, and Leigh's cherished front row haystack – born September 1979, it says in the programme, so he is thirty-five – has been off the field for much of this opening half. But now he's back, and the second half begins with what's undoubtedly the most popular event that could possibly happen here: a second try by Moimoi-sponsored-by-Atico's-Hair-and-Beauty, and then in no time at all, his third of the game, a wondrous example of pure strength and fearless determination. Most people at some time in life have come across the ancient speculation about what to expect if an irresistible force meets an immovable object. Moimoi is the answer to that. When he's around, there is no such thing as an immovable object. What kind of so-called immovable object, whether mustered by Featherstone Rovers or even, one begins to suspect, by the

Royal Armoured Corps, could possibly stand in the way? Soon he is
trotting back to the stand again amid huge adulation, leaving Brierley and
R.-Logistics Services Ltd to match him with their own third try.

At about which point I have to abandon my spectator experience,
hurry away from Leigh's ecstatic Sports Village and head back to
London. As I leave they are 44–12 ahead and could very well be heading
for a victory at the end of the game by, let us say, 52 points to 18. But
the challenge that Wigan Council has pasted up all round the town has
already been triumphantly met. Believe in Leigh? How after this could
anyone do otherwise? Though it has to be said that when in the round
of play-offs the top four teams in the lower division took on the bottom
four in the premiership, all of them failed; Leigh, though so vehemently
believed in, finished last.

9
THUS FAR, AND NO FURTHER

94 Carlisle–Crosby-on-Eden

ALMOST HALF-WAY THROUGH THIS UNDERTAKING, things are starting to
come unstuck. Bus routes that looked firmly established when I began
have been dropping away so fast that any day now I expect to find a
94 dead in a ditch. The 94 out of Nelson, Lancashire, was one casualty,
which is how I came to be rerouted to Leigh. And now my journey to
Brampton, Cumbria, a place which Nikolaus Pevsner, whose acquaintance
with English villages has rarely been equalled, found 'uncommonly
attractive', has been struck out as well. Not long before I was due to
go there, the behemoth bus provider Stagecoach ruthlessly chopped its
route 94 from Carlisle through Linstock, Crosby-on-Eden. Laversdale,
Irthington and Ruleholme (Golden Fleece), to Brampton, Market Place,
and sometimes even to Hallbankgate, down to Carlisle to Crosby only,
one bus a day, just before nine in the morning.

All of this has been part of a general amputation of services throughout
Cumbria, leaving some communities with no buses at all. Crosby can think

itself favoured in still having this curious remnant. This is not, as I said at the start, a book about buses, but a book about the places where buses take you; or in some cases, don't. Yet the continuing decline of the rural bus seems to me very much a part of any picture of Britain in the early years of the twenty-first century, and how it came to be as it is.

Carlisle, once county town of Cumberland and now, since the merger with Westmorland in 1974, the capital of Cumbria, where my diminished journey begins, is a place about which I have mixed feelings. The responsibility for that lies with my great topographer hero Ian Nairn. In *Outrage*, that condemnation of the dreary, increasingly uniform world we were now creating, which made his name (he was twenty-four), he famously complained of a process where the outer stretches of one town were becoming indistinguishable from those of most others. That he chose Carlisle and Southampton as his examples was hard on Carlisle (as on Southampton) since most towns of any great size were becoming equally blighted. Then in 1972 he made a film for BBC television in which he travelled on the celebrated railway from Leeds to Carlisle, breaking his journey at places such as Skipton, Settle, Dent and Appleby, whose rich local character delighted him. And then he came to Carlisle, where he stood by a railing in the market place and despaired of what he saw: a place that had lost its identity, that was being destroyed by traffic, that was cluttered with clumsy street furniture and prissy flowerbeds.

Yet on this visit I take to Carlisle. There's a pleasing sweep in the main shopping street from the market place through to the Citadel, especially when the sun is shining as enthusiastically as it is this morning, and the crowds are flowing across the market place to the shops and cafés in a way that would not have been possible when the traffic was still in command. Two years after Nairn's programme, Carlisle got its ring road; the market place and the street beyond were pedestrianized in 1989, six years after his death.

The city's principal buildings, as celebrated and enumerated in a remarkable guide to the county by William Pinnock almost 200 years ago, give it a real sense of occasion. There's the uncompromising castle, built by William Rufus when he drove the Scots out of Cumberland, improved by Henry I to deter attempts to retake it, chosen as a suitable stronghold to keep Mary Queen of Scots out of Scotland and captured by Jacobites in their doomed adventure of 1745. Then the Citadel, the intimidatingly solid sequence of towers commanding access to the southern city gate, built by Henry VIII against a feared retaliation by Catholic nations after his defiance of Rome.

Both buildings are powerful reminders that for centuries this was a place that lived on the edge, where even times of peace were full of apprehension. That may have persisted even after open hostilities ceased. Another of Pinnock's attractions, the eighteenth-century town hall, endearingly simple and unostentatious, stands at the head of the market place by the corner of English Street. Pinnock also salutes the cathedral (though regretting that it never fully recovered from what was done to it during the Civil War), to which I would add William Tite's Citadel railway station, built in 1847 as a general station, equipped to accommodate seven railway providers, some of which had till then clung on to their own scattered stations – not a match for the glory of Huddersfield, or for the joy of somewhere like Tynemouth station of 1882, with its riot of glass and filigree ironwork, but nonetheless grandly and Gothically imposing.

The city at night, with its busy bars and restaurants, not all with the chain names you find everywhere, is far livelier than I'd remembered from some dull evening long ago. And ranging out from the centre, substantial, serious streets of the 1820s and 1830s with names – Lonsdale, Lowther, Howard – that evoke the days of aristocratic dominance, sometimes benign, sometimes reprehensible. I wouldn't quite say that those who love cities would be 'gratified even to satiety' (as Pinnock puts it), but what he would call 'this vicinity' seems pleasant to wander in.

I came across Pinnock while plotting my doomed journey from Carlisle to Brampton. Born in 1782, so approaching forty when he came to anatomize the county of Cumberland, Pinnock was a writer and publisher, famous enough for Maggie Tulliver to speak disparagingly of his schoolbooks in George Eliot's *The Mill on the Floss*; also a manufacturer and salesman of musical instruments, and a marketer of works to be played on or sung to them: *The Musical Moralist*, for instance, containing a choice collection of songs and hymns, or *New and Admired Glees*. But above all he was a writer of catechisms, the question and answer exercises which children were required to learn by heart.

Some of Pinnock's catechisms – he published more than eighty – were concerned with religious belief, or the requirements of morality and duty to one's parents. But many weren't. Among the subjects he covered were algebra, chemistry, chronology, heraldry, ichthyology, ornithology and the use of globes. And even when it came to writing a guidebook, he fell naturally into the rhythms of catechism. In *The History and Topography of Cumberland with Biographical Sketches &c & c.*, published in 1822, he begins with a preface that foams as lavishly as the Cumbrian waterfalls and torrents:

To the admirer of Nature in her boldest dress, the rugged rocks, the aspiring mountains, the roaring torrents, and the wide-spreading dreary heaths of Cumberland, will afford scenes of the deepest interest; while the beautiful lakes, fertile vallies [*sic*] and lovely woodlands, with which some parts of the county are adorned, will afford high gratification to him who delights to view her milder and more simple features.

Thereafter, though, apart from the odd instruction ('proceed with your enumeration'; 'proceed with your description') it is all invigilation. The Romans used to ask two kinds of question: those expecting the answer 'yes' – prefaced with *nonne* – and those expecting a no, which opened with *num*. Pinnock's your man for the *nonne* question. 'Is there not a remarkable monument of antiquity here?' 'Are there not some anecdotes relating to a former lord of this castle?' 'Are there not some interesting objects near Egremont?' I suspect any child answering 'no' to such questions would have been sent to bed with no supper.

What Pinnock likes most of all is the stately home of some stately person. Armathwaite Castle, for instance, the seat of H. Milbourne, Esq., where the surrounding scenery is 'highly beautiful and romantic', with the river 'spreading itself here into a broad and tranquil expanse like a lake', until at some distance it assumes a different character, and 'rushing down a cataract, pours with impetuous fury over the crag which opposes its progress'.

*****

Just before nine in the morning, Carlisle bus station, and the 94 arrives to pick up its solitary passenger. The journey to Crosby lasts a mere fourteen minutes, but it starts very pleasingly: hurrying on past Debenhams to open up a fine view of the glowering castle, crossing the River Eden, passing a pretty cricket ground, and then choosing a road that skirts a park that runs down to the river. At first there's the usual trail of houses, though before long splashes of countryside first interrupt them and then take over. There's a good-looking pub at Whiteclosegate called the Near Boot, apparently because if you were riding out of Carlisle, it was on the side of the road to which your boot would be nearer.

The road surges over the motorway and now there's a working farm and the sun is in charge of the weather and the day feels promising. We come to what the timetable bleakly describes as Linstock, Road End. The real 94s were happy to take you into the village, but this one can't be bothered and skims along the A689 that runs on towards Brampton, Bishop Auckland and

Hartlepool, until it reaches the turn for the Crosbys, the High and the Low. There's not a lot to High Crosby, though what there is looks substantially built and potentially pricey: the most substantial house is now a hotel. And then, just past the church, the bus arrives at a little green, and its solitary passenger leaves it. Though I know it's not up to him to make these decisions, I ask the driver what this new 94 is for, when the last bus of the day back to Carlisle is the one I've just come on, which is due to depart for the city in four minutes' time, it doesn't give the traveller much of a chance to investigate Crosby. He says the bus will return by a different route, so maybe the purpose here is to pick up people who want to shop or catch trains in Carlisle; but then how can they ever get back?

*****

And what has Pinnock to tell us about Crosby-on-Eden? Not very much. Travelling west from Brampton, the catechist puts to his charge one of the catch-all questions he favours from time to time: 'Do we find any thing remarkable as we progress?' To which the respondent can only reply: 'Passing through the village of Crosby, and near that of Linstock, neither possessing any thing remarkable, we arrive at Carlisle, already described.'

Pretty disdainful, that. But I think Mr Pinnock simply got there too early. When he wrote the village off in this disobliging fashion, the present church of St John the Evangelist and the neighbouring national school had yet to be built, and although a local directory published in 1829 listed no fewer than four pubs in the village, perhaps none of them was the Stag, which this morning looks so mellow, warm and inviting. Today this place is delightful. Green Lane, where the bus puts one down, runs down to a gate which leads to the River Eden, where you may find the kind of riverside walk which would make the would-be improvers in Milnsbridge expire from sheer envy. There are one or two houses in Low Crosby that would not seem out of place in High Crosby. But the small new estates that have been tacked on, and even most of the infillings, chime nicely with the general scene, and some of the older cottages near the church and the school are enchanting.

The school, though mostly recent, has managed to incorporate the original national school of 1844, stately and designed for scholarship yet, as the latest edition of Pevsner says, sweet, from which as I arrive a joyous procession of children is tripping out into the sunshine. And the church of St John the Evangelist, alongside the school, is equally pleasing. It's a boldly eccentric concoction, built in 1854 as a replacement for a medieval building. Pevsner even described it as 'very inventive, rather naughty', before evaluating the naughtiness in his scholarly way.

On the far side of the church there's a bench where you may sit and reflect, and behind it gates put up by the local community to honour the local flood manager, Glyn Williams, for his 'tireless efforts'; the work of the Low Crosby Flood Action Group is recognized too. It all seems very tranquil and well behaved in Crosby, though that does not means it is free from the occasional scandal. As recently as 1303, the vicar was placed under an interdict by the bishop, fined four shillings for his offence, and made to promise that he would not be guilty of any further incontinency 'with Maude, a parishioner, or with any other woman'.

It is, sadly, time to leave Crosby, and as I do so, I sense a final inquiry from William Pinnock.

Q *What conclusions might be drawn from an observation of this vicinity? Enumerate them.*

A Very well: first, I think it is lovely. But, second, it could do with a better bus service.

*****

Back home in London, I read that the budget which George Osborne was delivering even while I was making my way back to Carlisle pointed, according to the Office of Budget Responsibility, to real cuts in public services of more than 5 per cent in 2016–7 and 2017–18, more than twice as tough as any cuts seen so far, foreshadowing what they called 'a rollercoaster profile for implied public service spending through the next parliament'. In that context, local buses on the lines of a service established at Langwathby near Penrith may increasingly be the only available way of offsetting the further swingeing cuts that are bound to come, and even in some ways, it has to be said, deserve to come, when one computes the number of buses trundling around carrying only one or two passengers – of which several occur in this book. (And in the case of the 94 Carlisle to Crosby occur no more: this ludicrous service was predictably scrapped within months.)

One last question: how did our author succeed in regaining Carlisle? By walking though lovely country in glorious early spring sunshine to a place called Newby East, where a kindly woman who, hearing her dog barking, came to her cottage door and advised me to make my way to the Haywain pub at Little Corby – unfortunately, it was shut – and so to the Co-op store at Warwick Bridge, from where there is still a half-hourly bus service back to the city. Recommended, providing the weather is anywhere near as good as it was today. But walkers, be warned: you won't get much change out of five miles.

IO
TRANSFORMATIVE TIMES

94 Maryhill–Anniesland–Knightswood

SOMEWHERE JUST EAST OF GRETNA, the northbound train races across the border, which, had 191,969 people voted the other way on 18 September 2014, would have been a more epic moment than it is today, for then we would have been crossing into a different land. As it was, Scotland voted no to independence by a margin of 55 to 45 per cent, thus preserving its buses for inclusion in this book, of which my first starts in a place that I found, to my surprise, described as the 'Venice of Scotland'. More conventional people call it Maryhill, Glasgow, from where a 94 bus runs west to Anniesland and then on to Knightswood, all places involved in the explosion that didn't quite happen in September 2014, and even more in the one that did, in the general election eight months later, when the Scottish National Party took 50 per cent of the vote and all but three of the seats in Scotland.

What Walter Scott called the land of mountain and flood had, it seemed, become the land of Salmond and Sturgeon, leaving the once dominant Labour Party a blood-splattered mess on the pavements of traditionally loyal Glasgow. The swing from Labour to SNP broke every known record, and the increase in the Nationalist vote was highest of all in two of the constituencies that include this route: Glasgow North East (up 43.9 per cent) and Glasgow North (up 41.2 per cent) with Glasgow North West, which takes in Anniesland and Knightswood, close behind (up 39.3 per cent). In electoral terms, this was nothing less than a revolution.

The year 2014 was remarkable too for another explosion that didn't take place: the planned blowing up of a line of Glasgow's high flats, which the city had planned as a celebration of the start of the Commonwealth Games, serving too as a super-sized apology for decades of chronic misjudgements in public housing. 'The skyline of Glasgow', the council had signalled eight years earlier when this repentance took shape, 'is set to be radically transformed, as swatches of high-rise tower blocks make way for thousands of new homes across the city. Glasgow is enjoying a renaissance . . . This is an announcement that looks to the future and we are determined that we will not repeat the mistakes of the past.'

The blocks awaiting execution were part of a group of eight at a place called Red Road, north-east of the city centre, two of which had already gone, in 2012 and 2013. There were thousands of people in Glasgow, though, who were old enough to recall how the building of mighty towers like these had been heralded back in the sixties in much the same self-satisfied terms as animated this new announcement. A wave of protests began, directed not against the decision of Glasgow Housing Association, which now controls the housing stock that used to be the responsibility of the council, to demolish the Red Road blocks – few doubted that this was necessary – but against making it the occasion for a celebratory jamboree. The Association retreated. The Red Road flats would still come down, but without attendant palaver. A first attempt was made in October 2015, but even then two of the doomed blocks survived it.

Red Road had become notorious over the years as a place of noise and disorder that made the lives of its flat dwellers barely tolerable. Blocks now under threat had ended their days as refuges for asylum seekers. That didn't apply on the same scale to the tower blocks along the route of the 94 out of Maryhill. Yet if Glasgow is to achieve this 'radical transformation' of the city's skyline, will these join the reject class too? And – remembering subsequent mourning for old tenement blocks in the Gorbals which might have been saved – a further question arises: would they deserve to?

*****

The bus from the centre of Glasgow puts me down at a big clumping building that calls itself Maryhill Shopping Centre, but in fact might be better described as a mildly augmented Tesco. Since what it confronts across the Maryhill Road is a branch of McDonald's, I take this to be the centre of town. If so, the centre has seeped southward. Up the hill heading out of the town is the heart of the Maryhill that burst into life at the end of the eighteenth century. It began as a little settlement around the canal, known in those days as Drydock. In those early days the place had a reputation for lawlessness, too often – in a hallowed Glasgow tradition – inflamed by drink. It is said that Britain's first temperance society was created here. Then a local grocer called Robert Craig picked it out as a suitable space on which to build a new town. The land belonged to an unsuccessful entrepreneur called Robert Graham, who had married a rich heiress. One or the other (versions differ) said the deal could only go through on one condition: that the town be named after Mrs Graham, whose maiden name had been Mary Hill. The project foundered, but Maryhill now developed as an industrial town, with an iron works, the building of iron barges, and calico printing.

Down the hill, back towards the city, you come to the kind of sandstone tenements which punctuate the townships round here, and in time to the home ground of Partick Thistle FC, best thought of as the top team in Glasgow that isn't Rangers or Celtic. Just off the main road, there's an area called the Butney (probably a corruption of the word Botany, the name of a school in this area), which was once the toughest place in a pretty tough district. As befits a component of Glasgow's 'West End', it has now been cleared away.

*****

The 94 bus sidles up in a street above Tesco, picks up a scatter of bag-laden shoppers, and takes one straightaway into a different world. 'You've come to look at Glasgow's high flats, have you?' it seems to be saying. 'Well, here you are: sate yourself.' Suddenly, high towers surround you. This area was once Wyndford Barracks, which opened in 1869. When the military moved out, Glasgow council got hold of it and built close and high. This was late in the 1960s, the decade when so many of the mistakes were made that the city now deplores, but this sector is nicely done, with towers of a welcome variance of size and shapes – thirteen of the blocks here are between eight and fifteen storeys high, but four reach twenty-two storeys. It is said that tenants from all over Glasgow initially clamoured to live here. This is one of the points on today's journey when one starts to wonder if the prevalent Glasgow self-flagellation goes further than it needs to. But that's the impression they make when you merely look at them. Living there may be a different matter. One Glasgow sociologist, Sean Damer, has picked them out as 'an exemplar of everything going that is wrong with social housing in Britain today'. Unemployment is part of the problem; another is drug dependency.

Why Glasgow built high, and persisted in doing so even when higher authority, right up to Whitehall, ordered otherwise, is simply explained. Here were some of the worst slums in Europe. In 1917, a year before Lloyd George pledged, after the armistice, to create a land fit for heroes to live in, approximately 38 per cent of Glaswegians lived three or four people to a room; the equivalent for English cities was just over 2 per cent. Nearly thirty years, and one further war, later, grotesque overcrowding, often in buildings long since condemned as unfit for occupation, persisted: around 700,000 people lived on 18,000 acres, with one-seventh of Scotland's population compressed into three square miles of central Glasgow.

Then in 1961 a man took charge for whom the eradication of desperately overcrowded, ill-maintained and dangerous housing amounted to a crusade. David Gibson was convener (in English terms, chairman) of the city's housing committee. His politics belonged to the years of Red

Clydeside after the First World War. He joined the ILP in his youth and remained in it until 1954, by which time it had almost faded away. There was no place in his calculations for private enterprise. As Carol Craig notes in her instructive book *The Tears that Made the Clyde,* in the middle years of the twentieth century Glasgow had the highest concentration of council tenants in Europe outside the old Soviet bloc.

Theoretically, Gibson had no right to do what he now did. He should have been bound by a policy established in 1957 by the council and the Department for Health for Scotland, which still had charge of housing policy then, that reflected the doctrines preached in the South by the hugely influential planner Patrick Abercrombie. This required the city to build 40,000 houses within its territory but 60,000 on overspill sites outside it. Some in Glasgow detected a sinister motive here. To go along with what was required of them by their political masters in London and Edinburgh, where the Scottish Office was involved, would mean letting the city's population drop and sacrificing desperately needed revenue to authorities outside the city boundary, while the city's own expansion would be blocked by the banning of building within the Green Belt. Gibson resolved to ignore the guidelines. In this endeavour he had a reliable and ruthless accomplice in a Yorkshireman, Lewis Cross, an engineer in the council's architectural and planning department whom Gibson elevated to the role of Housing Progress Officer. Gibson was the strategist, Cross the enforcer, and together they put in hand an extensive programme of high-tower building. In 1962, contracts were let for no fewer than thirty blocks of twenty storeys or more, some like Red Road reaching thirty. Between 1961 and 1968, high flats accounted for three-quarters of all new public housing.

What followed is chronicled by Miles Glendinning and Stefan Muthesius in a formidable book called *Tower Block: Modern Public Housing in England, Scotland, Wales and Northern Ireland.* 'The architectural results of Gibson's 1962 multi-storey revolution', they write, 'were blocks of an unfettered monumentality, unparalleled at that date not only in these islands but in Europe as a whole':

> Around 1965, Glasgow's housing had certainly undergone an extraordinary physical change . . . large areas of the slum belt had been demolished, and developments comprising high and low blocks of flats were in course of erection in their place. But beyond the Comprehensive Development Area zone, there was a startling and awesome sight. Away in the far distance, groups of colossal multi-storey blocks were rising – twenty, twenty-five, thirty or more

storeys high. These were not located in planned redevelopments but were thrown haphazardly on gap sites anywhere in the suburbs: on pockets of waste-ground, corners of golf-courses, redeveloped pre-fab sites. If Manchester had been the 'shock city' of the Industrial Revolution, Glasgow was the new 'shock city' of the Modern housing revolution. Nowhere else, at such an early date, were so many large, high blocks completed or under construction at once.

They rate Gibson as 'arguably the most remarkable of Western Europe's post-war municipal housing leaders'. He and Cross were not alone in this enterprise. An ebullient architect called Sam Bunton, working with the city's powerful Direct Labour Organization, was inciting and creating high building too. Neither enterprise consulted the intended beneficiaries: the urgency was too great for that. As Ian Jack wrote at about the time Red Road was due come down, 'there was, shall we say, very little agency in Glasgow at that time. Its citizens had things done to them and for them . . . "If you want to drain the swamp, you don't consult the frogs" was a saying among planners at the time.' Few at this point (though a Glasgow academic called Tom Brennan was a distinguished exception) said what many would argue later: that some of the solid old buildings that were now being torn down could instead have been refurbished, preserving a sense of community and continuity that comprehensive redevelopment, here as elsewhere, was never likely to sustain. The Red Road flats, now destroyed and doomed, were Bunton's expected monument. Yet the legacies of Gibson and Cross were also no longer certain: since 2006, more than a quarter of the high flats so proudly, so flamboyantly, added to Glasgow in the years of their supremacy have already gone, and more are destined to follow them.

Wyndford goes unmentioned on the timetable for this route, as does our next destination, Kelvindale, where the street names suggest aspiration – Dorchester Avenue, Weymouth Avenue, Colchester Drive, Manchester Drive, reflecting a time when English associations were thought to bestow a touch of class on a street; an attitude which seemed to assume an English superiority, which is not the way Scotland tends to think now. And then we turn westward on to one of the great roads out of Glasgow, the Great Western Road, which would bring us in time to the edge of Dumbarton, and then on, if we persisted that long, to Loch Lomond, Crianlarich, Glen Coe, Fort William and ultimately Inverness. But instead, soon after we pass under the railway bridge and enter the main street of Anniesland, we swing away from it, at least for the moment.

Maryhill got its name from Mary Hill, and Glasgow has other districts which take their name from those who created them. Anderston was originally Anderson Town after James Anderson of Stobcross, and Hutchesontown in the Gorbals reflects the influence of the powerful local Hutcheson family of the seventeenth century. Finnieston was named by one of its creators after his family's tutor. Dennistoun took its name not from a man called Dennis but from one called Dennistoun, who began it. One might therefore suppose that Anniesland had started as land that belonged to an Annie, but whatever the true explanation, it isn't that. It is variously ascribed to the term 'annual land' and to a Gaelic word meaning 'destitute'. The Great Western Road is the core of the place.

Anniesland has only one skyscraping tower block, Anniesland Cross, but it's among the most famous in the city. Its twenty-two storeys make it the tallest grade A listed (the Scots equivalent of Grade One listing in England) building in Scotland. It looms up alongside Crow Road ('crow' in this case being a corruption of 'craw', which denotes not birds but cattle) and dwarfs its other neighbour, the hefty sandstone Temple Anniesland Church of 1904–5, which as well as having acquired this Big Brother looks out today on the car park of a lavish Morrisons supermarket. There's an undeniable 'wow' factor about this high block, more so when seen from some angles rather than from others, but it makes an unforgettable landmark everywhere, all the more so because it's so solitary.

Back on Great Western Road the place still retains the feel of an older Anniesland. On either side of the road there's a substantial block of tenements of the kind which always seem to be given the designation Mansions, and that's the case here as well. The better block of the two, in powerful red sandstone, incorporating a mission hall, looks north across the road at what once must have been a matching counterpart, though now a chunk of it has gone (bomb damage perhaps? we're not far from Clydebank, which suffered some of the most terrible raids of the Second World War). The gap has been patched by some sad infilling, as if an otherwise healthy mouth had been invaded by a botched set of false teeth. Just up the road towards Dumbarton are groups of later tenement buildings in the same Glaswegian tradition, dating from 1937–42 and a credit to whoever designed them.

*****

The destination blind says my bus is going on to Knightswood, which the map suggests is a simple matter of pressing on down the Great Western Road. But that's not what it does. Instead it heads off past Anniesland Cross towards Bearsden, beyond which is Milngavie, pronounced, I'm advised,

Mil-guy. Both belong to one of Glasgow's more prosperous territories, but both are outwith, as the Scots say, the city boundary. That's a matter of some resentment in Glasgow, since these suburbs (which essentially is what Bearsden and Milngavie are, though it's not a description they would choose) depend heavily on the city of Glasgow but have their council taxes pocketed by East Dunbartonshire. From here the bus swings away into a territory which in its unspectacular way is an instructive guide to part of the troubled story of the city's housing. This scheme (the Scottish term for what England calls an estate) was created between the world wars, and it gives some indication of how Glasgow might have chosen to house its people, had the money stretched that far.

The buildings in Knightswood could hardly be called distinguished, but they're full of indications of an aspiration to do something better: little frills and decorations on the frontages to make householders think their homes are not just the same as everyone else's, and enough green space in the form of front and back gardens and shared interruptions to hint at the aim of creating a garden suburb. The prime minister, Stanley Baldwin, came to open it, for which service they named a street after him.

These streets, even so, hardly vary from one another, and the place where the 94 reaches its conclusion appears quite arbitrary, no different from anywhere else. 'So where', I ask the driver, 'is the centre of Knightswood?' At first, she finds this question baffling. Then she says, 'Oh, that's down the hill. This is Higher Knightswood. If you want the Tesco, you can take the number 6 bus.' But I don't take the number 6 bus. Instead I walk through even more identical houses until I find, perched on the hillside, a kind of park, but with uncropped grass, making it seem as much meadow as park. The word they use here is 'brae', meaning a steep bank or hillside. It's a glorious late summer afternoon, and a woman leading an uncooperative puppy comes over to say so. The puppy, out for only its second outing, is fascinated by the sights and sounds the brae has to offer: perching and swooping birds, the agitation of trees, clandestine movements among the bushes, every natural and human activity. Such a lovely view from here, the woman says; and indeed it is, looking out over mingled town and country to the hills beyond. She picks some of them out for me: those, she says, are the Kilpatrick Hills, out in Dunbartonshire. Take the car, and fifteen minutes from here you're already in gorgeous country; half an hour, and you've reached Loch Lomond . . .

But also down in the valley there's a stately parade of classic Glaswegian tower blocks, eleven, possibly twelve. Where exactly, I ask, is that? Oh, that's *Lower* Knightswood, she tells me. Up here, we're in *Higher*

Knightswood. She says this with a pride in her own patch which makes it sound like the highest of all possible Knightswoods . . . And as you discover walking back to the Great Western Road, they are indeed part of Lower Knightswood, some specifically ranged along Lincoln Avenue, others clustered nearby: the dreams of Gibson and Cross, made real by Wimpey, their most fecund contractor.

This is one aspect among many of replanned, and now in some ways repented of, Glasgow. The big, largely characterless, socially vacant schemes which were to become a byword for trouble – the inevitable consequence, some asserted, of bringing people who had always been housed in slums on to this newly created territory – belong more to the east of Glasgow than to the west, though Drumchapel, which to some extent shares the reputation of places like Easterhouse, Billy Connolly's 'desert wi windaes', is close to Knightswood; it is just out of sight from my bench on the brae.

*****

The communities on this 94 route have a settled feel to them, which perhaps enhanced their readiness to invest their futures in votes for independence (Maryhill more decidedly than Anniesland) and in the general election for the SNP rather than a Labour Party seen as dominated by Westminster. The impressive numbers who voted in the referendum and again at the general election make it clear that this seismic change went beyond a mere surge of protest.

From this bench on this brae, you might think that little had changed. I had rather expected a wholesale fluttering of saltires, but not so. Yet it's clear that the independence issue is nowhere near buried. Animosities that boiled up in the independence debate have not abated. Far from it: there are, old Glasgow friends tell me, continuing angers, augmented resentments, disrupted friendships and even families pulled apart. Among nationalists, the cause is sometimes pursued with a kind of religious fervour. A Durham theologian called D.J. Knowles, attending an SNP event at the Glasgow Hydra Arena, found himself in the presence, as he thought, of a counterpart to evangelical Christianity, 'an all-encompassing movement with faith at its core'.

No visitor for a day can be sure of the reasons when expert minds in Scotland have come up with such varied explanations. A crucial shift in the balance in that dual identity, Scottish/British, that the Scots have always lived with? The decay of institutions and practices that once upheld established authority and bound Scots, if often unthinkingly, to big brother England? Among these one might list the decline in established religion. The 2011 census showed that for the first time those saying they had no religion (1.9 million) outnumbered those who said they belonged to the Church of Scotland (1.7 million). There was also a perceptible fading of instinctive Labour support in the city's Roman Catholic communities. The elimination of so much of the country's industry in the latter part of the twentieth century, with grievous consequences for jobs, afflicting not only old bastions like shipbuilding on the Upper Clyde but relatively new rescue projects like Linwood and Ravenscraig, with governments in London unwilling or unable to save them – or even willing the process on – was a substantial destabilizing factor too.

All this must have undermined the old assumption that Scotland had a deep practical need of the Union. Increasing resentment of domination by a London that consistently failed to deliver was fuelled by disgust at the way the financial crisis of 2008 was dealt with and at Labour's apparent acceptance of an austerity regime that could only compound Scotland's difficulties. Why, people increasingly asked, is Scotland so often required to march to a distant drum?

All of these interpretations have circulated. And yet when you look at the figures, there is also the sense of another hidden but potent ingredient that would locate these events as a process of evolution, not revolution. They may be the culmination of a trend in which in political terms Scotland and England have drifted further and further apart. An element in that may be the peculiar phenomenon of seventy years without Britain being involved in a major war. It has long been accepted that the threat to a nation that comes with a war tends to bind its people together. In 1945, people across the whole kingdom, rejecting their greatest war hero, put into office a party that pledged to make a complete break with the way things were done before, to guarantee that Britain would never go back to the 1930s – and was believed.

What seems most striking is the widening discrepancy that developed thereafter between voting in England and voting in Scotland. In 1951, and again in 1955, the Conservatives/Unionists take a bigger share of the vote in Scotland than in England. In 1964, Scotland wants Labour, England (though only just) prefers the Conservatives, but it's Scotland that gets what it wants. But in four successive contests from 1979 to 1992, a Scotland which votes for a Labour government gets the Conservative government England prefers. That happens again in 2005 and 2010, by which time the Conservatives have so far alienated the Scots that their share of the vote is derisory. By now, Alex Salmond is offering what looks like a sure-fire remedy. The obvious way to break with the domination of a party that so few Scots want is to have a political system where the will of Scotland can be guaranteed to prevail. A year on, the Brexit referendum would expose this cleavage even more brutally, as Scotland voted to stay within Europe, while most of England voted to leave.

*****

So many unresolved questions . . . There's another question, though, that I've brought to Maryhill. Why should anyone have classed it as the Venice of Scotland? I found this exuberant concept in a blog by Ian Mitchell on a website called *Pat's Guide to Glasgow West End*. 'Anyone with a bit of knowledge of Maryhill', he explains, 'will probably be aware that I am suggesting that its position astride the nub of Central Scotland's canal system, where the Forth and Clyde joins the route to Port Dundas in Glasgow, renders Maryhill the Scottish Venice.' And then there's the aqueduct that carries the canal over the River Kelvin. 'The Kelvin Aqueduct', Mitchell says, 'was a wonder of the world, the mightiest built since Roman times, and tourists flocked to see it, including the crowned heads of Europe.'

It only takes a couple of minutes to walk from the Tesco to the canal. I have to say there's no immediate sense that any Venetian reaching this spot would from then on regard his city as the Maryhill of the Veneto. There's a notable absence of vaporetti. And there's no way of telling which way to walk to discover this wondrous aqueduct. But at least at the end of the day, swept back on the 94 past Anniesland Mansions and the couthie street names of Kelvindale and the high rise complex at Wyndford into early evening Maryhill, I manage to find it. At the top of the town close to the railway station I come to a chain of locks, created by Robert Whitworth between 1787 and 1790. And, as one always hopes, there's a boat going through: the *Hannah* from Cramond, just this side of Edinburgh. There's a tower block close by that seems to have escaped from the general cluster, and someone is watching the *Hannah*'s progress from a fifteenth-floor window.

And here at last is a signpost pointing the route down to the River Kelvin, above which Whitworth's aqueduct rises. It isn't, I have to say, quite the excitement Ian Mitchell suggests; it isn't really a match for the Dundas Aqueduct near Limpley Stoke, which I'll see later on (chapter 20). But maybe when boats are crossing high up on the canal you can still catch a hint of the tingle factor which caused one early visitor to term it 'one of the most stupendous works of its kind in the world', or moved another, in 1804, to wonder at the spectacle of 'square-rigged vessels . . . navigating at a height of seventy feet above the level of the spectators'.

And certainly worth what it hasn't yet got: a big boastful signpost somewhere in the centre of town.

II

OVER THE HILLS AND FAR AWAY

494 Tobermory–Dervaig–Calgary

NORTH AGAIN, this time to Oban (change for the Isle of Mull). There's a bus you can catch at Anniesland that will take you there, but it isn't a 94, and although, surprisingly, the journey by bus is quicker, I've come here by train. For the first forty miles out of Glasgow, the routes diverge, but thereafter road and rail stick close together through ravishing Highland scenery – mountain, rugged hillside and luxuriant lochs, their waters scintillating on this benevolent morning. From Oban, the mighty ferries of Caledonian MacBrayne will sweep you across the Firth of Lorne, past the gleaming white lighthouse of Eilean Musdile, to the ferry port of Craignure on the Isle of Mull, third largest of Scotland's myriad islands.

There are three regular bus routes on Mull: the 494, the 495, which is sometimes the 95, and the 496, which is sometimes the 96. You might think that three routes on a self-contained island might logically have been numbered 1, 2 and 3, but logic doesn't always prevail in busland. The preliminary number 4, as the driver of my 494 will explain to me, denotes a service subsidized by Argyll and Bute Council. The 95 that takes me from Craignure to Tobermory, capital of the island, is a jolly red double-decker over which West Coast Motors have plastered the legend 'Tobermory Topper' and which fends for itself without any subvention. But the rest of the journeys along this route only persist because Argyll and Bute is prepared to pay for them, and so they are numbered 495. The route from Tobermory to Calgary depends entirely on government largesse. You wouldn't, as the driver assures me, find a commercial organization taking on a route like this one.

In Tobermory, the only settlement of any appreciable size on this island, the accents of Scotland mingle in summer with those of all parts of England and perhaps even more today with those of America. There are something like 350 square miles of Mull, and a coastline that runs to 300 miles, and Tobermory is much the biggest place on it, though there are far fewer people living here now than there used to be. London created it. An imposingly if not exactly catchily named organization called the British Society for Extending the Fisheries and Improving the Sea Coasts of the Kingdom (hereinafter, where necessary, BSEFISCK), based in London but powered by Scots, established it in 1787 as part of a general plan to build some thirty or forty fishing ports. Few ever materialized – and except for Ullapool on the mainland and, for a time, Tobermory here, none ever flourished. In 1801, a mere fourteen years after the port was established, there were more than 8,000 people living on this island. The 1861 census found 7,300. But by 1961, that had fallen to 2,300, and though Mull has picked up since then, at the 2011 census the permanent population, as opposed to that swollen by tourism in the summer, was 2,800.

Today, the fishing has all but faded away and the town is all about tourism. It's a gleefully eye-catching, even eye-wrenching, scene, especially in weather like this, which seems to belong to the Mediterranean more than the Hebrides. A traveller here in 1702, when BSEFISCK had yet to begin operations, said of it: 'Italy itself, with all the assistance of art, can hardly afford anything more beautiful and diverting.' And like the 95 bus, the town is a double-decker. At sea level, it's a crescent of brightly coloured, occasionally garish, buildings. At one end is a sturdy distillery, with tourists queuing up to get in, and the Mull Aquarium ('Europe's first catch and release aquarium') alongside a car park and bus station. Thereafter there's a procession of cafés and restaurants and inns, craft shops and gift shops and one that sells fishing tackle but also books; a church that is still in use and another that's now a café and gallery; an ironmongers that also sells wines and spirits, a chandlers, a little museum, and to round it all off a big Fish Café. Beyond that there's a ferry station: not despatching boats over to Oban, which need the bigger berth at Craignure, but offering passages to Kilchoan on Ardnamurchan. Ardnamurchan Point, a name familiar from shipping forecasts, is the most westerly spot on the British mainland, whatever Cornwall may like to think.

A steep climb above all this brings you to Tobermory's top deck, a Victorian town (two principal streets are named for Victoria and Albert) where there's a church and an arts centre. Victoria came here, and before her, the composer Mendelssohn, which added a further air of romance. There is also the island's wildlife to draw people in: visitors taking to boats are promised basking sharks, minke whales, porpoises and dolphins, and for those on dry land, eagles, owls and hen harriers.

*****

I approach the evening ride on the 494 for Dervaig and Calgary with a tinge of apprehension. I've seen this road across the north of the island on a map. It looks like one of those squiggly lines you sometimes see in TV hospital dramas where machines are plotting the course of some life-or-death crisis.

Before I left London, my friend Doris Ker said she had ridden this route a while ago, and she too had been apprehensive. Before she left, a kindly official had offered what he obviously thought were words of reassurance. 'You may have every confidence,' he said. 'Your driver today is Dougal. He has the MA . . .' Significant pause: then, 'But he is a good driver.' Which he was, she says, and something of a polymath, too, it emerged.

The 494's driver today is a man from Dervaig whose name I will later discover is Pat Geall. Since I'm the only passenger whom Argyll and Bute Council is subsidizing this evening, I get a good chance to talk to him. He comes from Bognor Regis, an English south coast resort which resembles Tobermory hardly at all, and he used to drive buses through Sussex on routes of which much the same could be said. And certainly this moorland landscape – lonely, sometimes severe, with little or no habitation (a stone cottage along the way turns out when we reach it to be an abandoned ruin), but punctuated by lochs – is a vastly different territory from anything one might encounter between Horsham and Pulborough.

I say this road must be tricky – it is classed as 'challenging' for drivers – but Pat drives it five days a week, and says it's fine once you get used to it. You just have to take things steadily, and always be conscious that there's no way of telling what you might be about to meet around the next corner. Like almost all roads on Mull, this one is single track with passing places, but the allocation of passing places is generous, and most people he meets on the road know how the system works. The one potential menace here is drivers of camper vans: not the ones who own the vans they are driving, who are usually courteous and competent, but the ones who have hired them and don't always know which way to move when they meet you. And worst of all, often don't know how to reverse.

We pass, at a decorous speed, Loch Peallacht, Loch Meadhom and Loch Carnain an Amais in a chain known as the Mishnish Lochs, soft, benign and romantic in the evening sunshine; but although the odd signpost mentions Loch Frisa, it does not appear. Ah, but it will, Pat says, in a moment or two; and here indeed is Loch Frisa, stretching blue and languorous into the distance with mountains sealing if off at the end: the most beautiful sight by some distance on what is much the most beautiful route in this whole unlikely odyssey. Pat stops the bus for a moment to let me drink the view in. I just wish I could take it home with me.

But even a bus as laid back as this one has to work to a timetable, and now we are wiggling, wriggling and squiggling our way into Dervaig, the only place of any real consequence in the northern sector of Mull. Like Tobermory, it only really came into existence at the end of the eighteenth century. Before that this territory was classed as part of two parishes, Kilmore and Kilninian. The heart of the place is the street which runs north-west from the Bellachroy Hotel ('the oldest inn on Mull, established 1608', says a noticeboard) through a parade of low white cottages, interrupted by a small shop and post office in what was once the village reading room. This street is a kind of reversal of Glasgow – a defiantly low-rise place, as no doubt common sense dictates in such Hebridean settlements, with their Hebridean weather. Most of the cottages here are single storey or single storey with modest windows peeping out upstairs. Others are unconditionally two storeyed; a three-storey house around here would seem like an impertinence.

The population in 2011 was around 150, yet there seems to be quite a lot going on. The Dervaig Books Group will discuss *The Book Thief* by Marcus Zusak; Michelle's Hatha Yoga Class meets on Thursdays in the village hall; someone is setting up a computer and satellite club; and the village hall will also be hosting, a few days from now, a 'food extravaganza'. Extravaganza isn't a word you'd expect to find in Dervaig. When I walk back from the Bellachroy to my excellent bed and breakfast, the Tigh-na-Mara (the house by the sea), the loudest sound – indeed, almost the only sound – in the village is the rippling burn that bubbles under a bridge.

Below the church – still Kilmore church, as it was before Dervaig began – the road divides. One track goes straight ahead over an ancient bridge that spans Loch Cuin, where anglers ply their patient trade and otters now and then surface, and on towards Calgary; the other is signposted to Salen and Craignure – but with a warning that ice may make it impassable: a reminder that this landscape, so glorious in the September sunshine, may be alarmingly bleak in a few months' time.

At twenty past ten next day, Pat Geall arrives with his 494 and off we all go to Calgary; at least a dozen of us this morning, with a great deal of lively middle-aged chatter. 'Calgary' the 494 says on its destination board and it was refugees from the Highland Clearances here who arrived to form a new settlement in what's now Alberta, Canada, and gave it the name of their old homeland on Mull. We do get people from Canada come in search of their origins, Pat Geall says, and some are very surprised that this Calgary isn't bigger.

This isn't a tourist bus – West Coast Motors runs those as well, some of which have passed through Dervaig this morning. Yet in a sense that is just what it is, since Pat delivers an intermittent commentary pointing out what we might otherwise miss. As we catch a fine view of the sea, he explains that out there are a group that is known as the Small Isles: Rum, Eigg, Muck and Canna. Are they inhabited? Yes, though he isn't quite sure of the numbers. Had the average age of his customers been twenty rather than fifty-plus, there would have been a barrage of information within about forty seconds as passengers summoned up population statistics on their mobile phones. Had that happened, today's busload would have gone home safe in the knowledge that when the 2011 census was taken Eigg had 83 people, Rum 22, Muck 27 and Canna 12.

Now and then we are briefly delayed by some slow-moving vehicle that cannot be overtaken. At one point, there's a man operating a hedge-cutting trolley who signals our driver to stop. 'You seem to have got an oil leak,' he says; Pat says he's noticed that, but thanks him for pointing it out. 'Don't worry,' he assures his cargo, 'even if we break down, we'll get you back!' He has asked for a replacement bus, but this one will take them straight back to Tobermory, which is what most of those riding this 494 are intending to do. They've come for the scenic ride, not for any specific joys of Calgary.

The bus stops briefly at a spot known as Farmhouse: that was the name of a hotel, now gone out of business, though the stop now serves a café and gallery across the road, from where you may make your way through woods to Calgary Beach. It finally comes to rest outside a block of public toilets; some passengers disembark for a moment, but others stay put. Having come nearly 600 miles to get here, I'm not leaving Calgary until I've discovered what it's about.

*****

As someone says in my Dervaig bed and breakfast, Calgary may not be the best beach on Mull, but it's surely good enough for most visitors. The *Guardian*, gathering nominations for the best seaside places to camp, put Calgary at the top: 'the free wild campsite at Calgary in the north-west corner of Mull', a reader wrote, 'is what your tent was made for . . . Pristine white sand edges a crystal-clear bay, with the Treshnish Isles on the horizon. You will share the beach with otters, basking sharks and the odd sea eagle gliding past.' A young backpacker whom he'd brought here the previous night joins Pat's bus back to Tobermory, and he asks how her camping had gone. Otters, basking sharks and sea eagles don't get a mention: she says, with a remembering shudder, that the night was frightfully cold.

On the beach I meet two women who've come here by car from Stirling and we try to adjudge the sands: white at the nearest point, certainly, but beyond it, a kind of golden brown. And just look at the sea! they say. Such an array of colours, blue and turquoise and ultramarine, constantly changing.

They go off to explore the northern headland of Calgary Bay. I choose the southern side, along the main road that leads on down the coast and right round the island until it meets the more eminent road that runs west to the Ross of Mull. Before that, however, it runs out towards a dramatic headland. At first it's a mild affair that takes you past holiday cottages and a bigger holiday house and even a house which appears to have permanent residents, but before long the landscape and seascape are toughening, with rocks and boulders below, and craggy hills overhead conveying a mild sense of menace. The views open out: here clearly defined in the sunshine across the water is the Isle of Coll, thirteen miles long, three wide, where some 200 people live. It's a walk constantly interrupted by cars and camper vans and a great many bicycles – you can collect one at Calgary, while 'e-bicycles' (electric ones) are for hire in the street at Dervaig.

My time, and perhaps my stamina, have run out before I get to the headland, which you reach by a track where the road turns south-east just short of Ensay. It's time to return to Calgary, where there's said to be an ice cream kiosk 'down the beach', optimistically advertised as 'open daily, if sunny, 12 noon to 5 pm'. But I head for the café up the hill, and now the sky clouds over and there's just a minute or two of rain; a little later, it rains enough for people sitting outside the café to come hurrying in, but even then it lasts for less than five minutes before the sun reasserts itself. 'The best week we've had all year,' someone assures me; 'this has been our worst summer for over thirty years.'

Soon Pat will be back with his bus. It's one that only runs if people ask for it, which, at his suggestion, I've done. The arrangement is not the kind of thing that you'd find in the London borough of Sutton, where I live. This bus leaves Calgary just after half past one and goes at first only as far as Dervaig, which suits Pat fine since this means he can take the bus home and have an hour there for his midday meal. I meanwhile have time to look at the church. It's an ancient site, but the church you see now dates only from 1905. It's marked out by its distinctive tapering tower – which is causing trouble: it's disfigured now by algae growing on its limewash, and the church needs to raise a substantial sum to correct it. Inside, the list of ministers runs back to 1673. Appointments have not always been easy, especially since they need to find Gaelic speakers.

The altar, almost ostentatiously simple, is sheltered in an apse which has exuberant stained-glass windows. A Bible lies on the altar, open today at the end of the book of Ecclesiastes and the start of that rampantly unecclesiastical work, the Song of Solomon. 'Thy cheeks are comely with rows of jewels, thy neck with chains of gold,' enthuses the Song, chapter I, verse six, which one can't imagine being read out to a congregation in these chaste Presbyterian surroundings; likewise verse thirteen:

'a bundle of myrrh is my wellbeloved unto me; he shall lie all night betwixt my breasts.' There's a second bible on the desk of the pulpit, and that is open at Jeremiah, chapters six to twelve, which are full of the kind of warnings of the fate that awaits the ungodly that I've always imagined being thundered from Scottish pulpits.

Pat is back at three and setting off for the third time today for Tobermory. There's a heartening moment just out of Dervaig when, close to a congregation of standing stones, one of three clusters in this territory, a second, agreeably conversational passenger joins us. And that's the end of my travels on the Mull 494. At the car park by the distillery and the aquarium, I say goodbye to Pat, who over the past two days has come to assume the role of guide, philosopher and friend. The Tobermory Topper returns to take us back to Craignure. And from there it's back across the shimmering water to Oban. What was it that the eighteenth-century traveller said about Mull? 'Italy itself, with all the assistance of art, can hardly afford anything more beautiful and diverting.' On this blessed September evening that verdict needs no amendment.

12

SCHOOLS OF HARD KNOX

94 St Andrews–Cupar–Newburgh

EASTWARDS NOW TO A KINGDOM, which like many a bigger kingdom, has its quarters of easy affluence and pockets of crushing poverty; which thrived in the past on farming and fishing, and later on diverse heavy industries – most, like farming and fishing, no longer the force that they were; a land of abbeys, cathedrals and castles, many now ruins; one which has given the world two kings and one prime minister, and was the birthplace over the centuries of one of the greatest of all economists, one of the greatest philanthropists and the vocalist and lead guitarist of Jethro Tull. It has towns evolved over centuries and others grown substantial in a mere fifty years, forests and lakes and rolling hills and sea and two mighty rivers – all wrapped up here in some 500 square miles of land – a

third of them owned by forty people. We have reached the Kingdom of
Fife, a peninsula bounded by the Forth, the Tay and the sea and hemmed
in to the west by the Ochil Hills. 'Bid farewell to Scotland,' it used to be
said, 'and cross into Fife.' The extent to which Fife can be properly called
a kingdom is a matter for argument. It certainly seems to have been some
kind of sub-kingdom of Pictish Scotland. Thereafter the nearest things it
had to a king were the earls of Fife. But a kingdom is what it calls itself;
anyone who speaks of it as a county risks being marked down as English.

The 94 out of St Andrews pursues a slightly wandering course through
the northernmost swathe of this kingdom, by way of the old county town
of Cupar and westwards to Newburgh, perched on the very edge of the
kingdom, only a mile or so out of Perthshire.

It's a grey grumpy afternoon in St Andrews, but the town (or burgh
or city: some say one, some the others) is *en fête*. It's a place that is built
on three straight serious streets running east–west: North Street, South
Street, Market Street and parallel, with them, the Scores, where the ruined
castle presides; all linked by lesser lanes, known traditionally as wynds,
though here and there more formal names have replaced the old ones:
Granny Clark's Wynd remains faithful to Granny Clark, but Baxter's Wynd
has become the more Anglicized Baker Lane. Union Street (and what street
name could be more respectable?) was known until around 1830 as 'the
Foul Waste'.

The great determining institutions of St Andrews are all represented
here. At the east end, above the harbour, is the tower that is all that
remains of the church of St Regulus, also known as St Rule, alongside the
surviving fragments of what was once the greatest church in Scotland, St
Andrews Cathedral, the high headquarters of bishops and archbishops
until John Knox came here and denounced them in 1559, precipitating
their destruction, a process officially classed as 'cleansing'. God was the
dominant element in St Andrews; now it's the university, which, as in
Oxford and Cambridge, keeps cropping up everywhere, from its grand
ceremonial buildings to its student union and its University Shop. In places,
historic religion and modern scholarship are effectively intertwined: the
grizzled old chapel of St Salvator on North Street is part of the university,
as in a sense is the memorial on the pavement under its shadow. That
consists of the two initials, P.H. They commemorate Patrick Hamilton, one
of a little army of St Andrews martyrs, tried for heresy by Archbishop
James Beaton and burned at the stake. New students at St Andrews are
warned that stepping on this monogrammed stone may cause them to fail
their exams.

Beyond the three streets and the elegant terraces to which they lead, there's a further religious shrine: the Royal and Ancient course, the home of golf in Britain, though not, as is sometimes assumed, its birthplace – today, only three weeks away from staging the greatest of Britain's annual tournaments, the Open. However, it's not the golf that is causing today's excitement, but a graduation day at the university. The graduands are here in force in their bright coloured robes attended by flocks of friends and family, unsparingly notching up more and more pictures against the appropriate background of this old stone city. Some must have come long distances to be here. Among those honoured today, alongside James French from Newport-on-Tay, Angela Ward from Kirkcaldy, Ann Melnyk from Auchtermuchty, and Ben Jamieson and Kimberley Miller from St Andrews itself, are Stanca Barbara Bortos from Cluj-Napoca, Romania, Galina Netylko from Moscow, Minna Kristiina Emilia Kajaste from Espoo, Finland, Muneerah Ab Razak from Singapore, and Cynthia Fry from Steamboat Springs, Colorado. It's the kind of scene you might find in any university town, except that here quite a few men have improved on mere picturesque gowns by the wearing of kilts.

And yet there's a kind of mismatch here. I feel a strange sense of rebuke, as if ancient St Andrews is displeased with the new one. That may come from the names of the shopfronts. Names that insistently speak of the South: Rymans, Holland and Barrett, Subway, Boots, Pret a Manger, Costa, Paperchase, Carphone Warehouse. Or perhaps it is more the presence of a mood that so far fails to accord with the place's sombre traditions, as symbolized perhaps by the celebrations on the spot where Patrick Hamilton died his horrible death. There's an air of levity now, and the old frowning buildings seem to be saying: this is St Andrews! It isn't a place for levity.

But it's time to move on from St Andrews to a territory that rarely gets written about, let alone recorded in photographs on a thousand smartphones. The 94 takes a road that flirts with the sea and brings us through Guardbridge, Leuchars (where St Andrews goes to catch its trains to Edinburgh and London: its passenger service ceased in 1969) and Balmullo to a place that seems a little mysterious. Most people call it Dairsie, but it's also officially recorded as Osnaburgh, perhaps because it was occupied by linen weavers who migrated here from Osnabruck in Germany. Place names in these parts have a pleasing localness: Luthrie. Moonzie. Blebocraigs. Clatto. Craigfoodie and Wester Craigfoodie. Glenduckie. Dunbog.

And now, in gentle rain, we reach the outskirts of Cupar.

*****

It may be a kingdom and not a county, but Fife has always needed a county town, and this was it from some point in the eleventh century, when it took over from Crail, until 1975, when a Local Government Act brought in by the Conservatives was implemented – though by then it had fallen well behind bigger towns such as Dunfermline and the one that became world famous first as the home of Adam Smith, author of *The Wealth of Nations*, and then as the matchless source of linoleum: Kirkcaldy. The new choice was Glenrothes, then less than thirty years old, having been designated as Scotland's second new town in 1948.

Cupar had developed as a market centre and an administrative and legal hub. The sixteenth-century Latin scholar and historian George Buchanan defined it as 'a place in the middle region of the country where the rest of the people of Fife go to receive justice'. Its prosperity was built on grain and, from the 1720s onwards, on its linen industry. As the bus sweeps in, one gets the immediate sense of the kind of sober, serious, God-fearing place that I always used to expect in small towns in Scotland. Here at the centre is the Mercat Cross, once exiled to a local mansion, where it sojourned until Victoria celebrated her 1897 jubilee; at which point it was returned to its proper station. South from here, down what used to be High Street and today is Crossgate, or west along Bonnygate, or eastwards back towards St Andrews, churches proliferate, some still open for worship, some now recycled. Even buildings which weren't ever churches somehow contrive to look like them – notably the Duncan Institute, with its odd twisted spire, founded in 1870 with a legacy from Miss Duncan of Edengrove, 'for the education', and no doubt the moral improvement, 'of the working classes of Cupar, Dairsie and Kilconquhar'.

East of the centre on St Catherine Street the Corn Exchange has its tinge of the ecclesiastical too. Beyond it is a sector reconstructed by a local banker and decidedly dodgy provost, John Ferguson, without much regard for the rules he was meant to administer. Since it got in the way, he decided to knock down the tolbooth, an outcome he achieved by calling a council meeting, inviting only those likely to support him, and marshalling a workforce ready for action who moved straight in and destroyed it. Even so, Cupar named a square after him, perhaps in recognition of his success in giving the approach from the east a greater sense of occasion. Building where necessary on land that he did not own, he created the county hall. Hotels gathered around it, some like the Tontine, now gone, and others, like the Royal, now broken up into apartments, though it still displays the original name. The banks were here too, displaying architectural ambitions second only to those of the churches. God first, mammon runner-up, and often not by much.

Beyond is the old cattle market, with a crescent of houses behind it, none especially distinguished but nicely harmonious, though the scene is dominated now by parked cars and a block of public lavatories. Across the road is a splendid park, complete with what every splendid park needs to offer, a bandstand – more garishly painted now, I guess, than it was when Cupar installed it in 1924.

Then, south of the town, close to the railway station and just across from the park, there's a resolutely important classical building which prominently displays the name of William Watt, nurseryman and seedsman. You would hardly guess it was built as a prison, replacing the tolbooth in East Street that Ferguson in his reforming zeal had obliterated. It was never a popular prison, in the sense that local opinion felt it was far too grand for prisoners, so much so that Cupar was persuaded to think again. The military took it over until Watt bought it in 1898 for his eminently peaceful business, which lasted for more than a century. But Watt has gone, and today there are advertisements for a Full Monty breakfast only £7.49, including nine items plus tea and coffee.

Levity again? Certainly it looks like an invitation to self-indulgence. And what is this? Here, directly across the street from the Duncan Institute, there's a window of W.H. Smith that isn't likely to foster the education and moral improvement of Cupar, Dairsie, Kilkconquhar or anywhere else. It is full of advertisements for the new E.L. James, successor to *Fifty Shades of Grey*. Previous generations here would surely have feared retribution, a display of God's wrath, possibly featuring a thunderbolt or perhaps a murrain of frogs.

I'm struck by the warmth and friendliness with which Cupar greets strangers. But perhaps that's because the sun, breaking with recent practice, is shining with most of its might. It won't last, I tell myself as I get on the 94 for Newburgh. And it doesn't.

*****

The road to Newburgh runs through a string of largely unmemorable settlements. Past the railway junction town of Ladybank, the country becomes more dramatic, with low hills closing in. Much the best sight is the snug little church in a beautiful fold of country at Abdie: the place seems to exude a sense of changeless tranquillity. On the other hand, I've read that the congregation here was recently riven by the discovery that its woman minister was about to marry her girlfriend.

We pass a lake which, refreshingly, is really a lake rather than a spread of polytunnels resembling one. There used to be a Tironesian abbey (the Tironesians were followers of St Bernard of Abbeville, who sought to restore the original rigour of the Benedictine Order) not far on from here, at Lindores, though only the ruins are left. In the year that John Knox denounced St Andrews Cathedral and all its works, he ordered the monks of Lindores to be gone, advice he amplified by having his followers sack their abbey. People helped themselves to the stones, which they used for building in Newburgh.

The 94's run into the town begins with a perfunctory tack through minor streets, but soon we are in its long gently curving high street, which is where you are most likely to be if you're in Newburgh, since there's so much high street and not a lot else. It has half a mile or so on each side of nearly continuous housing, here and there interspersed with a shop (not many of those), a church, a side road leading up the hill to subsidiary streets or down the hill to the river, a dark alleyway – all welcome to break the monotony. Not that the buildings here are identical: indeed there's hardly one that matches its neighbour.

I remember this street from a visit, perhaps thirty years ago. It astonished me then, and still does now. We had come to visit relations who had lived in Newburgh all their lives and were proud and protective of it, extolling its merits as we drove down the high street. Until, that is, we reached a house occupied by a dentist. Oh, no one in Newburgh goes to that dentist, one of them said. We're none of us happy with him. At which point the dentist's door opened and a patient – it could only have been one of his customers – tripped down the steps. Our informant was wholly unfazed. 'Och, she's nae from Newburgh,' she said. 'Just look at those heels!'

What I did not see then, and do at last today, is the tract below the high street bordering the River Tay. This was once a busy port, shipping salmon from fisheries all around to important destinations like Billingsgate Market in London. Today there is little moving here, though a boat perched on the bank is ready for action when needed. It's called the *Sea Eagle* and offers river trips. Somewhere a dog is barking, and a wood pigeon coos as if in response. But otherwise, perfect peace. Across the broad Tay, beyond Mugdrum Island, are the gentle blue and green hills of Perthshire. A woman appears walking her dog; we enthuse together. And it's even better, she says, as you walk further, beyond the park, where it's been beautifully landscaped.

Had this been the end of this journey, as I'd originally planned, I'd have walked on as recommended. But by now I've resolved to add an indulgent coda. Not far from here is the township of Auchtermuchty. The 94 avoids it, but its deviant sibling, the 94A, which alternates with it hour by hour, leaves the main route to take it in. I know three things about Auchtermuchty. The first two – the allurements it holds out to visitors – come from the world of entertainment. One is a statue, larger than life, commemorating Jimmy Shand. That's not a name that resonates in Watford or Woking, but it still does in Scotland, and perhaps even more among Scots expatriates. He led a band, he played the accordion – in each case, with a minimum of flamboyance. His obituarist in the Guardian, Brian Wilson, described him when he died in 2000, aged ninety-two, as 'the musical icon of Scotland's tartan sub-culture'. You can catch Jimmy, frozen in posthumous musical action, near the top of Burnside, which is where the bus from Newburgh comes in and stops at a point which no publicist for the place could have chosen, by a disused church with shattered windows. But there's still life in Auchermuchty; this very night is due to see the opening of a production of Arsenic and Old Lace in the village hall.

The other tourist lure here is purely nostalgic too. In a celebrated television serial built around Dr Finlay of Tannochbrae, Auchtermuchty played Tannochbrae. But that wasn't the version that so many watched so avidly south of the border, in which young Dr Finlay was played by Bill Simpson, Andrew Cruikshank was cast as the kindly but sometimes caustic senior partner and the part of Tannochbrae was taken not by Auchtermuchty but initially by Milngavie, Glasgow, and thereafter Callander, Perthshire. That in a sense was the authorized version. The Auchtermuchty series was a kind of revised version put out on Scottish Television with the simplified title, Dr Finlay. David Rintoul was the now not-so-young Dr Finlay; Ian Bannen was Dr Cameron, now retired but not yet withdrawn from the action; and Auchtermuchty took over from Callander. It was never the craze that the earlier version became, but Auchtermuchty likes to remember it; there's a Tannochbrae Tearoom up in the square for devotees.

You reach the square up a steady slope off the A91 St Andrews–Cupar–Stirling trunk road that roars unrelentingly through the foothills of Auchtermuchty. The parish church is here, and the square beyond it, dominated the old tolbooth, enhanced by a clock tower: it is now the town hall and library. There aren't many people about and at two o'clock a man whom I take to be the tea room's proprietor is standing a little disconsolately on the doorstep, as if hoping that fans of the Rintoul and Bannen series may yet be on their way.

There's a second Auchtermuchty, though, which is also fictitious. It used to materialize, week after week, in columns in the Sunday Express, written by its editor, John Junor. 'One of the most disagreeable men in England', the Tory journalist Max Hastings called him; 'a world class legendary monster', said another.

His Auchtermuchty was a kind of Junoresque Utopia, a community as wedded to his curmudgeonly prejudices as he was himself. The term 'political correctness' did not exist in the 1950s, but he discerned it at regular intervals and ground it beneath his feet. One could imagine Junor – perhaps this was even how he imagined himself – riding sword in hand to smite the forces of lily-livered do-goodism with the people of Auchtermuchty arrayed behind him. 'I wanted a sort of Brigadoon,' he said, 'a place which had been bypassed by the modern world and in which old-fashioned virtues still persisted.'

Poor Junor. No statue for him; not even a tearoom. Auchtermuchty had never endorsed, let alone authorized, the picture he drew of it. It wasn't even a place he knew well: he stopped there from time to time on his way to watch golf at St Andrews. He never lived there; he wasn't born there. Indeed, if anywhere is to be blamed for having produced Sir John, that must be his birthplace. Which, as it happens, was a place I was in two journeys ago: that Venice of Scotland, Maryhill.

13
BLOTS ON THE LANDSCAPE

94 Gateshead–Team Valley–Low Fell– Felling–Heworth–Gateshead

FOR CENTURIES these two communities glowered at each other across the murky waters of the River Tyne. To the north, mighty Newcastle, a name famous far beyond England; to the south, its perpetual poor relation, unfavoured Gateshead. From the northern bank, Newcastle looked south with disdain and often disgust; from the south, Gateshead scowled back with a mixture of envy, resentment, and apprehension at the thought of what Big Brother might try to do next. And often with justified apprehension, for Newcastle had seemed from the earliest days of this dysfunctional relationship intent on doing its humbler neighbour down. It had sought at various times to annexe it, to reduce it to a dependency, in the hope of exploiting and living off its natural resources, especially its burgeoning coalfields. Its merchants argued their case not on the basis of the good it would do to their own economic fortunes, but as the best available means to deal with Gateshead's disorder and irreligion. But Gateshead in this controversy gave as good as it got. Gateshead people, it was argued on their behalf, were godly people, men of good wealth and upright behaviour, whereas Newcastle's were 'inflamed with ambition and malice', and, with one named exception, 'all Papists'.

At one point, in 1553, the bigger town seemed to have got what it wanted: John Dudley, Duke of Northumberland, Lord Protector to the fifteen-year-old Edward VI, pushed legislation through Parliament in the space of ten days to annexe Gateshead to Newcastle. But three months later, Edward was dead, Mary was on the throne, Dudley was on his way to his execution, and Gateshead was free of its powerful, bullying neighbour. Yet the pressure continued. In the 1570s, Newcastle acquired enough of the town to make it Gateshead's master. And as Gateshead's historian Francis Manders accepts, just as Newcastle had promised, Gateshead prospered under this new hegemony. Its wealth increased and, with it, its population. Once the former balance had been restored, Gateshead's progress began to falter – through this was largely due to a decline in the fortunes of its mining industry, which had begun while Newcastle was still in charge.

And Gateshead remained hereafter, in Newcastle's contemptuous eyes, a blighted place. It didn't help that looking across the Tyne it saw the worst of Gateshead. Two dreadful old streets, Pipewellgate and Hillgate, commanded the southern bank. Pipewellgate, 300 yards long and for much of its length no more than eight feet wide, was home to some 2,000 people, many of whom were immigrants, from Ireland especially, drawn here in the days of the town's prosperity by the hope of finding work. They lived in filthy lodging houses with only three privies to serve the whole street, no dependable water supply and wholly inadequate sewerage, amid the sights and smells of piggeries, slaughterhouses and tanneries. In 1835, an inspector for the Poor Law Enquiry Commission found a house in Pipewellgate where there were '34 persons – chiefly Irish – 1 child lying dead – whole party drinking spirits', while eight years later, another inspection recorded a mortality rate in this street far worse than any to be found in Newcastle, and almost as bad as the worst place of all, in Liverpool.

Not much flourished here, but typhus and cholera did. The first wave of cholera had surfaced in 1831 and lasted a year. In January 1849, an ailing tramp from Edinburgh arrived in a Pipewellgate lodging house where some fifty people were living, sleeping two to a bed. That set off a second wave which lasted till December, extinguishing nearly 200 lives. And Newcastle had other potent causes for resentment. One night in October 1854 fire broke out in a worsted mill, Watson's, on the south bank. It rapidly spread to a much more dangerous site – a warehouse next door where among the commodities stored were sulphur, nitrate of soda and other combustibles. Here the fire raged even more savagely, culminating in a mighty explosion heard at least thirty miles away. Gateshead suffered worst: a swathe of buildings east of the mill and warehouse were almost entirely destroyed – some of them squalid housing in streets such as Hillgate which should have been swept away long before, but also the parish church of St Mary, so extensively damaged that its wholesale replacement was considered.

But Newcastle suffered too. The fire damaged or even destroyed many buildings across the water, even beyond the quayside. Among the fifty-three who died in Gateshead's fire were Newcastle people, including Alexander, the twenty-six-year-old son of the great Tyneside architect John Dobson, whom his father had hoped would succeed him. These things were not forgotten in Newcastle. Yet Gateshead always had its collection of grievances too. In 1901, for instance, officials discovered that the master of Newcastle workhouse had been turning vagrants away, telling them to make their way to Gateshead.

Through the nineteenth century, reformers demanded that Gateshead must make much more determined attempts to better itself. But the town was in the control of people whose overwhelming priority was to keep down the rates, and who vehemently opposed any suggestion that the town should build houses. Some robustly maintained that the poor had only themselves to blame: dirty people made dirty houses, said Alderman Dunn. He would not interfere with their pleasure in filth. Yet the meanness did not only come from sheer bigotry. The town was so poor that a pound rate would raise at best only a quarter of what the equivalent levy would produce in Newcastle.

The outside world, if it considered Gateshead at all, tended to take a Newcastle view of it. Many travellers assumed it to be a mere suburb. Boswell reports Dr Johnson dismissing the place as 'a dirty lane leading to Newcastle', a sentiment echoed in a Lords debate in 1831 by the Marquess of Londonderry, a County Durham coal owner who, opposing the allocation of parliamentary seats to Gateshead, called it 'a mere suburb, a long, dirty lane, leading to Newcastle – a most filthy spot, containing the vilest class of society'.

When J.B. Priestley came to Gateshead on his *English Journey* (1934), his judgement was scarcely kinder than Johnson's. 'There seemed', he wrote of his arrival, 'a great deal of Gateshead and the whole town appeared to have been carefully planned by an enemy of the human race in its more exuberant aspects.' To which after further inspection, he added: 'It has fewer public buildings of any importance than any town of its size in the country. If there is any town of like size on the continent of Europe that can show a similar lack of civic dignity and all the evidences of an urban civilisation, I should like to know its name and quality . . . They used to build locomotives in Gateshead, very fine complicated powerful locomotives, but they never seem to have had time to build a town.' 'Every future historian of modern England', he concluded, 'should be compelled to take a good long slow walk round Gateshead. After that he can at his leisure fit it into his interpretation of our national growth and development.'

In other troubled towns and cities, people emerged, like Joe Chamberlain in Birmingham, Henry Bolckow in Middlesbrough or Richard Grainger in Newcastle, who understood the deficiencies and needs of their home towns and did something about them. The problem in Gateshead was that no such saviour appeared. And when rich industrialists here became rich enough, they preferred to move out to somewhere much more salubrious.

Those who expressed most concern were often more troubled by the moral state of the place than its physical conditions. In 1827 a charismatic preacher called Hodgson Casson, popularly known as Cumberland Hodge, arrived in the town from his native county. As his biographer-hagiographer Allen Steele wrote: 'Leaving the inhabitants of the dales in their scattered dwellings, where they were comparatively shut out from much of that contaminating influence, which, like a moral pestilence, stalks along in places more densely populated, poisoning the life-blood of society, he had now, in the order of Providence, to plant his battering rams on a place "where Satan's seat" was; where bold unblushing infidelity was not ashamed to show itself unmasked; and where vice in all its disgusting and hideous deformity, reigned on every hand.' Very soon, Casson was changing the climate: 'By many he was considered as one of the most popular preachers in the north of England; and that his ministry was highly appreciated, not because of his eccentricities, but for the rich and holy unction which attended it, appeared by the crowds that flocked over the water from Newcastle, to hear him, many of whom ranked high for intelligence and sound discrimination.'

On the less favoured side of the river, though, it may have been his eccentricities that scored as much as his unction. It's recorded of Casson that coming one evening to his chapel and finding it almost empty, he hurried up the high street as far as Sunderland Road, where 'suddenly turning round, he gathered the tails of his coat under his arms, took off his hat, and commenced running back as hard as he could, shouting at the highest pitch of his voice: "A fight! A fight!" An enthusiastic crowd mustered behind him and followed him to the chapel where he climbed the stairs to the pulpit and told his ungodly new adherents: "My friends, you have come to see a fight; you shall not be disappointed; for I am just going to have one with the devil."'

Casson left Gateshead for Durham in 1830. Almost thirty years later, William and Catherine Booth, then still aligned to the Methodist New Connexion and not yet engaged on creating the Salvation Army, were posted to Gateshead, where they discovered that Satan had not been entirely banished by Hodgson Casson, and where they had at least as great an immediate impact, not least because of a shared talent for godly showmanship, which may have given Catherine the courage she needed to insist on preaching herself. They were there for only three years, but maintained a close interest in its redemption. In 1879 they returned for a season with a kind of backing group known as the 'Hallelujah Lasses' and supporting acts which included men known as the One-eyed Captain, the Hallelujah Giant (he was thought to weigh thirty-three stone) and the Converted Sweep (a man called Elijah Cadman, who would rise to be a Salvation Army commissioner).

A reporter from the *Newcastle Chronicle* attended, with some trepidation, one of their all-night meetings where the congregation took up lines that William had introduced: 'the chorus might have been sung a dozen times when there was a shrill scream, a bustle round the platform, and a general rise of the audience. Seats were mounted; hands were raised in the air; the singing was mingled with loud "Hallelujahs", bursts of vociferous prayer, shouting and hysterical laughter.'

Many, including several described as 'known to the police', were said to have joined the ranks of God-fearing rectitude after these meetings. But the physical deficiencies of the town were not to be so swiftly amended. Despite sporadic mitigations, they persisted into the new century. In the 1930s, at about the time when Priestley was shaking his head over its general hopelessness, official figures confirmed Gateshead as one of the worst-housed communities in the land. There had been improvements, including the belated erasure of the old Pipewellgate, but there was not enough housing to take those who had been displaced. In the early 1990s,

Newcastle, a city that was trying to rehabilitate and relaunch itself in the wake of the Second World War, found one blight it was powerless to deal with, in the form of that far from distant and far from pleasing prospect across the water.

By this time, though, the borough council across the water was determined to sweep the worst of Gateshead away. The 1951 census showed how necessary this still was. One analysis showed that for housing, Gateshead was the worst provided and most overcrowded of all the large towns of England and Wales. Its rates of tuberculosis and its infant mortality were among the most distressing anywhere. But it needed central government to come up with money, and when that occurred, it set about reorganizing itself with all the destructive vigour that characterized the sixties in Britain. Old streets were razed, some of the better along with the worse; much of the Georgian legacy in the centre of town was lost. Fast roads were created that scythed their way through the centre, a move whose principal benefit, it was complained, was making it much easier to drive at speed to Newcastle. As affronted by Gateshead's progress as Priestley had been by the lack of it, Henry Thorold wrote, in his *Shell Guide to Durham*, published in 1980: 'Gateshead has in recent years been ruined by monstrous tower blocks, the ancient town torn apart by "relief" roads, dual carriage ways, roundabouts, flyovers, underpasses: a concrete jungle indeed.'

The first of Gateshead's tower blocks had appeared in the 1950s. Well before Thorold condemned them, the council was having second thoughts. In its zest for reform, the council now created a shopping centre, hailed by some, Ian Nairn among them, as a brave and imaginative piece of pioneering, and by others as the town's newest and most prominent eyesore: Trinity Square. But the square's subsequent fate must be kept till later, since it's now time to take a circular tour of latterday Gateshead aboard a 94 bus.

*****

This route – they call it The Loop; a 93 does the same journey the other way round – provides a kind of accidental summary of Gateshead's troubles and imperfections over the centuries, some now redeemed, others not. What we now call Gateshead, it has to be said, is greatly enlarged from the one that Hodgson Casson and William and Catherine Booth knew. In 1974 the old county borough became a metropolitan borough, roping in the former townships and villages of Felling, Whickham, Blaydon and Ryton, Birtley and Lamesley.

The bus leaves town down the Lobley Hill Road, passing the edge of the formerly derelict site where in 1990 the town, having won the right to do so against twenty-seven other contenders in a competition instituted in 1980 by Michael Heseltine, staged its garden festival, the fourth in a succession of national festivals, following Liverpool, Stoke and Glasgow – all, like this one, places requiring urgent resuscitation. There were several sites to choose from, since so many of the town's old core industries had gone. The loss of some – notably glue manufacturing, a notoriously stench-ridden enterprise – was something of a relief, but it cost valued jobs. Gateshead's economy had at first depended most of all upon coal, but increasingly it came to owe more to the railway, which became its largest employer, ahead of chemicals, engineering and metal manufacturing, ship- and boat-building, and in the hills round about, quarrying. The loss in 1910 to Darlington, some thirty-five miles further south, of locomotive-building was hurtful and damaging, but what Manders calls 'the single most telling blow to the town' came with the closure of the railway works in 1932, again snatched by Darlington.

In its previous existence the 200 acres now allotted to the garden festival had been home to a gasworks, a coal depot and coking plant, and a railway sidings. They found £37 million to stage the show – £22 million from private sources – and brought some three million visitors to the place, some of whom would have barely heard of it before. Then, and perhaps even more now, the town regarded the festival as a triumph and a possible turning point. And when it was cleared away, it provided room for the spread of new houses that now border Lobley Hill Road.

From here the 94 proceeds to Kingsway, the broad core thoroughfare of another, earlier bid to bring about Gateshead's redemption: the Team Valley Trading Estate. It emanates from an era of want which is nowadays often summed up by a single place name: Jarrow, though Jarrow, some eight miles from central Gateshead, was only one of a great many places across the North East grievously blighted by recession in the 1930s. Gateshead, too, had privations not far behind it.

But while national government declined to intervene to save Jarrow, that determination relented when it came to Gateshead. A scheme unlike anything instigated by government in Britain before – such enterprises had until now been left to private providers – set about creating a trading estate which it hoped would provide employment for 15,000 people. Streets were established on a strict grid pattern. Some flaunted aspirational names – Kingsway, Queensway, Dukesway – while others echoed the place's utilitarian purpose: First Avenue, Second Avenue and so on. It began to take shape in 1936; but in 1939, when King George VI formally declared it open, it was still well short of the hoped-for employment target, and by that time the imminence of the Second World War denied it any immediate chance of growing further.

Today, it's a mixture of trading enterprise and domestic extras, its original company buildings interspersed with shops. A Team Valley Shopping Village (there isn't much of it) is sandwiched between Rosewood Packaging and the more comprehensive Enterprise House. Later on there's a bigger affair called Retail World which has stores in the Argos/Asda/PC World/M&S Simply Food league. Beyond, with the A1 trunk road roaring past them, are the respectable brick homes of Chowdene, a settlement where John Wesley once came to preach. 'Twenty or thirty wild children ran around us,' he wrote in his journal. 'They could not properly be said to be either clothed or naked. One of the largest (a girl, about fifteen) had a piece of a ragged, dirty blanket, some way hung about her, and a kind of cap on her head, of the same cloth and colour. My heart was exceedingly enlarged towards them.'

*****

We are now on the edge of Gateshead Fell, which constitutes yet another kind of local redemption. This was once a bleak and dangerous territory. The intrepid Wesley came here in February 1745 and found 'a pathless waste of snow'. 'Many a rough journey had I before, but one like this I never had; between wind, and hail, and rain, and ice, and snow, and driving sleet and piercing cold.' It wasn't that hospitable in dry weather either. In 1827 the local historian Eneas Mackenzie recalled the state of the fell as it had been fifty years after Wesley's visit: 'Thirty years ago, the Fell was studded with miserable mud cottages, inhabited by tinkers, cloggers, travelling potters, besom-makers.' The fell in those days was a notorious haunt of criminals, including the occasional highwayman, and a place of some terror for travellers.

All that changed when the land was enclosed and above all when a new road was driven through it, which became the main link between Durham and Newcastle – the old A1. Now a tract of land that respectable people had sought to steer clear of became a positive lure. Here, high above industrial Tyneside, successful manufacturers, from the northern side of the Tyne as well as the south, built sturdy villas with gardens where they could taste pure air. Today, Low Fell, on the edge of the fell, is a village where good northern stone is mixed with brick and where there's a sense of decent prosperity elusive in much of Gateshead.

From here, the bus begins the climb up Beacon Lough Road, which will bring it high up on the hill to the Queen Elizabeth Hospital in a district called Sheriff Hill; the next one's called Windy Nook, a potent reminder of what life was like on the ancient fell. But here we turn northward, past the church of St Alban in the district once known as High Felling, and the bus plunges down to the valley, delivering us to Felling.

In 1936, the year of the Jarrow march, Felling was an independent town run by its own urban district council, but part of the Jarrow parliamentary constituency, which had recently elected a tiny left-wing Labour firebrand called Ellen Wilkinson. After years of failing fortunes, a shipyard called Palmer's, by far its greatest employer, had collapsed. The town had appealed for help to the national government, where the issue was handled by one of its Liberal ministers, Walter Runciman, president of the Board of Trade. He knew the area well – he was born only four miles away in South Shields, and although Ellen Wilkinson described him as 'icy cold', he was said to have warm passion for Northumbrian folk song. But here, he was bleak. 'Jarrow', he ruled, 'must work out its own salvation.' That response, Ellen Wilkinson said, 'kindled the town'. The unemployed workers of Jarrow, together with those of neighbouring Felling and Hebburn, resolved to march on London, carrying a petition.

There were many such marches out of similarly stricken places. Most were organized by the National Unemployed Workers Movement. Wal Hannington, who led it, was a Communist, one of the British party's founding members, so the Labour movement would have nothing to with events he organized.

Jarrow was not alone in the calamities that had overtaken it, yet in this case Jarrow was different. Ellen Wilkinson, though she too had once been a Communist, was a mainstream Labour MP. The newspapers, whether friendly or, in most cases, hostile, tracked them as they marched the 290 miles south to London. These 200 men from Jarrow, Felling and Hebburn, marching for twenty-six days, and greeted in London by appreciative crowds and tea at the House of Commons, engaged the sympathies of a far wider public than the NUWM marches had met with. In the sense that, despite all this, nothing immediate was done to help Jarrow, the march was a failure. In a wider and deeper sense, it made its mark.

Today, Felling looks once again like a place fallen on hard times: not on the scale of the 1930s certainly, but enough to give it a place among the communities in this area rated highest on the 2015 Index of Multiple Deprivation. Gateshead overall has improved in the past five years, but some of its wards are still down near the foot of the table, Felling most of all, with nearly two-thirds of its people living within one of England's most deprived districts.

Felling feels no more like a suburb of Gateshead than Gateshead feels like suburb of Newcastle. Perched on the side of the fell, it has two levels. The first, where Split Crow Road and Crowhall Road meet at the square, is just about holding its own. There is certainly no shortage of pubs: around the square, the Greyhound, the Victoria Jubilee, the Blue Bell at Felling and, lurking a little beyond, the Portland Arms – nearly all busy on this wet and windswept County Durham afternoon. But there's no such cheer to be found in High Street, which takes you down to the lower level of Felling. It's like walking into a mortuary; so many dead shops, some empty, others where shops of general usefulness have been replaced by ones you wouldn't need every day: 'Posh But Common', second-hand furniture; 'Spiritual Insight', shuttered; 'Pimp My Mutts', dog grooming. (I thought I must have copied the name down wrongly: surely mutts came here to be primped rather than pimped? But 'pimp' is what it says on their website.) There's what may have once been a grocery shop, its three windows full of the kind of goods you might have seen displayed in High Street's better days – but they're only pictures.

Down at the foot of the hill on the old Sunderland road, one is just as sharply aware of what this place has lost. Two almost anonymous buildings, each once intended to signal the importance of Felling, face each other across the main road: a faded inscription on one shows it to be the old police station; the other tells you only that it's protected by Securitas, but it must have been the town hall. A council heritage notice confirms that this spot was once indeed the centre of Felling, with the town hall, a major Co-op, a police station and the Newcastle tram; also, the station, still open, one of the stops on the Brandling Junction railway established by the coal-owning Brandling family, lords of the manor here since the sixteenth century, to run from Gateshead to Monkwearmouth near Sunderland with a spur to South Shields.

A relief after this to come back to the square where in front of a hulking building, mildly suggesting an aircraft hangar, a typical afternoon queue, all women except for me, are awaiting buses, some of them running modestly late. The ones at my end of the queue have lived here or hereabouts for most of their lives and they mourn the Felling that's gone. High Street especially: they still remember it as a street that you could be proud of, with shops where you wanted to go. The one most missed seems to be the shoe shop, which is talked of with something like love. They miss Woolworth's too, but everywhere has lost those. But they're pleased that the hangar-like building is being converted; it used to be a Co-op but it's now going to be an Asda; the Co-op, they say, 'could be a bit pricey'.

*****

It begins to rain even harder. Now and then it's been reduced to mere drizzle, but mostly it's reached every level above that, up to serious vehemence. Felling melts almost imperceptibly into the 94's next destination, Heworth, where the bus stops in a square in front of the road and rail interchange which suggests that Heworth may be experiencing better times than Felling. It's a coherent scene, the church of St Mary, the Swan public house, the dutiful buses circulating, the trains running by in the background; yet the place has traces of Felling about it. In the graveyard of St Mary's there's a celebrated tomb under a canopy with effigies of three children, dead in a four-poster bed. But also here is another solemn reminder of the unforgiving pattern of life in places like this. St Mary's is also the burial place of all but one of the ninety-two men who died in a pit disaster at Felling in 1812 (the last body was never found). As a notice by the wall in the churchyard records, they were victims of explosions – probably caused, as so many mining disasters were, by firedamp. The rector, John Hodgson, it says, 'took up the cause of mine safety, and as a direct result of his efforts, the miners' safety lamp was delivered'.

This was one of three fatal events over thirty-five years at Felling, and much the worst. More than half the victims were aged between eleven and twenty; ten, including six ten-year-olds, were even younger. The average age of the victims was twenty-four. And the names indicate how often several deaths must have occurred within the same family.

And now the 94 turns back towards Gateshead, at first steering a complex course through new estates and past industrial parks and schools, off the A184, the new Gateshead–Sunderland road. It has rained so long and so resolutely, leaving the windows so steamed up and spattered, that it's hard to see where we're going. I even fail to make out Gateshead International Stadium, another crucial element in Gateshead's long campaign to reinvent itself.

From here, the bus swings into town, passes Gateshead College, and comes to rest at the neat, clean and convenient Interchange, which brings together the town's copious buses and the metro line which takes you through to Newcastle. (There's yet another indignity here: mainline trains from London and Edinburgh pass through Gateshead but do not have a station at which they could stop. You have to get off at Newcastle and finish the journey by metro train or bus.)

But any suspicion that Gateshead remains Newcastle's humble subordinate is dispelled when you leave the interchange and walk east through the town. Where the slums of Hillgate once festered, you will find a way through first to St Mary's Church, now a visitor centre, and then to the celebrated latter-day glories of Tyneside: Norman Foster's Sage Gateshead music centre; the BALTIC Centre for Contemporary Art, converted from a disused flour mill which, though it looks older, dates only from 1950; and Wilkinson Eyre's inspired Millennium Bridge. These, as I say, are Tyneside's glories, gathered together, now that the old animosities have died away (at the official level at least) under the designation of NewcastleGateshead, a kind of typographical equivalent of a civil partnership, adopted when in 2002 the two places made a joint bid to become Britain's City of Culture.

But let it not be forgotten (and Gateshead will keep reminding you) that the town that inspired these attractions was not Newcastle but Gateshead, out of its Labour council's insistence on redeeming the town's dingy and battered image. Even before these enterprises, there had been that garden festival. There was also the commissioning from Antony Gormley of the flying figure over the A1 now known as the Angel of the North, extensively disparaged before it was raised in 1998 as a waste of precious public money, but once the wider world began to take notice acclaimed almost universally, even by those who had once been against it. All the more so since it was paid for largely out of National Lottery funds rather than out of Gateshead's coffers.

To that you could add a telling private initiative: the creation in 1986 by the Newcastle entrepreneur Sir John Hall of the massive Metrocentre, the biggest shopping centre in Britain: a place that attracts all Tyneside, with huge car parks and its own rail and bus interchange, but firmly moored in Gateshead, not Newcastle. As for the bridge, every day around noon you can watch the graceful manoeuvre where the bridge opens and tilts to let shipping though. I watch, in one of today's more drenching torrents with a huddle of umbrella'ed and raincoated admirers, one of whom explains that the apparent ease and simplicity of the process was a tribute to its ingenious hydraulics. And at either end of the bridge, the Newcastle side as much as the Gateshead, the attribution is unqualified. This glorious addition to the great range of bridges that unroll before you as the train from London comes into Newcastle station is the *Gateshead* Millennium Bridge.

*****

I had come to Gateshead ten years before for a previous book, and been saddened by it. The best of the place was clearly a tribute to enlightened, adventurous local government, espousing the very opposite philosophy to that of the many years when spending the least you could was the watchword.

But the core of the town was hardly a match for its ambitiously revamped periphery. How many, I wondered then, of those who walked across the bridge to hear the Northern Sinfonia in its brilliant new headquarters would go for a meal or a drink or an hour or two's shopping in Gateshead? How many would even give the rest of Gateshead a thought? The shopping streets remained mean and dismal, with takeaways and charity shops and amusement arcades, but since Snowball's department store, estab. 1850, had folded in the 1940s, no shops of any great substance.

And it still does not, cannot, never will, come anywhere near to matching the glamour or range of Newcastle. Even so, there's been some advance, as is immediately evident when you cross from the interchange to the new pulsating heart of Gateshead's shopping experience; or, as people seem frequently to refer to it here, 'Tesco's'. But first, to retain some sense of balance, a deviation, to a building tucked away just beyond this gleaming new world.

Here is the Gateshead Advice Centre, the home to that often undervalued and undercelebrated national institution, Citizens Advice. One of its functions now is to house another essential volunteer organization: a food bank, one of at least a thousand that have multiplied across our lop-sided land since 2010, when food banks were still rare enough for no one to know how many there were. As is so often the case, the churches, of all denominations, have been at the heart of it; fifty-five of some seventy churches in the borough have become involved since this one was launched in September 2012, after two local churchpeople visited a food bank in Durham and decided that Gateshead needed one too.

Ian Britton, secretary of Beacon Lough Baptist Church, one of the prime movers in this enterprise, calculates in August 2015, when I am there, that the bank has in the past three years helped over 8,000 people, with the numbers accelerating year by year. They've also analysed the factors which drive them, often reluctantly, even shamefacedly, to seek help. By far the great single cause, however much the Department for Work and Pensions disputes this, is being let down or directly deprived by these principal agents and arbiters of welfare. Of 4,228 vouchers issued to the 5,582 adults and 2,628 children whom the Gateshead bank has helped at this point, 31 per cent were needed because of delays in paying benefits whose justification no one disputed. A further 15 per cent were attributable to the DWP changing arrangements – for instance, switching from weekly payments to fortnightly, leaving its clients stranded. A further 15 per cent were classed as the result of low income, and 13 per cent as the result of debt.

There's no doubt at all that the sanctions regime as tightened under the stewardship of Iain Duncan Smith exacerbated problems of poverty. The chief executive of Citizens Advice, Gillian Guy, says their research shows the impact of the 'tough and often poorly applied new sanctions regime' ranking alongside delays in DWP payments and shortfall in incomes as the principal reasons nationally for making use of emergency aid. And it's certainly not the case, as some critics of food banks allege, that they're simply an easy option for people who prefer to have others pay for their basic requirements. You don't get vouchers for the Gateshead food bank unless you've been referred by some qualified organization: Citizens Advice especially, but also care professionals and family doctors. And not many applicants, Ian Britton says, come for help more than once; the organizations that issue the vouchers try to follow their stories through and find ways of helping that go well beyond emergency handouts.

Collections in stores account for some 40 per cent of the 90 tonnes of emergency aid they've distributed up to this point; 30 per cent more comes from churches. There's a massive bin at the entrance to the new Tesco in Trinity Square, and the weight of donations inside leaves no doubt that Gateshead shoppers – and not only the better-off shoppers – are keen to help.

*****

Tesco is here in all its majesty because eventually Gateshead Council did what it had long been eager to do, and in 2010 ripped out the heart of the 1960s Trinity Square shopping centre, obliterating its shops and especially its attendant car park. This action was much attacked. The complex was the work of a brutalist school of architects: the firm that designed it was the Owen Luder partnership, where the shaping hand was that of Rodney Gordon. It was hailed at the outset with great enthusiasm by some architectural writers, a response largely unmatched in Gateshead. True, when the decision was made to remove it, there were local protests at the plans to get rid of the multi-storey car park, but less on aesthetic grounds than because it had featured in the 1971 film *Get Carter*, during which Jack Carter (Michael Caine) propels Cliff Brumby (Bryan Mosley) off the top of the car park to a horrible death. So powerfully had this image seized the imagination and even stirred the pride of Gateshead that the place was popularly known as the Get Carter car park.

The objections of others, however, went far beyond cinema history. The architectural critic Jonathan Meades, in one of those moods which make him sound like the Jeremy Clarkson of architectural analysis, was well to the fore in the ranks of calumny. The three finest works of British brutalism, he wrote in the *Guardian* in February 2014, had been designed by Rodney Gordon of the Owen Luder Partnership. They were Eros House in Catford, London; the Tricorn in Portsmouth; and the Trinity in Gateshead. Eros House had been 'disfigured'; the other two had been destroyed in 'acts of petty-minded provincial vandalism'. 'One can have nothing but contempt', he went on, 'for the scum-of-the-earth councillors, blind planners and toady local journalists who conspired to effect the demolition of such masterpieces.'

And yet there are powerful considerations which, for all their petty-minded provincialism, understandably tend to weigh with your scum-of-the-earth local councillor more than they do with visiting aesthetes. They have to take into account local wishes and local opinion. That's especially true of the art of the architect, whose work you may have to experience whether you wish to or not. People who don't like van Gogh or Jack Vettriano don't have to go and look at what they've produced. Those who don't like Dostoevsky or E.L. James don't have to read them; people who don't like Bartók or One Direction are not required to listen. But public architecture may leave you with no alternative. What Gateshead councillors, in their crass and untutored way, knew that their critics didn't was that Gateshead wanted a far better shopping centre and was happy to sacrifice what Jonathan Meades considered a masterpiece if that was the way to get it.

The doomed Trinity Square has been replaced by a centre dominated by a bumper branch of Tesco, and filled out with secondary shops, cafés and restaurants with student flats above. Tesco's hegemony here is hardly surprising: the company that rebuilt the Trinity Centre is called Spenhill Developments, and Spenhill Developments is Tesco by another name. The development finished second in the 2014 Carbuncle Cup, organized by the magazine *Building Design*, which aims to select the ugliest building erected in the past year in Britain. The 'winner', built at Woolwich in London, was brought into the world by the same developer, Spenhill, was designed by the same architects, Sheppard Fidler, and again featured a massive Tesco. The awards were made by three judges, only one of whom was Owen Luder.

Yet I guess local opinion, regrettably not as sensitive to architectural merit as *Building Design*, is happy with Tesco's replacement of Luder's creation. It never warmed to the square as over the years it has come to do to the Angel. The main sense of what was said on the Internet by local contributors after the deed was done was one of relief; and the general verdict in my dripping wet bus queue in Felling seemed to be that at last they now had a place they looked forward to shopping in.

But what do they know? They merely live there.

14
TRAIL OF BLOOD

494 Selby–Saxton–Towton–Tadcaster

PRESUMABLY IN THE HOPE OF LURING PEOPLE ABOARD, some companies garnish their buses with what they believe are irresistible names. In honour of the witches of Pendle, Transdev's express service buses from Manchester to Nelson, through territory in which these ill-fated women were thought to practise, are labelled Witch Way. The same company's local buses from Burnley are labelled Starship, threatening disappointment for children when they discover that they remain earthbound, with destination boards promising Pike Hill and Stoops Estate rather than Mars or Jupiter.

So, what name, I wonder, might a more ostentatious, more market and PR conscious, operator than this one – Just Travel – choose for the bus that travels on Mondays only at 12.15 from Selby across North Yorkshire to Tadcaster? The bus this morning is all white hair and convivial chatter. Nearly all those aboard are elderly women with shopping bags, many of whom, I deduce from the conversation, are widows; and, as is the way with widows, those who have lived longest in widowhood are gently protective of those for whom the blow has more recently fallen. If you wanted to sum up the customers, you'd perhaps invoke some legendary widow like Naomi and her widowed daughter-in-law, Ruth, in the Old Testament. If you wanted a catchy name for this journey through fifteen miles of gentle, peaceable Yorkshire countryside, though, what about Trail of Blood?

This is a sector of England over which in less civilized centuries great, ugly and slaughterous combat has taken place, including what is generally held to be the most bloody, and bloodthirsty, battle on English soil. Selby, where we embark, might seem to be an exception. True, it made its contribution to the toll of death and destruction. In April 1644, the forces of Parliament, heading for the Royalist stronghold of York, had first to eliminate resistance in Selby, leaving perhaps as many as 1,500 Royalists dead. But this battle is not much remembered, for in the circumstances of those times that death toll could be regarded as modest. If you've heard of Selby, it's more likely to be for its abbey, founded by William I and distinguished in its subsequent history by a series of scandals, serving as a reminder that Henry VIII's dissolution of the monasteries in some ways reflected the dissolution of monks.

A commission that visited Selby in 1275 found several, their abbot among them, guilty of loose living and misconduct with women. The next visitation uncovered a trail of neglect with the abbot consistently guilty of flouting the rules he was meant to enforce and of enriching himself by the unauthorized distribution of his abbey's lands and assets to his family and friends – finding time meanwhile to consort in distinctly impious fashion with at least two named women, one of whom was said to have given him offspring.

Further visitations in 1306, 1322 and 1324 showed that Selby was still far from a model monastery, while yet another in 1335 uncovered still worse excesses: Adam le Breuer had misbehaved with one Alice Smith and her sister, was commonly drunk and riotous and a sower of discord, and using clothes he'd designed for the purpose, had made off with some of the abbey's property. Another monk was making regular gifts to women of the town and was guilty of lascivious conduct and theft; three more had engaged in illicit conduct with women, raising suspicions of carnal connection. The following year uncovered further malpractice, but that was the last visitation for which records survive. Perhaps from then on the monks of Selby led holy and blameless lives.

Robert Selby, otherwise known as Robert Roger, who was abbot of Selby at the time of the dissolution, was treated with some leniency by the King, no doubt his reward for having come to Parliament and supported the break with Rome. This perhaps explains why this abbey survived when so many were ravaged and left as ruins, and can still be explored today. Encased as it is in the town, it looks more like a large parish church than a once separate abbey with green lands about it like Rievaulx, Bolton or Fountains. Yet in spite of Henry's forbearance, the abbot fled to France, taking with him, it was said, as much of the abbey's property as he could manage – perhaps for safe keeping. But four years later he had found his way back and was living in one of the town's principal streets, then as now named Gowthorpe.

*****

The future Henry I was born here in this town to William the Conqueror's queen, Matilda, an event it was apparently hoped might help reconcile the truculent North to its Norman invaders. But ask what it was that had brought Matilda to Selby, and the potential of a Trail of Blood bus begins to resurface. William had parked her here while he set about punishing the

North in the manner that came so naturally to him: systematic slaughter. This, of course, was a game it took two to play. Atrocity was traded for atrocity. In 1069, the rebels rose against the Norman garrison and killed the governor. Then, reinforced by the Scots and the Danes, they took control of the city and burned a great part of it, savaging the Norman garrison, putting some 3,000 people to death. William in turn made for York, leaving a trail of devastation and killing countless numbers of men on his way, obtained its surrender, and razed the place to the ground. 'So terrible was the visitation', the historian D.C. Douglas wrote in his book *The Norman Impact Upon England*, 'that its results were still apparent twenty years later.'

In a history of these times an eleventh-century Norman monk called Orderic Vitalis purports to record the dying words of the King: 'I have persecuted the natives of England beyond all reason, whether gentle or simple. I have cruelly oppressed them and unjustly disinherited them, killed innumerable multitudes by famine or the sword, and become the barbarous murderer of many thousands both young and old of that fine race of people.' Guilty as charged, Your Majesty; but it surely owes very much more to the writer's imagination than to any deathbed repentance.

*****

One of the themes of conversation on today's bus to Tadcaster is self-denial: a recitation of goods, particularly clothes, which this congregation had been tempted to buy in the Selby shops but in the end had held back from. The other, even more dominant, is the future of these Monday journeys. There is apprehension that North Yorkshire Council, which like all the rest has to come to terms with a severely reduced budget, will now withdraw the subsidy without which this service could not run. 'Have you heard anything about these buses?' someone asks. 'Nothing positive,' says her friend, which, in effect, means 'nothing'. Gentle attempts are made to engage the driver, but he does not respond, no doubt because he too knows nothing. As drivers will tell you, they are often the last to hear. It's clear that if the 494 is lost, it will mean a great deal more to these customers than just an empty space in the timetable. These journeys to Selby market are part of their way of life. If this route is axed, it will still be possible to ride in from Tadcaster and the villages along the route, but you'd have to change, which would mean waiting about, perhaps in the cold and rain, at Sherburn-in-Elmet.

Still, the bus is running today, and it's soon on its way through flat, almost fen-like fields – quite a few of them flooded this January morning

– by way of Biggin and Little Fenton, to Church Fenton, a much more substantial place with a couple of pubs and a station. Church Fenton too has its associations with war. The RAF established an airfield here in 1937, which became a fighter base during the Second World War and a training base thereafter.

All seems tranquil at Saxton, a very agreeable, unmessed-about and tucked-away village – some parts of this route even have to use single-track lanes with passing points – clustered around the church of All Saints and the Greyhound pub. And here is the village hall, the scene of the monthly gatherings of a society which meets to commemorate the gross and murderous battle which did so much to determine the course of the War of the Roses, the battle of Towton, fought in snow and blizzard on 29 March, Palm Sunday, 1461.

Eight weeks earlier, on 2 February, York had defeated Lancaster at Mortimer's Cross in Herefordshire. On the basis of that victory the eighteen-year-old Edward, Earl of March and son of Richard, Duke of York, who had died in the battle of Wakefield two months earlier, came to London and had himself proclaimed king. But though Edward had triumphed and Owen Tudor, one of his chief opponents, had been captured and taken away to be beheaded, Mortimer's Cross had not been decisive. Henry IV's queen, Margaret of Anjou, who had all the spirit and fury her husband lacked, had taken her revenge in the second battle of St Albans on 17 February. Henry, who had been till this point a prisoner of the Earl of Warwick, was recaptured and reunited with his queen. But even she could not maintain the momentum that the Lancastrians should have gained from this victory. And Towton would be a very different story.

The standard interpretation of Towton says that on 29 March the Lancastrian commander, the Duke of Somerset, twenty-four years old to Edward's nineteen, drew up his forces on marshy heathland close to the present-day villages of Saxton and Towton. The terrain was of Somerset's choosing, but the ground was treacherous. His forces, though they outnumbered Edward's by a margin of perhaps five to four, coped far worse than their enemy with blizzards of snow and a marshy terrain, and were outfoxed by a cunning plan of the Yorkists. They fired a fusillade of arrows at their opponents and then swiftly retreated, so that the Lancastrians wasted hundreds of arrows by firing them into the spot that the Yorkists had left. The turning point was probably the arrival of reinforcements headed by the Duke of Norfolk. By nightfall, the battle was over. No reliable count of the death toll exists, but contemporary estimates put it at 28,000. No one knows for sure how big the population of England was then, but most estimates put it a shade above two million, on which basis a death toll of 28,000 would amount to about 1.25 per cent. The equivalent figure for England now would be well over 650,000 lives.

For years these events were remembered for their particular horror. Daniel Defoe, who was here in the 1720s, recorded:

> On this road we pass'd over Towton, that famous field where the most cruel and bloody battle was fought between the two Houses of Lancaster and York, in the reign of Edward IV. I call it most cruel and bloody, because the animosity of the parties was so great, that tho' they were countrymen and Englishmen, neighbours, nay, as history says, relations; for here fathers kill'd their sons, and sons their fathers; yet for some time they fought with such obstinacy and such rancour that, devoid of all pity and compassion, they gave no quarter, and I call it the most bloody, because 'tis certain no such numbers were ever slain in one battle in England, since the great battle between King Harold and William of Normandy, call'd the Conqueror, at Battle in Sussex; for here, at Towton, fell six and thirty thousand men on both sides, beside the wounded and prisoners (if they took any).

Most later accounts scale down the numbers, but not the brutality. Edward had ordered that no Lancastrian should be spared, and as their opponents turned and fled, the Yorkists drove them back to a swollen stream called Cock Beck and beyond it into the deeper Wharfe, where a great many drowned and others still on land were joyfully slaughtered. 'Down the valley', wrote a local historian, Edmund Bogg, in 1904, 'ran the blood of the slain, changing the waters of the rivulet and the Wharfe to crimson, even the brown waters of the Ouse.' In May, Edward was back in London and being bestowed with God's blessing at his coronation.

If you want to look at the battle site – perhaps, one should say, the presumed site, since the evidence is sketchy – the place to get off the bus is Saxton. (You can't do this if you need, as I did, to complete the 494's journey, since there won't be another along for a week, but you still have the option of catching another bus back from Tadcaster later.) From the church at Saxton there's a pleasant walk through to the B1217 Towton to Garforth road. Here you may turn north towards Towton, which will bring you to Towton Cross, erected in 1929 to commemorate those who died in the battle. There is evidence to show that Edward planned to build a chantry as a memorial to the battle and to the slain, which his brother Richard of Gloucester, succeeding Edward as king in 1483, was left to finish, but Richard, whom we will meet being disinterred in chapter 16 of this book, was killed two years later at Bosworth and the chantry was never completed.

Alternatively at the end of the road from Saxton you can turn southwards and walk through the area where the battle is thought to have taken place. This will bring you in time to a pub called the Crooked Billet, beyond which is a tiny church which may or may not have had something to do with the battle, but is strange enough to make the walk there worthwhile. This is Lead Church, which I'd read about in the 2013 diaries of Alan Bennett, where, after reflecting a little sourly over the Richard III's bones excitement, he writes:

> Just east of Leeds and not far from Towton and its bloody battlefield is Lead Church, a medieval cell of a chapel which possibly served as a refuge or a dressing station after the battle in 1461. I have known the chapel since I was a boy when I used to go out there on my bike. It stands in the middle of a field, the grass grazed by sheep right up to the south door and has latterly been in the care of the Churches Conservation Trust . . . However, calling there a few years ago we found that the grass outside the south door had been replaced or supplemented by a patio not even in York stone but in some fake composition. Inside, draped in front of the altar was a gaudy banner advertising the Richard III Society. This I rolled up and had I had the means would have destroyed. I wrote to the CCT, who generally do a decent job, but was told the patio had been there for many years. It hadn't and I suspect the culprits were the Richard III Society, who see the church as a Yorkist site on which they can lavish their presumably ample funds. So had the last of the Yorkist kings been left under the car park I would not have grieved.

Despite this reservation, I squelch across the waterlogged field to the chapel door where I find a sign that says: 'This church is cared for by the Churches Conservation Trust, the national charity protecting historic churches at risk. Although no longer used for regular worship, our churches remain consecrated and open to all.' Four essential words were missing from this encouraging statement. It should have said 'remain open to all, except when they're shut.' Today the door is implacably locked and I squelch back to the road disappointed.

*****

From Saxton the 494 presses on along the kind of rural lane which doesn't make much allowance for buses to the village of Towton, which no longer has the air of a place where blood was abundantly shed, except in one fairly harmless (I hope) respect: an advertisement for a murder mystery weekend due to be staged here. We are now closing in on Tadcaster, a brewing town, famous for that and for the smell that went with it, though otherwise, I fear, a largely unmemorable place. Perhaps the most attractive spot is close to the bus station, where the 494 puts me down: the bridge over the Wharfe, which will very soon merge into the River Ouse. (I'm able to cross it today, though in December 2015 floods would damage it so severely that one end of the town was cut off from the rest for several months. A temporary footbridge was installed while a new bridge was designed – despite the opposition of Humphrey Smith, aged seventy-one, described by the *Daily Mail Online* as 'the hereditary ruler of the Samuel Smith brewery empire'. A town councillor was reported as saying: 'If Humphrey Smith were bumped off tomorrow, you'd have about 6,000 suspects.')

Of the three brewing operations at work today, one (the Tower Brewery) is now owned by the big American company Coors, who bought it from Bass; the other two still bear the name of Smith. They are John Smith's (famous for their Magnet and Taddy Ales, advertised match after match in the Leeds United programmes of my youth), which is now part of another big brewing conglomerate; and Samuel Smith's, whose Old Brewery business remains independent. Are these Smiths by any chance related? Indeed they are: these were Smiths from a single family who fell out and went their separate, rivalrous ways. Mercifully, there does not appear to have been any bloodshed.

Of course, as you'd expect in this territory, Tadcaster had its battle: the King v. Parliament (a comfortable win for Parliament) in December 1642, sixteen months before Selby's event. It was not, though, a very serious battle, not many dead, certainly in nowhere near the same league as Towton or Marston Moor, twelve miles away, the scene of one of the greatest Civil War battles. For a Trail of Blood bus route, it has to be said, Tadcaster bus station would make a limp ending. But that could be simply remedied. Were the 494 to push on for a mere three miles, it would come to a place called Wighill, which is the likeliest nomination for the scene of yet another barbarous outrage.

The victim this time was a powerful Northumbrian magnate called Uhtred, son-in-law and champion of the Anglo-Saxon King Ethelred. His butcher was a man called Thurbrand the Hold, whom Uhtred had tried but failed to kill years before, acting now at the behest of King Cnut (more commonly known as Canute). Having driven out Ethelred, Cnut sent for Uhtred, promising him safe conduct and the chance to settle peace terms between them. Uhtred arrived with a party of forty men. At some point in the evening a group of Cnut's soldiers who had been hiding behind a curtain closed in on Uhtred and those he'd brought with him, and slaughtered the lot. After his father's murder, Uhtred's son Eldred sought out Thurbrand and killed him, only to be murdered in turn by Thurbrand's son Carl. That is how things were done in those days.

Add a very small deviation from route 37, and the revised 494 would carry you on to Long Marston, near where occurred the battle of Marston Moor, in which the forces of Parliament and their Scottish allies met the Royalists led by the hopelessly impetuous Prince Rupert of the Rhine. This would, the prince announced before the two sides engaged, be a glorious day. As it was – for his opponents. The Royalists were broken across the North thereafter. On the Parliament side, a few hundred died; among the Royalists, around 4,000. Quite a mild event, compared with Towton, yet enough of a corpse count even so to justify a further extension to the Trail of Blood bus service. Come on, Transdev: you already run Witch Way and Starship: what are you waiting for?

15
WHERE LITTLE TROY ONCE STOOD

94 Brigg–Hibaldstow–Gainsthorpe

MY 94 BUS out of Brigg, North Lincolnshire, is heading towards a place less remarkable for what is there than for what isn't. Gainsthorpe is a very small village, scarcely more than a hamlet, on a road that runs west from the A15. A sign at the boundary says it welcomes slow drivers, but the road is so temptingly straight and direct that in my brief experience there, it tends not to get them. They race past a traffic sign which vainly asserts a limit of 40, past a tidy line of cottages, and over a railway bridge beneath which there runs, though less often now than it did, the Sheffield to Lincolnshire railway. Alongside the railway there's a site which was once a cement works; the works have gone, and haulage contractors have taken it over. The bus waits here for five minutes or so before it heads back to Brigg. Three buses a day run out of Gainsthorpe; only two run into it. Not many people live there; there is not much to see. Yet devotees flock here: not for what Gainsthorpe is, but for what, as discovered almost a century back, it once must have been.

The 94 out of Brigg is what moments before had been the 95 out of Scunthorpe, transmogrified as it reaches the Cary Lane bus station. Brigg used to be called Glanford Brigg, the 'Brigg' simply meaning the bridge which in the fourteenth century replaced the ford across the River Ancholme. It's a market town, and Cary Lane gives on to the market place, which still has a good market place feel about it. In the forefront is the building, once Brigg Town Hall, now known as the Buttercross, put there in 1817 by a prominent local family, the Elweses, to provide the town with a suitable meeting place.

Brigg is often disparaged, or awarded only faint praise. In Arthur Mee's volume on Lincolnshire in the *King's England* series, first published at the end of the 1940s, it is designated as 'quaint', a term perhaps used with more approval then than it is now. 'Not very old or interesting', says the *Shell Guide to Lincolnshire* (1965).

Yet I like it. Beyond the Buttercross, the road divides. On the right is Bigby Street, where beyond the Lord Nelson Hotel and the Dying Gladiator pub, whose dedicatee is crudely sculpted dying in bloody agony over the porch, you pass the church of St John the Evangelist, 'squeezed in' as the 1964 edition of Pevsner's *Buildings of England* says, and the Exchange coach house inn. There's a gentle curve to this street which denies you full sight of what's coming next and draws you on. If you persist, you will come to the road that leads to what's left of the railway station, where trains on the line from Sheffield to seaside Cleethorpes still stop – though only on Saturdays.

Turn left, and you may find your way back into town by the other street that leaves the Buttercross, which is Wrawby Street, which you join near a pub called the Britannia. It sports a sign which shows Britannia all decked out to do battle with some intrusive opponent, with a set of patriotic white cliffs in the background. Nearby, and apparently thriving, is the White Horse.

Intruder supermarkets apart, Wrawby Street remains the main shopping street of the town, with a pleasing scatter of local names over the doors. Back in the market place, past the Angel Hotel, whose 'Tudor' frontage dates from the 1890s, and the Woolpack, you come to the bridge which was once the main purpose of Brigg, beyond which is a broad street encompassing a former riverside mill. Here you will find the Nelthorpe Arms, the White Hart and the Yarborough Hunt. I saw a sign which wistfully claimed that Brigg once had twenty-six pubs or related hostelries. Yet it's not doing badly now.

If I had to choose one word for the appeal of Brigg, it would probably be 'unhurried'; a quality you particularly value if you're here on a day out of frantic London. And clearly it's not always as tranquil as it seemed on this spring morning. 'Brigg robber attacks woman, 90', a newspaper billboard announces, and this week's *Scunthorpe Telegraph* has no shortage of instances of less eye-catching criminal acts perpetrated in Brigg.

The composer Percy Grainger came here more than once in the first decade of the twentieth century and noted down some of the local folk songs. He later recalled George Gouldthorpe, who since the death of his wife had lived much of the time in the workhouse, and was sixty-six when the composer first heard him: 'Though his face and figure were gaunt and sharp-cornered (closely akin to those seen on certain types of Norwegian upland peasants) and his singing voice somewhat grating, he yet contrived to breathe a spirit of almost caressing tenderness into all he sang, said and did – though a hint of the tragic was ever-present also. A life of drudgery, ending, in old age, in want and hardship, had not shorn his manners of a degree of humble nobility and dignity exceptional even amongst English peasants.'

Later Grainger's friend and fellow composer Delius incorporated one of the songs that Grainger recorded, this time sung by the seventy-one-year-old Joseph Taylor, in his English rhapsody *Brigg Fair*. The fair, one of the country's largest horse fairs, still takes place every August, as it has since the thirteenth century, though the site near the river where it used to be staged is now occupied by Tesco.

*****

And now we are scudding away across the bridge towards Scawby – 'the favoured village of Scawby' in estate agent speak. Those of us already aboard this bus when it was still a mere 95 have been treated to a tour of Scawby already this morning, and now we're in for another. The old place doesn't seem to have changed much in our absence. There is still the inviting gateway that leads through well-nurtured gardens to Scawby Hall, the grandest house in the village, early seventeenth century, open to the public on some days, but not today; a shop, a pub, the China Red takeaway, the village hall, and a certain amount of bungaloid straggle.

The next port of call is Hibaldstow – the 'stow' or burial place of a seventh-century Saxon saint, St Hibald (or Hybald or Higbald), a popular figure round here: the church at Scawby is named for him too, as is another a few miles away at Manton. His village looks staid, settled, seasoned.

The RAF had a wartime base which now houses, perhaps a little incongruously in the context of gentle Hibaldstow, a skydiving centre. And though the place still speaks of a placid past, the future is looking over its shoulder, in the form of a giant wind turbine, only recently established away to the east on the banks of the River Ancholme, reaching higher into the Lincolnshire sky, the company who created it claims, than even that great county icon, Lincoln Cathedral.

From Hibaldstow, the logical course for my bus might seem to be to continue along the road we have taken since Scawby to Redbourne. But the 94 leaves that till later, on its way back to Brigg.

*****

The very good-natured man at the wheel of my 95-turned-94 bus knows where Gainsthorpe is, since that is his destination and turning-round point. But the medieval village? There he is not quite sure. 'But it sounds worth seeing,' he says. 'Do you know, I drive along this route every day and I've never looked at it.' Fortunately there's a signpost, so he drops me off, and I plod down a farm track until I come to a field with an English Heritage sign. 'The first medieval village to be identified from the air,' it says. The village plots, it explains, follow the medieval pattern of toft – a building with a rear yard – and croft – an enclosed paddock behind it. Later, it says, there were courtyard farms, indicating changes in later medieval agricultural practice, which eventually killed many communities. Including, presumably, this one.

That's about all. To understand what you're about to see, you really need to have read up the sources beforehand, or come with someone who knows. What you see is a meadow of irregular shape with a bumpy terrain of hillocks and hollows and trackways. That something eventful happened here has long been evident. That the place has yielded its secrets up is attributable to the vigilance of three men, one of whom had been dead at the time for more than 300 years. The first was the vicar of Welton, a village fifteen miles down the A15 towards Lincoln, who thought he had detected the signs of a Roman settlement. He brought this to the attention of the second, an archaeologist and geographer called Osbert Guy Stanhope Crawford. On 3 April 1925, Crawford, a pioneer of the newly born practice of aerial archaeology, flew over the site, and immediately saw that the vicar was on to something – but even so, had been wrong about what he saw.

Here Crawford had the formidable advantage of already being acquainted with the writings of the third of this trio: Abraham de la Pryme, curate of Broughton, a village now horribly bloated, but then modestly gathered around the church of St Mary, who in 1697 noted down in his diary a visit he'd made to Gainsthorpe:

> This day I took my horse and went to a place called Gainstrop which lies in the hollow on the right hand, and about the middle way as you come from Kirton to Scawby. Tradition says that the aforesaid Gainstrop was once a pretty large town, though now there is nothing but some of the foundations. Being upon the place I easily counted the foundations of about two hundred buildings and beheld three streets very fair . . .
>
> Tradition says that the town was, in times of yore, exceeding infamous for robberies, and that nobody inhabited there but thieves, and that the country having for a long while endured all their villainies they at last, when they could suffer them no longer, rose with one consent and pulled the same down about their ears.
>
> But I fancy that the town has been eaten up with time, poverty and pasturage.

This was a moment of some significance in the history of archaeology. 'The modern traveller', Maurice Beresford wrote in his ground-breaking book, *The Lost Villages of England* (1954), 'has the advantage of the air photograph, which under favourable conditions offers information about the village plan only equalled by a visit to the ruins in the months immediately following their destruction . . . for many sites the air photograph has been the means of returning for a moment to the conditions of the sixteenth century.' In *The Lost Villages of Britain*, published in 1982, a later practitioner on this territory, Richard Muir, calls Crawford's detection of Gainsthorpe 'a landmark in the hunt for deserted medieval villages'.

Yet neither Crawford, in his plodding autobiography ('At the risk of being tedious . . .' – p. 158) *Said and Done* (1955), nor Kitty Hauser, whose wonderfully spirited account of Crawford, *Bloody Old Britain*, was published in 2008, treats it as that kind of turning point. Crawford's own sense of his moment of breakthrough is recorded in a piece he wrote for the *Observer* in July 1923, two years before he flew over Gainsthorpe. 'Sensational revelations', he wrote, 'do not often appeal to archaeologists. But when an Air Force friend showed me some photographs taken for practice near Winchester I realized instantly that they marked the beginning of a new epoch in archaeology.' The invention of aerial photography, he forecast, would do for archaeology what the telescope had done for astronomy.

Crawford was born in 1886 in India, where his father was a high court judge. His mother died soon after his birth and the boy was packed off to England and entrusted first to the care of two aunts and later to the rather less tender attention of Marlborough College. Marlborough was an ideal base from which he could walk or ride on his bike to sites of archaeological interest.

He moved on to Oxford, but failed to complete his geography course. At a loss for what to do next, he signed up for an expedition to Easter Island, but finding its leaders intolerable, got off the boat at St Vincent and came home. An assignment in Sudan served him better. On the outbreak of war he enlisted with the London Scottish regiment, was despatched to the trenches and invalided home, less, apparently, because of an episode in which he was found to have fired on his own side than because he had malaria. When he returned to action, it was in the more appropriate role of a mapping officer – contributing to maps rather than making them – an expertise he developed first by studying aerial pictures taken by pilots of the Royal Flying Corps and then by flying with them as an observer.

Crawford's time with the RFC was a preparation for what he would later become: a kind of gifted airborne detective who could construe what he saw from the air with rare perception. Ogs, as everyone called him, was devoted to cats, and defined the advantage of aerial archaeology over the conventional kind with an appropriately feline analogy. Put a cat on a carpet and from its position low on the ground it will observe a certain sense of it. But have a man, towering above it, looking down on it from a height and he will see and understand very much more. From Winchester onwards, he applied that test and fathered a new archaeology.

He did not dig much himself. Others could wield the spade. Instead his essential tools were his eyes, his feet, his bike and his constant companion, his camera. Like Beresford and W.G. Hoskins, whose book *The Making of the English Landscape* taught a generation how to observe and understand their country's heritage, his watchword was: go there and see for yourself. And it isn't enough to see; you need to *look* as penetratingly as you can at what you are seeing. He built up a formidable archive of pictures. And since he could find no regular publication in which to promulgate his findings and his ideas, he launched one himself, which he named *Antiquity*.

Crawford was a born maverick, though sometimes in a way that tinctured the word with menace. He was misanthropic ('generally speaking, I prefer things to people') and, even more, misogynistic, impetuous, argumentative and, in a general sense, often a 'difficult' man. And though he exalted science above all other human concerns, contrasting it with the erosive delusions of superstition, religion and tribalism, he himself could be swept away by a wholly unscientific, impulsive fervour. He became early on an apostle of the cause of world government, as preached by H.G. Wells, whom he knew and admired. And in 1932, this man so adept at teasing out the distant past began to discern with even more passion and certainty a not far distant future. He went in that year to Soviet Russia, and marvelled at what he saw.

Here was a system that exalted science, and looked on religion, along with superstition and tribalism, as the delusions that they indisputably were. Here was the road to world government, since when other nations knew and understood what the Communists were achieving, they would find the chance of doing the same irresistible. That applied not least to poor broken Britain, a land where in his judgement no one one ever did anything properly – an indictment he would one day expand into a book of angry prose interrupted by bursts of equally angry verse which he called *Bloody Old Britain*. That remained unpublished, since this was the darkest point of the war and, as the publishers Methuen told him, to print such an indictment now would be like kicking a man when he was down.

Another book had preceded it, one written in the white heat of his Russian epiphany. He called it *A Tour in Bolshevy*. This too had been deemed unpublishable, leaving him to distribute it only to like-minded friends. Where he would not have resiled from *Bloody Old Britain* in later life, the fact that this earlier book remained largely unknown must in retrospect have felt like a lucky escape. The great exponent of not only seeing but looking, and looking with the vigilant and unsparing eye of a Sherlock Holmes, had here closed his eyes to every indication that this new world might not be perfect. The great disparager of faith had been led astray by his faith, as he later came to acknowledge. Disillusion developed slowly, but the Russian invasion of Hungary probably finished him. By the end of his life he declared himself 'fanatically' anti-Soviet and anti-Communist.

Yet none of this detracts from what he achieved in the service of archaeology. You can see his legacy in the story of Beresford's identification of the lost village of Wharram Percy in Yorkshire, setting off the most comprehensive excavations of any such site, and abundantly in television series like Tony Robinson's *Time Team* or Ben Robinson's series for BBC 4, *The Flying Archaeologist*. Archaeology had largely concerned itself until now with prehistory and with the Romans. As late as 1949, the doyen of British economic historians, Sir John Clapham, had decreed that lost villages in Britain were 'rare', and some subsequent estimates put the number in the low hundreds. By the end of the twentieth century some 2,000 sites had been listed. English Heritage now knows of around 3,000; Richard Muir thinks the number of identified sites is now about 7,000.

*****

So what today can be safely said about the lost village that this progenitor deconstructed in Lincolnshire? There's a definite pointer about how it began. The name Gainsthorpe derives from Gamelstorp, which is how it appears in Domesday Book. So it's likely to have started life as the 'thorp', or secondary estate, of Gamal, whose first settlement may have been at Hibaldstow. There are no written records, of course, but one has to assume that Gamal and his dependants and associates saw this spot as a fair field for occupation and exploitation. And thereafter? How did Gamal's successors fare here, and how in the end did they vanish, and why? There is very little to go on. But as Sir Thomas Browne so hauntingly says in his book *Urn-Burial* (1658), 'What song the sirens sang, or what name Achilles assumed when he hid himself among women, though puzzling questions, are not beyond conjecture'; and of that, there is plenty.

The causes of this kind of rural depopulation are now largely agreed. Once, countryside legend blamed Cromwell, the great destroyer, or even the devil. And no doubt people living around lost Gainsthorpe would not have been alone in imagining houses 'pulled down', as Abraham de la Pryme described it, 'around their inhabitants' ears' as punishment for their past villainies. Latterly, the standard assumption was that places like these were lost to the plague, and especially to the plague that reached Britain in 1348, which we now call the Black Death, when according to some estimates a third of the population of England perished.

But in general, the verdict of experts now is that the legacy of the plague was more complex and slower to take effect. Because so many common labourers died, labour became harder for landowners to find, and consequently more costly and more ready to move elsewhere for what we would nowadays call better terms and conditions. That was alarming enough to engender the Statute of Labourers (1351), which tried, without much success, to prevent such migrations. So landowners – their ranks now being augmented by new money — hit on a smarter, more dependable solution. The cost of hiring men might be becoming prohibitive: not so the cost of hiring sheep. Sheep were not as fractious as men, and all you needed to keep them disciplined and obedient was a shepherd and a sheepdog. Bishop Latimer, preaching before Edward VI in 1549, complains that because of the work of enclosers, 'where there have been a great many householders and inhabitants there is now but a shepherd and his dog.' So the plough was left to rust; the annual harvest of grain was no longer there to be celebrated. And the village died.

Centuries later, when Otmoor rioted (chapter 2), parliamentary approval was required before common land could become private enclosure. There were no such strictures for medieval enclosers. Their ranks had been swollen in years of prosperity, as a government Bill of 1514 observed, by 'many merchant adventurers, clothmakers, goldsmiths, butchers, tanners and other artificers and unreasonable covetous persons'. They installed themselves as lords of the manor and eradicated land that till then had given the people grain, and turned it over to sheep. The more enlightened landlords bought the previous occupants out and even relocated them. Others simply evicted them. One or two cases fell between. Monasteries were among them. Where the terms they offered were not accepted, they simply drove the occupants out.

The fate of poor people evicted in the Highlands to make way for sheep in the Clearances of the eighteenth and nineteenth centuries has been widely documented and denounced. The clearances of the later Middle Ages are much less commemorated. They have no John Prebble to write their memorial. Yet some even then were scandalized. A Warwickshire priest, John Rous, writing a history of England at the end of the fifteenth century, chronicled the ruthless large-scale destruction inflicted on the North by William the Conqueror (see chapter 14), and asked what now should be said of the 'modern' destruction of villages. 'The root of this evil', he said, 'is greed. The plague of avarice infects these times and it blinds men. They are not the sons of God, but of Mammon.'

From 1489 onwards, the state sought to curb their excesses, not on the grounds of morality, as Rous had done at about the same time, but because it was feared that driving the population off these territories might make them more vulnerable to military attack, and that would directly affect the interests of the King. Then, too, as in our own times, there was fear of what might result if men were left idle. The preamble to the general statute of 1489 pulsated with alarm at the threat if such things continued not just to the Crown, but even to God.

> Great inconveniences daily doth increase by desolation and pulling
> down and wilfull waste of houses and Town ... and laying to pasture
> lands which customarily have been used on tillage where idleness
> – ground and beginning of all mischiefs – daily doth increase, for
> where in some Towns two hundred persons were occupied and lived
> by their lawful labours, now be there occupied two or three herdmen
> and the residue fallen in idleness; the husbandry, which is one of
> the greatest commodities of the realm, is greatly decayed; churches
> destroyed; the service of God withdrawn; the bodies there buried
> not prayed for; the patron and curate wronged; the defence of this
> land against our enemies outward greatly enfeebled and impaired;
> to the great displeasure of God, to the subversion of the policy and
> good rule of this land.

Even the wealthy, even the landowners, met with unwanted consequences
when they travelled the roads. Dispossessed villagers took to the
highways and lived sometimes by begging, sometimes by vagabondage
and sometimes by violent attack. This too must have contributed to the
sense that the state had to intervene. By the time of the 1489 legislation,
though, the tides were abating, and the worst depredations were passing
into history.

And in time the laws of supply and demand began to alter the balance.
There was now a surfeit of wool and a shortage of grain. To remedy that,
the pasture so long surrendered to sheep would have to be restored to the
ploughman. But the threat to farmland was far from over. Behind the march
of the sheep came the march of the emparker: the landlord who wished
to enhance or enlarge his estate and found the cottages on it, and even
sometimes the church, a tiresome encumbrance, impeding the vistas he
wished to show off to visiting friends. Again, there were those who dealt
with the matter sensitively, in that they built new homes for the evicted,
while others simply banished them and left them to find new lives.

While we do not know what settled the fate of Gainsthorpe, the probable
explanation is some kind of human agency, whether driven by ambition,
a sense of self-preservation, or simply by Rous's 'plague of avarice'. But
there could have been other factors: the exhaustion, in an age yet to be
tutored in sensible agricultural practices, of never highly productive land.
It's clear that the communities most vulnerable to extinction were those
that were working poor land or unable to find new land around them
which might be more promising. The deterioration of the climate from the
fifteenth century onwards may be another culprit.

Later, more civilized centuries would knowingly eliminate villages too: to bring water to great cities, with old settlements sunk under reservoirs. The requirements of the military closed down or disposed of villages such as Imber on Salisbury Plain and Tyneham on the Dorset coast, from both of which every family was abruptly evicted on the grounds of national necessity in 1943. And easy assumptions that the days of clearances of the poor by the rich are nowadays wholly unthinkable may look less dependable when we arrive in London at the end of this book. Were John Rous to return, I think he would say of twenty-first-century London very much what he said of the Midlands then: 'The root of this evil is greed. The plague of avarice infects these times and it blinds men. They are not the sons of God, but of Mammon.'

Whatever determined its fate, the original Gainsthorpe was gone, according to the Medieval Settlements Research Group, by 1383, taking its place in a roll call of lost communities that also includes Hungry Bentley in Derbyshire; Archdeacon Newton in Durham; Hartley Maudit in Hampshire; Lobthorpe and Goltho elsewhere in Lincolnshire; Kepwick in Cocklaw, Northumberland; Sock Dennis, Somerset; and Cowlam and Rotsea, Ousethorpe and Eddlethorpe, Waplington and Waudby, Bilham, Stotfold, Little Edstone and Hutton Hang from Beresford's toll of casualties in Yorkshire. Today you must bring to this place not just the product of your research but, above all, your imagination. Its modern surroundings don't help. You cannot escape the sight and sound of the traffic that races along the A15, the great juggernauts hurrying north and south in the service of Mammon. And away to the west, across the now largely silent railway, the remains of the old cement works loom.

And yet what I shall remember from Gainsthorpe is not the distracting traffic or the abandoned works so much as the tranquil greenness of this once busy, populous field and, on this glorious morning, the birdsong: inexplicable yet surely not without meaning; an expression of joy but also, I suppose, resembling in a curious way what 'twitter' means to most of us now – an exchange of news and gossip, sometimes happy and sometimes ominous, but on a spring morning like this, sounding overwhelmingly, infectiously joyful.

Some things never change.

16
BEASTLY PLACE, LEICESTER

94 *Leicester–Frog Island–Glenfield*

AT DADLINGTON, schools mounted a guard of honour, and morris dancers and handbell ringers performed. At Sutton Cheney, a recorder group played medieval music; at Market Bosworth, falcons were flown and the Bishop of Leicester preached. The procession moved on: Newbold Verdon, then Desford. Wherever it stopped on the route the king had once taken, there were prayers. All this before the cortege even reached the old city boundary, Bow Bridge, spanning the River Soar, where the Lord Mayor was waiting to usher it in. At the church of St Nicholas, more prayers were said before the procession moved on through the thronged teatime streets to its terminus at the cathedral.

Everywhere great numbers turned out: 20,000 people at least, it was said at the end of the day. Big screens had been erected in Jubilee Square and at the Clock Tower, the centre point of this city. Next morning long queues had begun to assemble from 4.30 am onwards at the cathedral door, which persisted through to Thursday, the day set for the king's reinterment. The service then was full of glittering uniform, lavish sentiment and high pageantry. The Queen didn't come, though she sent a daughter-in-law and a cousin, but the crowds were somewhat consoled by the presence of Benedict Cumberbatch. In every sense, the entry of King Richard into what it now saw as his city could not have been more of a contrast with his previous arrival, half a millennium earlier: defeated, dead, his naked corpse slung over a horse, to be buried with a minimal and perfunctory ceremony.

For years the city of Leicester had usually thought of the body of Richard III as lost, as having been dug up from its first resting place at Greyfriars when the friary was eradicated in 1538, and pitched contemptuously into the Soar at Bow Bridge. That was how the respected historian and cartographer John Speed had told it in 1611. A plaque posted on the bridge in 1856 recorded it; even the *Oxford History of England* had accepted it as a fact.

Some others didn't believe it. In the 1930s one local historian suggested that the body might still be in its original burial place, but little notice was taken. In 1975, a contributor to the magazine of the Richard III Society, Audrey Strange, again argued that the body might still be where it had been so casually laid after Bosworth, perhaps under land that was now a council car park. In the early 2000s, an alliance of diligent people, some driven by their allegiance to Richard III, others by a disinterested wish to establish the truth – with the historical novelist Philippa Gregory, an official of the Scottish Richard III Society, and the medieval historian John Ashdown-Hill prominent among them – resolved to test these theories. It took some time to enlist others with greater clout and more money to draw on. Even the University of Leicester, which now likes to claim it led the search for Richard III, seemed to some of these pioneers slow to respond. But gradually interest accrued, and the enterprise was joined by the city council, the cathedral authorities, the tourism organization Leicester Promotions and an eager TV production company.

The archaeologists started digging in August 2012 and on the very first day uncovered bones which subsequent analysis showed were those of a man in his thirties (Richard was thirty-two when he died) who had suffered brutal injuries. The university won the assent of the Ministry of Justice for the exhumation of six sets of remains, including those that just might be Richard's. Now a wider group of experts, on bone structure and facial reconstruction and especially on DNA tracing, became involved, and the first tentative identification became steadily more persuasive. Finally, in February 2013, the university teams declared themselves satisfied that beyond any reasonable doubt the dead king had been found.

By this time, interest had spread far beyond Leicester. Almost five million people watched a Channel 4 documentary, *The King in the Car Park*. Now the reinterment could be planned – though that meant fighting rival claims to the bones, not least from York, where some argued that Richard, undeniably a son of the house of York who had lived for a time at Middleham in North Yorkshire, had wanted his obsequies. A group who claimed to be relatives of the king, mustered under the title, The Plantagenet Alliance, started legal action designed to thwart Leicester. But the courts found in Leicester's favour, as did public opinion, where 34,000 people signed a petition for Leicester against 31,000 backing York. The fact that the whole endeavour had been so overwhelmingly set up and financed by Leicester no doubt swayed support.

Of course, there were sceptics: there always are – and rightly so. Had it not been for sceptics, Leicester would still believe that Richard's body was dumped in the River Soar. Some academics complained that the university's 'proof' that the bones were the king's was inadequate. In the *Guardian*, Polly Toynbee ridiculed the whole endeavour: 'The nation mourns its most reviled monster of a king. Never was adulation of monarchy taken to such transcendently absurd heights. It's comical, but tragic too, as a reminder of the indignity the British accept in their accustomed role as subjects, not citizens. Here are church, royalty and army revering a child-killing, wife-slaughtering tyrant who would be on trial if he weren't 500 years dead.'

But this exercise wasn't really built around reverence. It was built around revenue. Revenue for public authorities but for commercial interests too. Now in early June there are banners everywhere brandishing Richard's name in various contexts. Today I'm no sooner out of the station than I'm confronted with a big Wetherspoon pub called The Last Plantagenet, recently refurbished, or in other words, Richardized. A knitted Richard III woolly doll will cost you a mere £2.50. Leicestershire Aero Club is offering the Richard III Flying Experience – a trip in a four-seater plane over the route he took to his fatal encounter at Bosworth Field. And guess which play by Shakespeare the Curve Theatre will be staging in one month's time? . . . He wasn't here very often in his lifetime, but after 500 years of being dead, he is everywhere.

Two months on from the reinterment, official statistics were published that showed that people in Leicester had less disposable income than those in any other city in the United Kingdom. The city's elected mayor, Sir Peter Soulsby, said Leicester could and would put that right. And here, at this very moment, the evidence was emerging that the Richard III bonanza was doing just that. The exercise had cost a small fortune: the *Leicester Mercury* estimated the cost at more than £3 million: £2.5 million expended by the cathedral on making the building fit to house the recovered monarch; more than £250,000 incurred by the city council, almost £200,000 falling on Leicestershire county council, a modest £32,000 on Leicester University and £86,500 on Leicestershire police.

But that could be looked on as money well spent. A firm of consultants hired by the city estimated the boost to the local economy at £60 million, of which £4.5 million came in during the two weeks of the reinterment. The 'Richard III effect' had brought in some 600,000 visitors. They came from all over Britain and from overseas. One of the first in the queue when the cathedral opened its doors to the public was a sixty-two-year-old man from Atlanta, Georgia. Later, more typical, pilgrims included Rose and Michael McNichols from Widnes. 'I've been watching all the programmes on TV,' Rose told the *Mercury*, 'and I was watching the funeral while doing the ironing when I decided I really wanted to come.'

So now, in March 2015, Leicester could make claims previously denied to it. It had given a king of England the kind of funeral that monarchs deserved; it had used this event to catch the nation's attention – even, as the *Mercury* said, 'global attention'. Though on some counts the tenth biggest city in England, Leicester had rarely managed to interest either audience before. The city had been routinely dismissed with the faintest of praise, or roundly disparaged. Harold Nicolson, writer and diplomat, who was one of the city's MPs for ten years till swept out by the Labour landslide of 1945, looked in on his way to Nottingham nine years later. 'I gazed on that ugly and featureless city,' he wrote to his wife, Vita Sackville-West, 'thinking how strange it was that I had for so long been identified with those brick houses with their ironwork railings and their clean little steps.' Winston Churchill had come over to sympathize when in 1950 he learned that Harold's son Nigel had gone down to defeat in his father's old seat. Birmingham, was it? the old man asked. No, Leicester, Nicolson said. 'Well I knew it was a hopeless seat,' Churchill said. 'Beastly place, Leicester.' (Churchill had stood as a Liberal there in the twenties, and lost.)

'Beastly' was a harsher judgement than most. A more common insult was 'boring'. Even Leicester's distinguished historians accepted that. Jack Simmons, for many years professor of history at its university (then still a university college), says in his history of the city that it has nothing grand, nothing dramatic, nothing exciting. The reliably readable blogger who calls himself 'Jones the Planner' – real name Adrian Jones; he was once Nottingham's director of planning and transport – comes to much the same conclusion: 'Leicester has an image problem,' he wrote in 2007. 'It hasn't got one.'

Often such conclusions involved unflattering comparisons with the city of Nottingham, twenty-five miles away, and usually much the best rated of the three old industrial cities entrapped in an eternal East Midlands triangle along with Derby. 'Leicester', the mayor of the city commented, 'is a city that has historically lacked self-confidence and far too often we've looked up the road and assumed that everything is better there.'

Part of that may have been its absence of local heroes. Robin Hood may not have existed, but his name, and that of Maid Marian, give Nottingham a romantic allure that Leicester cannot match. Simon de Montfort, whom Leicester likes to describe as the founding father of modern democracy, held the earldom of Leicester and today has a university, a hall, several streets, a square, five companies and a doctors' surgery named after him, but there's no firm evidence that he spent any great time in the place. There is no name that signals Leicester as Jesse Boot does Nottingham. Perhaps the nearest is Thomas Cook, the great promoter of home and overseas travel, whose statue stands near the station, loaded with luggage and armed with a vengeful umbrella; but even he is not quite ideal, since he came from Nottingham. As Jack Simmons noted, the kind of local industrialist who moved on to direct a town's fortunes, became perhaps a Member of Parliament and established a reputation well beyond his city was never apparent here. Leicester industrialists shunned ostentatious houses and life styles, contenting themselves with running efficient companies and with purely local activity.

Leicester's sporting achievements – one of the most successful rugby union clubs in the land, far outstripping anything Nottingham ever produced, and a soccer team, Leicester City, which in the 2015–16 season would outstrip far richer and more famous rivals to win the premiership – top Nottingham's, though Nottinghamshire is way ahead when it comes to cricket.

Leicester has another distinction with which not everyone there is happy, let alone eager to brag about. This is the first English city where the ethnic group classed as white British is in a minority. The figures in the 2011 census showed 45 per cent of the population as white British and the total white population as 51 per cent. That figure is bound to reduce, since the non-white British populations have higher birth rates. For the rest, 37 per cent were categorized as Asian, with 28 per cent as Indian, and 6.3 per cent as black. That is nothing new for Leicester. In its high manufacturing days it drew in immigrants both from less prosperous tracts of Britain and from abroad. Over the years, people from Ireland and Poland, Latvia and Lithuania, Germany, Italy, Serbia and Ukraine established communities here.

From the 1960s onwards, though, the new arrivals came above all from Asia. Their numbers were greatly augmented when in 1972 Idi Amin drove Asians out of Uganda. Leicester became so alarmed at this point that advertisements were inserted in Ugandan newspapers warning that Leicester would not be able to take them. Later analysis showed that this had in fact suggested a possible new destination for many who had never till then known that it existed. Since that time, the numbers have grown so mightily that on the city's own calculations in 2008, around seventy different languages and dialects were in use here, while for as many as 45 per cent of school pupils, English was not their first language.

That might on some popular calculations have promised serious trouble, even in some people's language, rivers of blood. And there have indeed at times been disturbances, sometimes mounting to riot, chiefly in 1981, a year of widespread rioting in the UK, which though not always ascribable to inter-race tension was inflamed by it.

Yet on the whole the city has settled down amicably and in relative peace. Its politics tell the story. There hasn't been the boost to political groups dead set against immigration that's occurred in some places where immigrant numbers are slighter. Parties campaigning explicitly on the issue of immigration, the National Front until 1979, the British National Party in 1983, rarely exceeded 5 per cent of the vote and were mostly well below that. In the 2010 election the BNP reached 6 per cent in Leicester West, 3.5 in the East and 3 in the South constituency. Five years later they did not field candidates. Now those who wanted to protest over levels of immigration were turning to UKIP, who took 17.2 per cent of the vote in Leicester West and 8.9 in the South. But with such a mixed electorate, their scope was limited. And the kind of burning resentment apparent in some other towns had been dampened down here, not least by good public management.

Here, too, is a side to Leicester that, because it is hard to quantify, has been underrated. Ian Nairn savoured this place above all for its sense of tolerance. Richard Hoggart, who taught at Leicester University in the early 1960s, warmed to it in much the same way: 'almost everything in Leicester fits its chosen mode,' he wrote in his autobiography: 'nothing dramatic, everything as it should be in a reasonable person.' He found the whole East Midlands region 'above all mild and friendly'. Though I may not have encountered a representative sample, I was struck on my day here by the friendliness and helpfulness of people. 'Are you lost?' when I stood bemused at what proved to be the wrong bus stop, 'where are you trying to get to? Can I help?' And that, despite their initial admissions that Leicester was seen as boring, rings through the pages of Simmons and Hoskins too. It might be small and modest and self-effacing, but this, they said, was a place that grew on you, which in time you might come (as they did) to love.

This understatedness is an aspect of Leicester exemplified by its town hall – begun in 1874 to supersede the medieval Guildhall alongside the cathedral: a pleasantly modest building which shuns the kind of swagger so often displayed in great municipal buildings. It calmly presides over a square with fountains, with away to one side the Wesleyan Methodist church of 1815 on Bishop Street. Which makes it all the more refreshing to find close by in Granby Street a building of way out and whacky exuberance: the Turkey Café, a riotous Art Nouveau concoction, fanciful and fantastic, with a gorgeous multi-coloured fowl installed at the top, built by the local architect Arthur Wakerley. This was Wakerley letting his hair down. Other buildings he has left in the city can't be accused of such unLeicesterly showiness.

*****

Yet moderation did not always rule in Leicester. Anyone who stopped off at the church of St Nicholas during the Richard III festivities will have been conscious of that. The great inner ring road hammered through here in the sixties hemmed it in and sliced it off from the city centre. To compound the insult, the roadway which accomplished it was given his name: St Nicholas Circle. Today this sector north-west of the city is all overpass and underpass and racing traffic and indifferent modern buildings dominated by a massive Holiday Inn (architect: William Bond of Memphis, Tennessee). This was the heart of Roman Leicester and of medieval Leicester, all swept away by bright-eyed planners.

In 1962 this became only the second city in England to appoint a full-time planning officer. This was an era when traffic was king. Birmingham had Herbert Manzoni (see chapter 4). Leeds designated itself in the sixties 'Motorway City of the Seventies', but fortunately failed to carry it all through. Elsewhere too there were powerful chief officers who liked to think they were visionaries and sometimes treated the cities that they commanded almost as if they were personal playthings. Great towns did not merely try to come to terms with traffic; they capitulated to it. The man Leicester chose was Konrad Smigielski, born in Poland, and until his appointment in 1962 an academic at Leeds University. Looking around the city on his arrival he valued the castle, the Guildhall and New Walk, a pedestrian boulevard that runs from the centre towards the university, but apparently not much else. His dreams for the transformation of Leicester were hailed then – and by some, are still – as visionary. Some of what he advocated – the installation, notably, of a city monorail – was too much for the city council. In the end, he left in frustration at having his schemes rejected.

There is still controversy in the city about what he did to it during his ten years in office, as over how much of the blame for the worst of it more truly belongs to his predecessor, John Beckett. Had Beckett's will prevailed, even New Walk, then grown shabby and squalid, would have been disrupted too. Smigielski halted that and began to restore it. The now much hated roads that he built, with all their attendant destruction, came from his recognition that the centre was being asphyxiated by traffic. He wanted to restore the space to the people, and to do that, he calculated, you needed to build fast and efficient roads close in. These solutions are now almost universally recognized as a disaster. As Professor Simon Gunn, of the Centre for Urban History at Leicester University, who on the whole deals sympathetically with Smigielski, accepts, some of the worst that happened to Leicester, while not directly his fault, was done on his watch.

Even the mild and moderate Jack Simmons could not forgive what was done to it in the sixties. 'In the last fifteen years', he wrote in his history of Leicester, completed in 1974, 'the Old Town of Leicester has been almost completely destroyed. In the late 1950s its medieval street plan was clearly visible, and it was dominated by the industrial buildings that summarised and embodied the town's Victorian prosperity . . . In their place we have a huge swath of concrete, taking the traffic of the city north and south, with windy and desolate stretches, of concrete again, on either side of it. The Old Town in its former state was grimy, and in many respects an inefficient anachronism. Nevertheless it was full of interest, of oddity; it was lovable and contained surprises.'

But where the1960s are remembered most of all for what they destroyed, recent years have brought some redemption. Near the top of what's left of Highcross Street (the old High Cross was long ago cleared out of the way) is a new shopping centre, remodelled and expanded in 2008 to replace an older, drabber affair called the Shires, and renamed the Highcross Centre. Compared with so many of the shopping malls to be found nowadays all over the land, it's a triumph. Inside the main entrance, on the edge of the city centre, there's a Debenhams and a House of Fraser. So far, so good; but what we hardened inspectors of this kind of enterprise always ask at this point is: have they managed to land a John Lewis? Then you climb the gentle slope towards the end of the sequence and there is the shimmering, glowing, affirmative answer. And in a fine bit of theatre reflecting the architects' use of split levels, you enter it over a bridge with a further shop-windowed street below. Nottingham has nothing to match this. Lucky Leicester! And luckier still when you come close by to the open market, arrayed before the imposing Corn Exchange, with all the ancillary stands that a market should offer, from haberdashery to ironmongery and books and assorted bits of electronic gear; but above all, a riot of fruit and veg, all gleaming in today's sunshine, superintended by cheery vociferous people, white and brown. There's a café in one corner where you can sit and gaze at this great gleaming natural panoply while sipping your cappuccino.

The 94 bus that runs from the city of Leicester to Glenfield, where the headquarters of the county council is now established, goes first to Frog Island. When I first listed the routes that might make up this book I discarded this one as a mere 25-minute potter though a string of suburbs to its ultimate suburb. But the name Frog Island lingered, and arriving here I am glad that I did. A journey of less than a mile from the bus station takes one from Leicester that is to the Leicester that was: a proud and practical manufacturing town.

Man, not nature, made this an island. A canal was engineered in a loop of the River Soar, and Frog Island is the bit between them. It seems generally agreed nowadays that it's an eyesore, a wretchedly inappropriate introduction to Leicester as you come in on the A50 Warrington to Leicester road, and needs to be swept away. The city says so: many, perhaps even most, of the people who live around it say so. It's not for a transient visitor to dispute that judgement: it's easy to see why they find it demeaning. Yet the buildings on and around the island tell a story that nowhere else does. This was a town that made things: shoes and hosiery (socks, stockings and tights), later developing new lines in engineering. Many of its most important factories or mills produced some line of everyday routine essentials. Theirs were not always, not often, household names. Corah's, the exemplar of Leicester endeavour, began as a very small company, the creation of Noah Corah, born in one of the outlying villages, imprisoned early in his business career for debt, but soon back in business buying up clothing from Leicester manufacturers and selling it on to markets in Birmingham. He prospered, enough to start his own factory on the edge of the city in the parish of St Margaret's. In time he caught the attention of Marks & Spencer. Where Corah had adopted the brand name St Margaret, Marks & Spencer began in time to sell Corah's goods using the name St Michael.

This relationship became the centrepiece of Corah's operations, beneficial for many years but fatal in the end. M&S grew mightier, and put ever-growing pressure on Corah's, and when times grew hard began to turn to cheaper suppliers abroad. The firm changed hands, falling under the control of an Australian company of the kind skilled at exploiting recessions, from the stable that became known as 'corporate raiders', who bought it up promising 'conservative management' and soon after, went bust. And that was the end of Corah's.

The firms that worked and for some time thrived on and around Frog Island were mostly far smaller and more obscure than Corah's, but they were still an essential part of the life of the city. The street which crosses first the canal and then the river here is also called Frog Island. Westward along the canal new outfits have taken over abandoned works: Stayfree Music, music studios and practice rooms; Igloo, transport consultants; Fischer-Futureheat UK, electrical heating engineers; Cahill Plastics, plastic injection moulding . . . but nearly all the rest are ruins, some with enough surviving structure to let you imagine what they must have been like in their prime, others as mere jagged wrecks. The locks carry visiting long boats along the canal, watched today by people with time on their hands and a very attentive dog.

It's hard as you stand on the bridge not to imagine the echoes of tramping feet approaching on their way to these workplaces or leaving at the end of the day with perhaps a stop at the tavern. Again, I tell myself, as I did at Tyldesley, that one must not be too romantic in such matters. These working men and their families lived hard and restricted lives in what must have been a polluted and unhealthy place. The Soar, rated one of the city's attractions now, was once best known for its stench. Yet as I felt when passing a much smaller array of industrial ruins in Birmingham, there's a case for preserving such relics, just as we do with religious houses long ago ravaged and then deserted, as reminders of once dominant institutions and the way we lived then. If you value these things, go to Frog Island. Soon there'll be nothing left.

Woodgate, on the far side of the island, has an Aldi store, where my next 94 arrives. It skirts a place called Newfound Pool, where, as Leicester burgeoned and more and more workers came in to seize its opportunities, a builder furnished a network of streets whose names spelled out his own, which was I. (for Isaac) Harrison: Ingle Street, Hawthorne Street, Alma Street, Rowland and Ruby, Ivanhoe, Sylvan, Oban, Newport. We're now entering one of the greatest post-war estates: New Parks – green and spacious, uniform and monotonous, characteristic of the great spreading Almost Anywhere of twentieth-century Britain.

And then in a break with the prevailing monotony we come to the border: the spot, by a vet's, where the city gives way to the county. How apart from these administrative designations does the pattern alter? Barely at all. Greater Leicester – a term that Jack Simmons used forty years ago – makes far more sense than an arbitrary line drawn on a bureaucrat's map. In 2005 the Office of National Statistics published tables of what were designated 'urban areas', showing Leicester's had a population of 441,000. But Nottingham's was 666,000. On that basis, the people who replied in a *Leicester Mercury* poll that Nottingham was the bigger city were right.

*****

Perhaps Glenfield, like the city, grows on you when you live there. But for most of the time it's all neat, clean, decent, often (in estate agent terms) desirable homes, and no local flavour whatever. The bus ends its journey at that part of Glenfield which still has some justification in claiming to be a village. The centre, around The Square, has a sense of the Glenfield that used to be. An elderly woman in a wheelchair on my bus says this part of it is little changed from her childhood, though as for the rest of the place . . . she sighs, and falls silent. On the way to the square there's the first of three pubs, the Forge; the Nag's Head and the Railway Arms are on Station Road, though as so often now with Station Roads, there isn't a station. Tucked away up a hill is the church of St Peter, completed in 1876, with alongside it, shrouded in ivy, the site of an earlier St Peter's which became too dilapidated to repair.

Where the station once stood there's a sizeable Co-op. Further on is Progress Works, which may sound like a slogan used to justify what was done in Leicester in the sixties, but in fact is a sturdy building of 1925, erected for the manufacture of boots and shoes by the Glenfield Progress Co-operative Society. Now it's the home of something more twenty-first century: Sole Fitness (spin, Zumba, legs, bums and tums, pump, and more.) And beyond, there's a side street of smart modern homes which bears the significant name Stephenson Close.

No passenger train has run into Glenfield since 1928. Already then the passenger usage must have been slight: 'the public', a local paper said, 'will not be seriously inconvenienced by the deprivation of a passenger service.' Yet if Glenfield had a Richard III, a man remembered for putting it on the map, he would surely be Robert Stephenson, son of the even more famous rail pioneer George. George was originally asked to take on the project, and found most of the money to pay for it, but it was Robert who superintended the coming of the railway here.

This was an early venture, in 1832, so well in hand even before the railway mania of the 1840s. To get a sense of how the Leicester to Swannington – in coalfield territory near Ashby-de-la-Zouch – came about, you need to walk north of the village as far as the A50 trunk road. Here on a nicely landscaped sequence, widened to cater for ever-increasing traffic, you will find the new County Hall: decent, restrained – in Leicester fashion, understated. Across the road is an overgrown path which leads to a flight of steps, at the foot of which is the track of the Leicester to Swannington. And immediately on the left is what was once Glenfield's great claim to attention: the end of what when it was built was, at 1,796 yards (just over a mile), the longest railway tunnel in the world. It is not quite as Robert Stephenson envisaged it; he designed stately portals which because of their threatened cost were never built. But in essence this was Robert Stephenson's project, executed by others but supervised by him.

These enterprises were dangerous: most of all for the turbulent navvies who moved in to build them, though here a director of one of the contractor companies fell down a newly dug shaft to his death. Had Stephenson not come to inspect it and ordered improvements, there might have been worse disasters on the service than the one that afflicted the very first train. The chimney on the engine was too tall for the tunnel and struck the roof, showering its distinguished passengers in soot; the train had to be stopped while they cleaned themselves up with water from a nearby brook. Yet passengers were an afterthought. The lines had been built to shift coal, and the early travellers had to cram into coaches tacked on the back of the train.

The line served its purpose for more than a century. But the last freight train clattered through the echoing tunnel in 1985, and in 1989 Leicester City Council paid £5 to acquire it, though it wasn't clear what they could use it for. Now someone has decorated the entrance with a swastika. Westward from here, the old railway track has become the Ivanhoe Trail (Sir Walter Scott's Ivanhoe makes much of Ashby-de-la-Zouch) open to cyclists and walkers. Also, it seems, to powered wheelchairs: 'I speed down there!' the elderly lady ensconced in her chair tells me gleefully as our bus rattles back towards Leicester.

So it's back through interminable Greater Glenfield and New Parks and over sad, evocative, doomed Frog Island to look at last at refurbished Leicester Cathedral, the parish church of St Martin until the town was promoted to city status in 1919. It's not so busy today, though the greeter at the door says there's now a one-way system in operation as you make your way to the tomb. Here there are notices begging visitors not to take photographs of themselves posing with Richard III, though no doubt, in this age of the selfie, hundreds still do.

All round the cathedral there are notices, best thought of perhaps as homilies, taking aspects of Richard's story and drawing morals in much the way that they do on 'Thought for the Day' on BBC Radio 4. 'The view of Richard III as a ruthless and ambitious schemer', says one on the way to the tomb, 'is a powerful myth . . . Was he good or bad? The answer is, he was both, as are we all.' Another pictures Richard as one who had to flee his country for a while to find refuge, and finds a parallel here with Leicester as a city of immigrant sanctuary.

Across the square in front of the cathedral, where people are sitting in the early evening sun, is the visitor centre set up as a further Richard III tourist allurement, which incorporates the place where the diggers had their success, and even such relics as the wellington boots that Philippa Gregory wore during these proceedings. Round the corner, by today's Greyfriars, is a mighty building up for sale for use perhaps as a café or restaurant, which was one of the city's banks, created by Parr's Leicestershire Banking, later acquired by National Westminster. Leicester built its banks well – there's another fine example not far from the Turkey Café in Granby Street, built for the Leicestershire Bank by Joseph Goddard, patiently waiting for some appropriate new purpose today. And here is Loseby Lane, not a place on most tourist itineraries, but gentle, withdrawn, cloister-like, the kind of minor street people find and enthuse about in continental towns, and one of the moments as I came to its crossroads with St Martin's that I found most endearing in Leicester. And one which, it has to be said, the city was asked to dispose of when Konrad Smigielski was king; by pulling it down the council could treat the city to a capacious multi-storey car park. Mercifully, the council knew better.

There's something about this street which solidifies my day's impressions of Leicester. People talk about this place as though it fails to measure up to the competition. Even Jones the Planner, who often writes about cities as tellingly as anyone since Ian Nairn, seems to endorse that. 'In both its character and its scale,' he says, 'the city centre is disconcertingly uncertain if it is that of a big city or not.' With Richardization, that is to some extent changing. Yet I think it misses the point. Leicester will never be Milan, nor reconstituted Manchester, nor indeed Nottingham. But that isn't what matters. The whole point about this city, and one it ought to be happy to settle for, is that it's good at being Leicester.

17
BATTLING BOADICEA AND
BATTLING MRS BYRNE

94 Colchester–East Bergholt–Hadleigh (94A)

I THINK I KNOW where I first set eyes on Queen Boadicea: in a children's book called *Our Island Story* by H.E. Marshall, published in 1905, as its preface says, not a history lesson but a storybook, designed to awaken children to the excitement of history. It certainly did with me. Henrietta Elizabeth Marshall – to prise her out from behind her austere initials – makes the story of her 'warrior queen' sound reassuringly straightforward. The Romans, she says, were a greedy people who wanted to take the freedom of Britain away and make it into a Roman province. When Boadicea's husband died, he left half his money to the emperor and half to his wife and children, but the greedy Romans wanted the lot. Yet they failed to see that many of the women of Britain were quite as brave and wise as the men. Boadicea rallied her people, telling them: 'We will fight, and if we cannot conquer, then let us die, every one of us – die rather than submit.'

Her artist-collaborator, A.S. Forrest, pictures the scene. Boadicea is addressing a group of hairy men in what look like togas. Tall and commanding, wielding a vicious knife and with vivid red hair, she seems for a twenty-first-century audience reminiscent of Rebekah Brooks, beleaguered editor of the *News of the World* and the *Sun*, facing down those who wanted to send her into imprisonment. 'Queen Boadicea looked so beautiful and fierce as she stood there,' Marshall writes, 'with her blue eyes flashing, and her golden hair blowing around her in the wind, that the hearts of her people were filled with love for her, and anger against the Romans.' Thus enthused, her men go out to do battle; and in terrible encounters that follow, the might of Rome is crushed and humbled.

So discovering that the 94 bus out of Colchester would take me in just under an hour to another town, across the border in Suffolk, where local rebels, less ruthless than the forces of Boadicea yet no less committed, had quite recently humbled another mighty, imperialistic invader seemed almost too good to be true.

As indeed, in one crucial respect, it was.

*****

The popular, vulgarized story of Boadicea is irresistibly linked with three places that she destroyed: Camulodunum (Colchester), Londinium (London) and Verulanium (now St Albans). Curiously, Marshall does not mention Colchester; yet this is a place long built into the story, and you can't be long in the town without becoming aware of her. They don't milk Boadicea (or Boudicca, as generations of more rigorous historians have taught us to call her) in the way that a place like Rochester keeps hurling Charles Dickens at you; she doesn't keep cropping up around the next corner as the Butes do in Cardiff. There's a Boadicea Way south-west of the centre, and a Queen Boudica Primary School of 2009, and a metal statue, in a style very far removed from A.S. Forrest's, on a roundabout close to the main station. She's one of the worthies whose effigies appears on the outside of 1902 town hall. And within the hall there's a stained-glass window with a picture that makes her look less as a warrior queen than something out of a nineteenth-century ad for Pears' Soap. In the museum at Colchester Castle, built by the Normans on the site once occupied by the massive temple to Claudius which the warrior queen destroyed, she takes her place in a sequence that begins with Cunobelin, Shakespeare's Cymbeline, whom the Roman historian Suetonius called the king of the Britons, and who made his capital here. The Romans, invading after Cunobelin's death, made it their capital too.

Boudicca is treated in the museum with a kind of respectful scepticism, reflecting an essential truth about her, which is that we know a great deal less than Marshall and Forrest might have you suppose. But like many museums today, it's as eager as Marshall was to fire the imagination of children. Where museums in my youth were full of notices saying 'don't this' and 'don't that', here they keep saying 'please do'; do touch, do handle, do please dress up as a Roman or warlike Briton. And not only children; while I am there one elderly man takes his chance to drive a simulated four-horse chariot, and when he's had a go his place is taken, after a furtive glance around, by an apparently even older one.

There's a film that runs continuously on a big screen at Colchester Castle in which someone dressed as an ancient Briton glories in the defeat of the Romans. 'She', he proclaims, evoking her in terms which echo Marshall and Forrest – her height, fierce appearance, long golden hair and powerful voice – 'was our queen, Boudicca. And we . . . were the Iceni.' And below there's a chance to vote on the question: was Boudicca right to destroy Camulodunum? Press this button for yes and that one for no.

Restrained though the presentation may be, it's still in some ways contentious. What right, it is asked in some places north of here, has Colchester to parade itself as Boudicca's town? What, after, all did she ever do for Camulodunum? She destroyed it, along it seems with all the Romans she found there. Norwich Museum claims her for Norfolk. 'Her story is told in Colchester and London,' John Davies, Chief Curator and Keeper of Archaeology at this museum, has said, 'but she was only there because she sacked them. There is nothing wrong with them telling the story there, but it is our story, this is where she lived. We are reclaiming Boudicca as a local heroine and trying to tell the story in the place it should be told in.'

And beyond all that, there's an even more troubling question: did she (some have doubted it) even exist? There are two main historical sources: the writings of Tacitus, in his *Agricola* and his *Annals* (the two accounts don't always square), and the writings of Cassius Dio, some 150 years after the events he's describing. According to Tacitus, Boudicca was the widow of Prasutagus, King of the Iceni, who to safeguard his family's interests had made the emperor his co-heir with his two daughters. When he died, their share was seized; Boudicca was flogged, and the two girls raped. The kingdom was treated as a mere province. The humiliated Iceni rebelled, joined by a neighbouring tribe, the Trinovantes, and others. The Romans built a temple in honour of Claudius – a blatant symbol of alien rule – and the subjugated Britons were made to pay for it.

But their town had no effective defences; it did not even have walls. The battle was prefaced by portents – outlandish shrieks and yells, a phantom settlement seen in ruins at the mouth of the Thames, a blood-red sea, corpse-like shapes washed up by the tide – terrifying the settlers, whose appeals for help went largely unanswered. They retreated to the temple, but that was seized too, and destroyed, along with all those found within it. Here and at Londinium and Verulanium, the natives looted, plundered and took a terrible vengeance, cutting throats, hanging, burning and crucifying. Gaius Suetonius Paulinus, governor of Britain, mustered a force of nearly 10,000 to subdue the rebellion. Boudicca defied him, driving round all the tribes in a chariot with her daughters before her. 'I am descended from mighty men,' she told them. 'But now I am not fighting for my kingdom and wealth. I am fighting now as an ordinary person for my lost freedom, my bruised body and my outraged daughters. Nowadays Roman rapacity does not even spare our bodies. Old people are killed, virgins raped. But the gods will grant us the vengeance we deserve . . . You will win the battle, or perish. That is what I, a woman, plan to do! – let the men live in slavery if they will.' But this time Boudicca failed. The Romans, says Tacitus, won a glorious victory. According to one report, almost 80,000 Britons were slain; the Roman death toll was around 400. Boudicca took poison and died.

Cassius Dio has Boudicca making a speech just as impassioned, even longer and probably no more authentic. Such accounts belong to a venerable category of inventive history writing which basically tells us what their authors think might have been said, had the protagonists been up to it. But here was Tacitus, an aristocratic Roman, writing out of sympathy for these near-barbarians, misused and cheated by Rome. As one might nowadays say, he felt their pain.

There isn't much else to go on. There is good archaeological evidence about the burning down of the towns, but that is as far as it goes. No one knows where the final battle was fought – suggestions range from 'near London' – possibly Hampstead – to Mancetter in Warwickshire, and Flintshire. One sixteenth-century Scottish historian had the whole sequence taking place in Scotland. No one knows quite how Boudicca died. No one knows where she was buried; some once thought it explained Stonehenge; others had her being interred at what is now King's Cross station, specifically under its platform eight, not far from Harry Potter's platform nine and three quarters.

And because we know so little about her, she's become a kind of blank page on which anyone who chooses can write their own version. You can make her a prototype British national leader, though that doesn't make even minimal sense when in her day neither Britain nor England existed: only a loose aggregation of tribes. There's a statue by Thomas Thornycroft on the Embankment at the end of Westminster Bridge, close to the Houses of Parliament, where she seems to be posed to defend them, which again belongs to romance and not to reality. She's sometimes portrayed as a fighter for feminism; the Suffragists adopted her as a forerunner.

Elizabeth I was presented as a modern Boudicca, as a warrior queen; her speech at Tilbury in 1588, dressed for the occasion as the Armada threatened, seems as reported (and many serious historians believe that to be authentic) to echo the (wholly invented) rallying cry of Boudicca: 'I know I have the body of a weak, feeble woman; but I have the heart and stomach of a king, and of a king of England too, and think foul scorn that Parma or Spain, or any prince of Europe, should dare to invade the borders of my realm, to which rather than any dishonour shall grow by me.'

A cult of Boudicca developed under Victoria (the name Boudicca means victory) even to the extent of portraying the Iceni queen as some kind of proto-empress. It grew, if anything, stronger after Victoria's death. Thornycroft's reverential depiction wasn't installed at Westminster until 1902, long after the sculptor's death and a year after Victoria's.

There's much to be said for Colchester – especially when it's compared with the county's other principal town. Colchester, once a capital, is now not even a county town; that honour has long belonged to Chelmsford, which is larger and more central, and which in 2012 was elevated to the status of city, leaving Colchester among the also-rans. There's a much greater sense of occasion here than in Chelmsford. Colchester has the longer, deeper and more absorbing history, the more celebrated university, and even a better football team. It also has a high reputation for oysters, and a zoo. It is happier in its geography. This is a town set on a hill: 'It has that characteristic of all the best towns from Rome to Dublin, from Warwick to Edinburgh,' says Norman Scarfe in his *Shell Guide to Essex*, 'you can see the open country from the middle of the town.'

It is into that open country that my 94 bus is due to take me today, with a break on my way to Hadleigh at East Bergholt, a place whose local hero few can have doubts about: John Constable glorified the place with which he's associated, whereas Boudicca merely ravaged hers. But now my bus has arrived with a disquieting message on its front: *Ipswich*. Suddenly my project seems to be facing disaster. The timetable I downloaded in London plainly states that the 94 runs through East Bergholt to Hadleigh. But this bus claims – and the driver confirms it – to have nothing to do with Hadleigh. Between them, Carters Coach Services (Ipswich based) and Suffolk County Council, whose funding keeps many such routes on the road, have denied the people of Essex and Suffolk the right they have long enjoyed of making the journey direct. East Bergholt, they say, yes, by all means: but Hadleigh, no.

*****

Having extricated itself from Colchester, the 94 bus initially sticks slavishly to the A12, the main route to Ipswich. Still, at least we are permitted a deviation when the bus turns down Gun Hill (where Constable painted) on its way to the village of Stratford St Mary, which has houses full of character and sometimes, as is often the case in this part of the world, of a pleasant eccentricity.

Rambling enough to have five pubs distributed through it (not all of which, I'm happy to say, have gone gastro), East Bergholt this morning is a decorous, prosperous-looking place, and unexpectedly quiet. That is no doubt because this is winter, and the people you pass in the streets are here because they live here, not because they've come looking for Constable, as they inevitably do as the year progresses. The village lives on invasions which must sometimes seem oppressive. Their true destination is less Bergholt than Flatford, on the road that leads down to the Stour; for though Constable drew and painted a good deal in Bergholt, it was Flatford where he did so to the point of obsession, the mill and the lock and Willy Lott's cottage and the meadows and the trees in their various seasons under the Suffolk skies: Constable scenes that those who come on pilgrimage here already have, if not on their walls, on their coasters and tea towels and table mats.

All are now in the care of the National Trust, who also offer an introductory exhibition at Bridge Cottage, guided tours which will take you where Constable walked and painted and no doubt show you the precise point at which he painted *The Haywain*, and a riverside tea room, and of course a shop. All closed today, since in winter it's weekend opening only.

The artist's father owned Flatford Mill, and prospered from it; John's oldest siblings were born there. Then the family moved to the more capacious property, East Bergholt House, where John was born in 1776. That was demolished in the 1840s; there's a plaque on the wall to establish its Constable connection. And right alongside is the church, which still awaits the tower it was promised almost 500 years ago, only for the project to fall along with Cardinal Wolsey. The bells, which are famously heavy as well as sonorous, have been housed ever since in the cage in the churchyard that was installed as a temporary expedient in 1531.

You won't find the graves of Constable and his wife, Maria, in Bergholt churchyard; they died and were buried in Hampstead in London. But you will find a stained-glass window erected by the parish in his honour, in part of which Mary, nursing the infant Jesus, is having her portrait done by a venerable painter. Below are short excerpts from John Constable's writings, one of which catches the sense of an identification with this swathe of England that never lost its hold on him all his life – even when he had long left Suffolk for London and the visits he so compulsively made to this cherished territory became ever rarer and briefer: 'Painting is with me but another word for feeling, and I associate my "careless boyhood" with all that lies on the banks of the Stour. These scenes made me a painter, and I am grateful.'

There are agitations in East Bergholt in 2015 over what is claimed to be a potential threat to Constable's legacy. Posters displayed through the village seek to rally its people against another alien invasion, this time from developers wanting to add nearly 150 homes to the village. 'We will not allow the tranquil images so famously depicted by Constable to be permanently destroyed,' the chairman of Action East Bergholt has declared. Not exactly rhetoric worthy of Boudicca, but showing a bit of her spirit, even so.

I walk back to the village, sit on a wall in momentary sunshine munching a sandwich and ponder the dilemma inflicted on me by Carters Coach Services and Suffolk Council. There's a 94 bus due in twenty minutes or so set on running to Ipswich. Yet a timetable displayed outside the Red Lion pub suggests there's also a route, number 94A, and so not wholly divorced from the route number on which these adventures are founded, which still (though not very often) makes the intended journey to Hadleigh. And in view of the morning's events, I now ask myself: what would Queen Boudicca do in such circumstances? Undoubtedly, just what she'd first intended to do.

And what would East Bergholt's local hero have done? Constable was no ruthless red-haired warrior in the manner of Queen Boudicca. He was through most of his life politically an instinctive conservative who reacted with deep alarm to the parliamentary Reform Bill of 1831. Yet, as visiting the church of St Mary has reminded me, he did not obediently bow to the will of those who were out to thwart him. At thirty (she was eighteen) he met Maria Bicknell, daughter of a London solicitor and granddaughter of Durand Rhudde, rector of St Mary's, then in his early seventies. Three years later, when she turned twenty-one, they officially started their courtship. Her parents discouraged their association; so even more vehemently, for reasons which have never been fully explained, did the rector.

Not only were they forbidden to meet; Dr Rhudde also said that if she did not bow to his will, she would be disinherited. For several years, marriage remained impossible. But in 1816 Constable's father died, and left him enough of a legacy to kill off the argument that as a mere artist he could never sustain a wife to the standard that Maria's family demanded. So they were married and would no doubt have remained so for many years had they not doted so much on children; she had to sustain pregnancy after pregnancy, the last of which, in 1828, weakened her to a point where she succumbed to tuberculosis and died.

So even peaceable Constable seemed to be saying: do just what you planned to do, and don't let the bus companies grind you down. So, spurning the Ipswich interloper, I climb aboard the 94A – otherwise empty, as it remains until we enter small but pretty and flavoursome Hadleigh. Two essential ingredients immediately signal themselves. One is the quirkiness of the houses, full of lines no more faithful to straightness than the route of my bus from East Bergholt, and in a variety of colours which made me wish I had a paintbox to check out their designations. Here, for instance, is a pub, the Old Shoulder: no longer a pub, but preserving the name picked out over the door. I suppose you might call it grass green: one of its neighbours is yellow, the other a curious pink: in places, even an angry pink, a pink with a sense of grievance. (That may sound unlikely, but this is Suffolk.) The other straightway evokes the late great battle of Hadleigh against an alien invading force: the local individual names on the shops. Boots, Greggs, Ladbrokes, certainly, but Andrews, quality butchers, and the Jolly Meat Company and Partridge ironmongers and Tatty Broyds (clothes): and the Idler bookshop – these and a string of others, intermixed with pubs and tea rooms, aren't names that you find everywhere. 'Anger Holbrows', says the sign on a small car showroom. 'Prop: Mr A. Breitsprecher.'

*****

And so to twenty-first-century Hadleigh's resistance to intrusive imperial power. For almost a quarter of the past century, supermarkets, and conspicuously Tesco, had been eager to wake up, shake up, sleepy old

Hadleigh. This wasn't quite how they proclaimed it; their plans, they said, were certain to benefit Hadleigh, not only by bringing the famed benefits of cheap, convenient shopping complete with spacious car parks to a place that was struggling without them, but by luring in out-of-town shoppers, who would patronize the old shops as well. The traders in the High Street did not believe them, and neither did a sizeable band of people who'd grown up, or long ago moved into, Hadleigh and preferred it to stay old-fashioned.

The company's first bid for the riverside site was refused by the local council in 2000, a decision endorsed by Whitehall the following year. A public inquiry into the future of the site, in 2004–5, left the way open for future applications, and in 2010, Tesco came back, only to be beaten off at a meeting of Babergh Council's development committee by a single vote. A determining issue here was the design of the building they were proposing. Very well, said Tesco: we'll revise it and try again, which they did in 2012. In the meantime, their rivals Morrisons had picked up the site of a former Tesco store a little way out of town and opened there in January 2013. The High Street traders were left with mixed feelings. That Morrisons was established might serve to undermine Tesco's claim that supermarket-deprived Hadleigh needed them; but doing their sums, they concluded that even out-of-town Morrisons had hurt them already.

The decisive battle of the campaign was fought in a meeting of the planning committee of Babergh Council at the town's Guildhall complex on 18 September 2013. Thirteen members were present; their deliberation lasted more than three hours. The council's economic development adviser had argued for rejection, as had English Heritage, which feared that the development would cause substantial harm to the significance of the designated conservation area and its important listed buildings, including St Mary's Church. Its planning officer, however, had recommended that Tesco's proposals should be accepted. He would have been well aware that local authorities have often spent substantial sums resisting applications that seemed certain to succeed in the end, a point strongly argued at the Guildhall by some councillors.

Once again the fate of the town turned on a single vote. For Tesco, six members – none of whom came from Hadleigh; two Conservatives, one Liberal Democrat and three Independents – against them, seven: four Conservatives and three Liberal Democrats. And this time, Tesco surrendered. They would not come back to Hadleigh again.

It's more difficult now, when the great days of Tesco appear to be over – and the strategy has changed from opening even more stores, big and small, to scrapping plans for new ones and closing some already in business – to appreciate how much this was local David defeating global Goliath, or primitive Boudicca trouncing mighty Rome. Perhaps it was even a portent of things to come. The retreat from Hadleigh came just at the moment when evidence was emerging that once invincible Tesco were coming unstuck.

The supermarkets, as agents of one of the most evident economic social and cultural changes that came over late twentieth-century Britain, have cropped up throughout these journeys and will do again. Tesco, which became the biggest and most successful of all, was created by an East End market trader, Jack Cohen (its name was formed of three letters from his tea supplier, T.E. Stockwell, with two of his own). It opened its first shop in Burnt Oak, between Hendon and Edgware, in 1929, and steadily expanded its range after the Second World War, buying up smaller competitors.

By 1970, new Tescos were springing up all over the land. In 1982 the company logged up sales of more than £2 billion and was threatening the supremacy of Sainsbury's. That achievement became certain when in 1995 it introduced its Clubcard, advertised as a way of rewarding good and faithful shoppers, but essentially designed to track consumers' preferences as a guide to where they might put their money next.

They were ceaselessly on the look-out for new worlds to conquer. At home, they launched a Tesco bank in 1995. They opened stores in Europe; they introduced a chain called Fresh & Easy in the US. By 2008 it was said there was now a Tesco – anywhere between a megastore and a more modest Express convenience store – in every post code (except, on some calculations, Harrogate). Tesco, the BBC reported in September 2013 – the month of the final trial of strength before Babergh Council – had become the nation's biggest employer, with 330,000 people at work in more than 3,000 stores. In 2011 the *Daily Mail* said Tesco accounted for close to one in three grocery purchases. The juggernaut seemed unstoppable.

But Tesco themselves knew by now that it wasn't. Shoppers' faith in the firm was ebbing away. Shoppers were defecting to the German companies, Aldi and Lidl, which were undercutting them as effectively as they had once undercut their rivals. The chief executive lost his job and was replaced, in a break with Tesco tradition, by an outsider. In September 2014, the firm was engulfed in a scandal over the publication of profits figures that appeared to involve a large and deliberate inflation of their true performance.

Yet if Tesco looked like a wounded beast, that certainly hadn't been the case when Hadleigh engaged with them. So why and how did Hadleigh succeed where so many other resistance movements had failed? Sheer determination was part of it; a sense of defending oneself and one's town against forces likely to blight it; the raising of money when money was urgently needed; also, a certain amount of slyness. Jan Byrne, retired nurse, town councillor, natural born campaigner, was in the thick of it all from 2000 – one of a troika (her husband, Joe, was another) from the Hadleigh Society who headed the first campaign, and today the only one who survives. At the outset, she says, the main aim was to warn local residents what Tesco was up to. 'We read [in one of their documents] that they were planning to "punch a hole in the High Street", and we were off.' Residents were leafleted. When a public meeting was called, the hall was full to overflowing and people who could not get in were loud in their protests. A town poll was organized which showed around 60 per cent of respondents opposed to Tesco's ambitions. Posters were distributed for window display. Marches and demonstrations were staged in the areas under threat.

Tesco's submissions were subjected to sceptical scrutiny. Activists went to the car parks of established Tesco stores, counted the traffic and compared it with what the company had forecast: the totals they found worked out at roughly twice the predicted numbers. They found a tactical ally in the Co-op, until now the dominant grocery store in the centre. Tesco would need additional land for access, which would mean demolishing a house that stood in its way. A compulsory purchase order was threatened; the Co-op moved in and bought it first. All this was prosecuted under a slogan as simple and catchy as 'Otmoor for ever' on the second of these journeys: 'Hands Off Hadleigh.'

But by the time Tesco returned to the fray in 2013, amateur passion was not enough. 'It is Tesco in their suits,' Jan Byrne said at one point, 'and we little souls in our jeans.' They needed compelling professional testimony, and that, in the crucial Guildhall meeting, was what they had got. From Andrew Cann, planning consultant; from Professor Alan Hallsworth, an academic expert on retailing; from Jonathan Glancey, former architectural critic of the *Guardian*; and from the barrister whom they retained, Paul Stinchcombe. That did not come cheap. Fortunately for them, Glancey lived in Hadleigh and was heavily involved in the protest long before that evening. He had been the one professional appearing for Hands off Hadleigh in the previous encounter, when he'd condemned the designs that Tesco proffered as 'patronising and banal'. He found the new ones no better; 'even more patronising than the first pink one', he snorted. The others were paid recruits. For all her own years of effort, Jan Byrne is adamant that the pros were crucial this time.

'Hadleigh United 3, Tesco 0', said a local newspaper headline. Yet Hadleigh was never wholly united. As Byrne accepts, the revolt against Tesco was far from wholly unanimous, and sometimes resented. There was even a Tesco supporters group, with which Hands Off Hadleigh did battle. 'Great fun,' says Byrne, 'and in retrospect, quite nasty.' The town has expanded – its population increased from 6,595 in 1991 to 8,253 twenty years on, a rise of almost 25 per cent – and there were those on the new estates, particularly, who thought supermarket shopping was sure to beat anything the existing High Street could offer. 'The Toffs have triumphed,' someone calling himself Polly's Dad complained on a newspaper website after Tesco's 2011 rejection.

But wandering round the town, and sitting for a while in its library among people searching out books, browsing, or even just quietly knitting, it is easy to understand what the anguish was all about. There's a rhythm to Hadleigh to which Tesco culture, big and brash and imperious, seems inherently alien. The church, calm and spacious in the way that churches in former wool towns so often are, is set about with good buildings: the timber-framed Guildhall; the fifteenth-century red brick Deanery Tower, originally the gatehouse, a survivor from the archdeacons' residence, the rest of which was obliterated in the nineteenth century; several deservedly listed private houses – all give it something of the air of a cathedral close. The site where the supermarket would have been built, once a joinery works, is scarcely a beauty spot, and though sheep graze placidly in the meadows close to the bridge, on the other side you're as much aware of the crowded car park. But the watermeadows would have been threatened, cherished allotments swept away, and wildlife sent into exile.

It's perhaps too soon to draw up any kind of final balance sheet for the rise (and now, the apparent fall) of the big supermarket. That it has demeaned and sometimes destroyed the old varied, companionable high street and the neighbourly shopping parade is indisputable. Yet for many it has been a liberation, and when set against what their parents found on offer, even an education, with a range of goods and services far more various, far more adventurous, than the cosier old stores offered. But that never meant that what was right for one town or suburb was right for everyone else. There must be many settled places, now blessed, as Tesco would argue, with supermarkets, which are as much aware of what they have lost as what they have gained. And perhaps regret that they were unable to summon the spirit of Boudicca/Boadicea or, failing her, Jan Byrne, to stand in the way of ruthless, relentless progress.

18
SONGS OF FAREWELL

594 Oxted–Limpsfield–Westerham

HAD I BEEN DEVISING THESE ROUTES, this one would have been different. This morning's bus proclaims its intention of going from Oxted in easternmost Surrey to Westerham in westernmost Kent. But which Oxted is that? There are two: one ancient, one modern; one cramped, one spacious; one spontaneous, evolved entirely by chance, the other contrived. The old one is more intriguing: a dark, narrow, close-knit street on a hill, for many years a sticky section of the A25, though happily now by-passed, overhung by ancient houses and accommodating pubs. It looks like something designed for a film set – on a grey winter's day, specifically for a melodrama; on a bright morning in spring, for a romance. Sadly, this bus – the 594 to Westerham via Limpsfield church, which alternates with the 595 to Westerham via Tatsfield (Old Ship) doesn't visit original Oxted. Instead it cleaves to the new one, a mile or so the north of it.

And soon we are into the heart – the severed heart, as it will shortly transpire – of that Oxted. Severed in effect by the railway, contemplated in the 1860s but not opened until 1884, the town's western and eastern components linked by a foot tunnel under the station. This is not because some ruthless railway entrepreneur bulldozed his line through the heart of a settled community, but because development started on either side of the line. The stop on Station Road East where the bus discharges the contingent who boarded it at the start – we have come down from a spot called Chalkpit Wood, tucked under the downs, on the northernmost edge of town – is close to Little Waitrose and Sainsbury's Local, nothing too out of scale with the shops around it, which display a pleasing collection of local names.

There's a sense of gentle affluence here compounded by an estate agent's window which has plenty of million-pound-plus homes. The Rightmove website is offering at this time sixteen houses for sale at a million or more, six in Oxted and ten beyond in Limpsfield and Limpsfield Chart.

Take the tunnel under the railway and the western side of the great divide is instructively different. Here for Oxted's occidentals is the fully grown supermarket denied to those on the eastern side, a monster edition of Morrisons. And the architectural identity west of the railway is more eye-catching, perhaps because it's more vulgar, than that to the east. 'Some of the terraces on the W side of the station', wrote Ian Nairn in the Surrey volume in the *Buildings of England* series, 'are possibly the most outrageously over-timbered in the county . . . Taken as far as this, it becomes interesting.'

But also on this side of the tracks are two encouraging dashes of culture. One is the Everyman Cinema, related to the famous ones in Hampstead and Baker Street, which today is offering something for the weekend in two sharply contrasting varieties. One is *Shaun the Sheep*. 'When Shaun decides to take the day off and have some fun he gets a little more action than he baa-gained for,' it says on the Everyman website; an experience which I gather also applies in the case of the heroine in the weekend's other option, the film version of E.L. James's *Fifty Shades of Grey*. The other is a second-hand bookshop modestly titled The Second Hand Bookshop.

Today's bus now turns down roads which appeal to a longer history than present day Oxted's: Gresham Road, Granville Road, names that relate to the Leveson-Gower family (they pronounced the name Luson-Gore), who lived just north of this route in a house called Titsey Place. Again these are streets where stockbroker Tudor dominates, until we come into Limpsfield, and there their pressure relents. And here the bus stops conveniently at the most alluring place on this route: St Peter's Church and, above all, its graveyard.

*****

This is the burial place of Fritz Delius, son of a German wool merchant settled in Bradford, who, shunning the chance to run the family business, became Frederick Delius, English composer. And what compelling connection did Delius have with Limpsfield? During his lifetime, hardly any. So how does he come to be here? That's explained in a booklet you can find in the church, and is further explained when the monthly St Peter's coffee morning kindly invite me in. He is here because, though he'd long been living in France, he had told his wife, Jelka, and repeated to a Limpsfield family, the Harrisons, that he wished to be buried in an English country churchyard; and specifically, one in the south, since his native Yorkshire was, he said, too distant and too cold.

Long paralysed and blind, he was able to continue composing at the end of his life only because he could pass on the thoughts in his head to a Yorkshire-born musician and aspiring composer called Eric Fenby, who came to work for him as an amanuensis and dutifully copied them down. Delius

died at Grez-sur-Loing near Fontainebleau in June 1934, and was buried
there. But the four Harrison sisters were determined that he be brought
back to Limpsfield. Delius had been close to them, as to their mother. All
four girls were musicians, their chosen instruments had been ones picked
out by their mother to enable them to play as a group. Beatrice, a cellist,
was the most distinguished: Delius's Cello Concerto and Cello Sonata, both
of which she premiered, are dedicated to her. May, her elder sister, was a
violinist: Delius wrote his double concerto for May and Beatrice. Monica,
whose health was indifferent, became a singer; Margaret, the youngest,
good enough to play at the Proms, was a pianist also.

They were known in the village not just for the music but also for their
curious ways. Beatrice liked to go into her garden at night and play the
cello in the hope of attracting nightingales, which she did to such good
effect that the BBC made an outside broadcast recording of her doing so. Her
more conventional accompanist Gerald Moore recalls in his memoir *Am I
Playing Too Loud?* a house full of animals: sixteen Aberdeen terriers, a fierce
Airedale, budgerigars, canaries and parrots, and two baby alligators.

Between them the sisters persuaded the rector, Charles Steer, to agree
to the composer's reburial. It's said in the village, and unconditionally
asserted in the *Delius Society Journal*, that Steer was initially reluctant –
had even, according to a writer in the *Journal,* to be 'coerced'. If so, that
is hardly surprising. Delius was not just some gentle agnostic who had
never taken to church-going but a proud atheist whose god if any was
Nietzsche. This was a source of great anguish to Fenby, not just on his
own behalf but also, as he saw it, on Delius's too. His master, he says in
his memoir of the composer, *Delius As I Knew Him*, was from his youth
a pagan at heart, but when he discovered Nietzsche, 'the poison entered
into him.' 'What was extraordinary in the man . . . was largely the fruit
of his unbelief and the secluded life he found it necessary to lead in
order to perfect his art, namely his intellectual isolation, his inhuman
aloofness, his penetrating truthfulness wholly indifferent to whether
he hurt people or not, his utter contempt for "the crowd", and his all-
embracing self-sufficiency.' His lack of faith, Fenby asserts, diminished
him as a composer: 'With belief there would have come that joy which
is not to be found in his music, and which constitutes its chief defect.'
They argued, Fenby sadly and Delius sometimes brutally. '"Look at
Elgar," he said. "He might have been a great composer if he had thrown
all the religious paraphernalia overboard."'

So some local concern at the admittance of such a man to a Christian
churchyard was to have been expected, but it went further than that.

The Protestant Truth Society had heard of the church's plans for reburial, and there were fears that they might attempt to disrupt the proceedings. Accordingly, Delius's body was conveyed by boat to Folkestone and thereafter to Limpsfield in a plain packing case which arrived in a van. The reinterment took place at night, in a darkness lit only by lanterns, with few, as they thought, apparently there to witness it; except that the news had somehow got through to the papers, and at the moment of the reburial, the scene round the grave was lit up by a fusillade of photographers' flashbulbs.

Next day all was decorous. The funeral service took place in the church, with admission by ticket only and hundreds of local people and admirers of Delius waiting outside. But when it was over, a concert was staged by the conductor who above all others had championed his work, Thomas Beecham, with players from the London Philharmonic Orchestra, after which Beecham, standing under an ancient yew tree in the churchyard, delivered the funeral oration. 'I say farewell to his mortal remains in no spirit of sorrow or regret. The most precious part of this man is the immortal part – his spirit as revealed in his work; and in whatever sphere that spirit is, I would like our greetings to pass beyond the confines of this earthly sphere and let him know that we are here not in a spirit of vain regret, but in a spirit of rejoicing that his work is with us and will remain with us for ever more.'

The composers Ralph Vaughan Williams, Herbert Howells and Balfour Gardiner, the conductor John Barbirolli, the violinist Albert Sammons, viola virtuoso Lionel Tertis, oboist Leon Goossens and artist William Rothenstein were among the congregation – Vaughan Williams somewhat reluctantly. He was no great admirer of Delius, whose music, he complained, lacked any sense of struggle. 'I think anyone who could write the wedding scene from *Romeo and Juliet* (not *The Paradise Garden*) entitles Delius to be a great composer,' he told his biographer Michael Kennedy. 'For the rest he smells rather too much of the restaurant.'

Eric Fenby was even more uneasy; he thought none of this should be happening. Delius would better have been left 'in that cold graveyard at Grez, over there by the wall among the peasants whom he had known'. Yet in this churchyard now, especially since later arrivals who had known and admired him were buried there too, he seems to be among friends. There are flowers on his grave this morning.

Beecham too is in Limpsfield churchyard – as is Delius's widow, Jelka, who died a few days after him. The great conductor died in March 1961 and was buried at Brookwood on the other side of the county. But his widow, Shirley, became concerned at plans to reorder the graveyard and arranged for him to be moved to St Peter's, close to Frederick and Jelka Delius. Beecham, in death as in life, is right there on the very front row. 'Nothing can cover his high fame but Heaven,' says the inscription, 'no pyramids set off his memories, but the eternal substance of greatness.' Close by are the pianist Eileen Joyce, who lived in the village; the conductor Norman del Mar, who succeeded Beecham as the leading champion of Delius; also the great clarinettist Jack Brymer, whom Beecham recruited for his Royal Philharmonic Orchestra, along with Joan, his wife, also a musician.

One other possible candidate for a place in this churchyard, who was at St Peter's for the funeral service but isn't here, is Michael Tippett, who lived in Limpsfield for several years while working as a teacher at a nearby preparatory school, while taking charge (for a modest remuneration) of the Oxted Singers, who in April 1930 staged a concert of his music that proved to be something of a turning point in his life. As he listened to the performances, he became convinced that much of what he had written so far was misconceived and would have to be ditched. In his autobiography, *Those Twentieth Century Blues*, Tippett recalls how he used to visit the home of the 'wonderfully eccentric' May and Beatrice Harrison, both to see them and to reacquaint himself with their pet alligator.

It's easy to see why Tippett liked Limpsfield. There's a long main street which begins as you come out of Oxted and climbs a hill through the village until it meets the A25, which before the M25 kindly abstracted some of its traffic was the main east–west route south of London. There's a diverse collection of shops, though in the way of these things, while the village store is still open, there are no longer butchers or bakers, but a bright and cheerful bookshop survives. There's a pub in the centre, the Bull, and a clutch of good upmarket houses, though the real joy of the place is the variegated cottages, some perhaps over-prettified but possessing bagfuls of character. There's an easy affluence here of an older vintage than Oxted's: an old notice displayed in the porch of St Peter's says: 'At morning prayers, all seats in this church are free when the bells cease tolling.' (Which is diplomatic rector-speak for 'if you want the best pews, you'll jolly well have to pay for them.')

From here it's on, by way of the entrancingly named Goodley Stock Road, to Westerham, over the border. This is a calm and peaceable place that epitomizes the small southern English country town, with a long main street punctuated by pubs.

And where the main street widens out on to a triangular green, you find Westerham's two local deities, both distinguished by their achievements in war. At the eastern end is General Wolfe, the hero of Quebec, born in Westerham, his sword raised above his head as if he were set on storming the charity shop across the main road. Beyond him, with his back turned on Wolfe, is Winston Churchill, the anniversary of whose death was observed just ten days ago: flowers have been laid at his feet. He is gazing with his customary resolution towards the last few houses on the edge of the green, or perhaps at the road which goes on towards Sevenoaks. It's disquieting to see at this moment, lumbering up the hill towards him, a red London bus, route 246, destined for Bromley. It feels like a mannerless intrusion on Kent. Westerham isn't London; it feels more like a repudiation of London.

The church feels impeccably Kentish too. General Wolfe is commemorated with a plaque above the south door, though you'd need better eyes than mine to make out what it says, and a stained-glass window by Burne-Jones. That the plaque says he is wholly local and wholly heroic can, I think, be taken for granted. The same cannot be said of Churchill. Heroic, yes – but local? Not really. His connection is his old house at Chartwell, now also in the hands of the National Trust, and performing reliable service in bringing visitors into the area.

East of the church the land falls away and the scene below on this sunny February afternoon is even more gratifying than the one down Limpsfield High Street towards the downs. There's a splendidly varied panoply of colourful rooftops stretching across to meadows and soft wooded hills. In all senses but one, Westerham makes an ideal end to my journey. Yet the omission is grievous. The second-hand bookshop that used to trade at the end of the green just out of Churchill's gaze (and is still advertised on a website) has gone.

Second-hand bookshops come (or we may soon have to say, used to come) in all shapes and sizes. The one in Station Road West in Oxted belongs to the orderly tendency: everything neatly arranged in well-marked sections. So does Limpsfield Bookshop, which trades in new books rather than second-hand. Westerham's bookshop, 'Barely Read', was not of that persuasion. 'This is no ordinary second hand bookshop!' a satisfied customer based in Newbury wrote on an internet site in 2009. 'Five steps in and I am at the back of the store, and I suddenly remember what it felt like to be a child rummaging in the depths of the understairs cupboard.' But like so many cherished second-hand bookshops, it's gone.

Of course, there is always Amazon, or a British newcomer such as Wordery. But that's a different kind of second-hand bookbuying. It may give you what you are looking for, but it's far less likely to give you what, as my shelves attest, a good second-hand bookshop can furnish: a book which you start to thumb through, sense that you like, acquire and will one day treasure.

You can't smell the books on Amazon. They don't on Amazon crowd companionably around you as they do (or did) in traditional shops. As in so much of life nowadays, the rule has to be: use it or lose it. And with second-hand bookshops, lose it is increasingly the likelier outcome.

The same goes for buses, of course.

19

CONK, CRANK, FLUTE, MULEWARD AND VAG WERE HERE

94 *Petersfield–Moggs Mead–Buriton–Petersfield*

THE HEART OF PETERSFIELD, a town of some 15,000 people under the downs, close to the Sussex border in easternmost Hampshire, is its friendly, pleasantly various square, full this morning of bustling shoppers. Others sit in the sun, catching up on the gossip or working their way through a novel by Agatha Christie, Dostoevsky or J.K. Rowling. And at the heart of the square, dressed as a Roman dignitary, with a laurel wreath on his head and a rolled-up scroll in his hand, sitting astride an elegant horse, is King William III, joint monarch with Mary, his wife, daughter of James II – after he'd evicted his father-in-law from that office in 1688. His proud and confident statue here is said to be modelled on one in Rome of the emperor and philosopher Marcus Aurelius, a figure whom biographies suggest William incompletely resembles. And the question that one feels tempted to ask him is this: what on earth are you doing here? For there's little indication that Petersfield played any notable part in his life.

As is so often the case, the presence of William is attributable to the will of a powerful local family: the Jolliffes, who dominated the town through the eighteenth and into the ninetieth century and furnished it with their hand-picked Members of Parliament, several of them called Jolliffe. Among the most formidable of the clan was William Jolliffe (1660–1749), who commissioned the statue, not out of any motive of artistic patronage (it was said that, rich as he was, he bragged that he had never bought a book, a picture or a print), but because he revered William III as the king who rescued England from the threat of a reign which might have reinstated a Catholic hegemony. He left £500 in his will to have the statue created. Originally it was stationed outside the family's home, Petersfield House. But in 1793, that house was demolished, leaving William homeless, as he remained until space was found for him in the square in 1812.

But he's hardly a local hero. Surely there must have been men and women born, brought up or later devoted to Petersfield with more deserving claims to its townspeople's subsequent attention? And indeed, had his family not abandoned Petersfield for a destination just down the road, there would have been a perfectly qualified candidate: a historian whose name became known across the civilized world for his charting of the empire over which Marcus Aurelius presided – Edward Gibbon, to whose one-time home a couple of miles away a 94 bus is due to take me later.

Or if you were looking for somebody local to honour today, what about Flora Twort? Twort was an artist who came here from London in 1918 and became the protégée of a considerable Petersfield figure called Harry Roberts. Once a much-loved radical doctor in London's East End, he had made his new home at Oakshott Hanger, a little way north of the town, which became a gathering place for writers and artists.

Roberts rented a sixteenth-century house on the edge of the square, originally a farmhouse, and opened it as a bookshop and craft shop, installing Flora Twort and two other young women to run it. True, Flora was not born in Petersfield, but she lived here for almost seventy years, and devoted much of her life to its greater glory. She might have become Flora Norway. In 1925 the novelist Nevil Shute, whose real name was Nevil Shute Norway, asked her to marry him. She refused.

The house in Church Path where she lived after she gave up the bookshop is now the Flora Twort Gallery. It is far too small to find a place on its walls for most of the works she left on her death in 1985 to Hampshire County Council, but the collection on show this morning is representative of them in that it's almost exclusively devoted to Petersfield. There's one glimpse of sunny Broadstairs, but otherwise the selection has nothing outside this town. There are pictures of its annual Taro Fair on the Heath, which in those days perpetuated its role as a place to buy and sell cattle ('taro' is a variant of a Welsh word, *tarw*, meaning a bull, which Welsh farmers used to shout as they steered their herds into town). There's also a sombre portrait of a mother and daughter with the title: *Before the Welfare State*. But mainly her pictures feature the Square: the Square on market day, the saddler's shop on the Square with the white-haired saddler sitting outside it. One picture shows children making their way unwillingly to school; a companion picture shows them bounding joyfully homewards. Some of the figures are curiously stylized. Old men leaning on sticks at the fair might almost have had the legend 'Yokel' plastered across them, and the children have a tinge of Mabel Lucie Attwell about them. There are miniatures in pen and ink and in pencil, which seem to me to do better justice to Flora's talent.

But some features of the town that were later torn down and replaced survive in the paintings, in which sense Flora too survives, as Petersfield's historian as well as its best-loved artist. And William Aurelius Imperator on his high horse is at the heart of nearly all of them.

*****

So, though the statue at the heart of Petersfield is something of an anomaly, it suits the place very well, melding in with a town that looks as you wander though it settled and confident; not ostentatiously affluent, but comfortable. The Square, especially on a Wednesday or a Saturday, which are market days still, is cheerful and spirited, with a kind of warm buzz in its shops and restaurants and cafés. Which makes it surprising to find, a little way down Swan Street, just beyond Morrisons, a food bank in a Salvation Army church. In Glasgow or Gateshead or several other stops in these journeys, that was entirely predictable, but in Petersfield?

Yet even here you're reminded that Petersfield is in general a place with money to spend. Brian Edwards, the Salvation Army man still running it when I call, though he's only days off retirement, says they've never been short of offers of food or money. And there's no doubt why people who are able to face the price of its houses would want to settle in a town that has so much going for it. There's the Square, presided over by the church of St Peter, its frontage opened up when two local luminaries gave their properties on the Square to the town on the condition that both were to be demolished so that full sight of their church should no longer be denied to Petersfield's townspeople. One or two of its buildings that later generations might have preserved were lost in the post-war years, but what's left remains an engaging mix of ancient and modern, formal and quirky, august and intimate. The High Street has suffered depredations too, with the saw-it-down sixties insouciantly disposing of hallowed buildings like the Dolphin Hotel. But the streets at right angles beyond, Dragon Street and College Street, have been rescued by the banishment of the London to Portsmouth traffic that used to fight its way down them, now despatched to the by-pass that opened in 1992.

And certainly not many towns of this size still maintain four separate bookshops: not just Waterstones and Oxfam, but two more that are independent and local: one selling new books, coupled with coffee and a sense of social occasion (One Tree Books in Lavant Street); the other, a rambling second-hand shop, the Petersfield Bookshop, with a kind of open-all-hours foyer where you can take what you like for 50p. This one is the direct successor to Flora's shop at 1–2 The Square.

Despite Flora's alarm that the essence of Petersfield might be in peril from avaricious developers, this is still a place to savour both for its streets and its unexpected byways and alleys and lanes and the discoveries to which they will lead you and, perhaps above all, the Heath and the lake, here modestly called Heath Pond, refreshingly close to the centre. The Heath is no longer really a heath but a carefully cultured park, while the lake on this generous August day is a feast of pleasures: walking, boating, fishing and picnicking. The road from the town to the edge of the Heath, lined with substantial and often attractive houses, might nowadays be classed as aspirational, though what it really suggests is aspiration satisfied.

But one other ingredient has been even more crucial to the Petersfield that has burgeoned and blossomed over the years: the railway station. It was built – by the same architect, William Tite, who designed the grand Citadel station at Carlisle – to furnish passengers for a new line from Guildford to Portsmouth, which came here in 1859. Today it will get you to Portsmouth in less than thirty minutes and to Waterloo in an hour, making this a happy location for such commuters as can splash out some £4,000 a year for the journey to London. When the station opened, Petersfield's population was around 5,000. By 1881 it was over 7,000; by 1911 it had topped 12,000. Through the eighteenth century the Portsmouth Road and the coaching inns had been the essence of Petersfield. Daniel Defoe, who was here in 1726, called it 'a town eminent for little but being full of good inns'. The railway changed all that. But here's no shortage of hostelries even now.

Yet the town itself is only one part of the attraction: what you find at no great distance outside enhances it too. Above all the downs, immediately to the south, which wherever you go in the town insistently remind you that they are there and awaiting your patronage. There are fine walking tracks: the South Downs Way, Winchester to Eastbourne; the Hangers Way, Alton to Petersfield by way of Gilbert White's Selborne and Edward Gibbon's Buriton; and the Shipwright's Way from the Alice Holt Forest, where the navy's trees were grown, to Portsmouth where they were built into ships. The South Downs National Park, established in 2011 after almost a century of campaigning, takes in the famous earthworks high up on the hill at Butser. Uppark, the romantic seventeeth-century house restored at colossal expense by the National Trust after fire substantially destroyed it in 1989, is five miles away. It's a mere eighteen miles to Portsmouth, twenty to Winchester, twenty-five to Chichester. And of course when the sun comes out, it take no time at all to get to the sea.

*****

I sit on a bench in the Square reading the *Petersfield Post* and contemplating the journey required of me by the 94, due to arrive in a moment. 'Circular town journey', the timetable says, which experience suggests may fall somewhere short of excitement. It's hard to say where a circular service starts, but this one takes in a Tesco superstore, the Square and the station, before embarking on an exploration of sectors into which the original town has spread eastward: Moggs Mead, Rival Moor, Penns Place, back to Moggs Mead, then again the old trinity: superstore, square and station. And sure enough, this, for most of its route, proves to be a memorably unmemorable excursion.

Moggs Mead ('mogg' is an ancient word for a marsh), which dates from the 1970s, is a creditable piece of development subscribing to the garden suburb teachings of Ebenezer Howard: a good judicious mix of detached homes, (fewer) semi-detacheds and the occasional outburst of terraces, all in green settings. And the pattern is here and there broken by some appropriate interruptions: a leisure centre with swimming baths and squash courts, a Co-op. But there's more to route 94 than Petersfield's suburbs. Every two hours or so, it is liberated from its previous urban monotony. Cows dance in the fields when first released from their winter incarceration and one feels the 94 bus should do much the same. After an episode of urban straggle, there are woods and open fields on either side of the road. We are in the country at last!

At least for the moment. But that seems is likely to change. The *Petersfield Post* is expecting the imminent confirmation of plans to build 200 homes on this land. That has worried the Petersfield Society, set up seventy years ago to safeguard the town from unwelcome development, which fears unprecedented growth in a very short space of time. It isn't only the loss of agricultural land that is causing apprehension; it is also concern about what it might presage for the centre of town. McDonald's, for instance, has a restaurant out on the by-pass next to a petrol station.

Let the town grow too much, and might they perhaps want to move into the High Street?

*****

It takes twenty minutes to get from the Square in Petersfield to a kind of square in front of the church at Buriton. The church is at the end of the High Street past two local pubs – the Village Inn and the Five Bells – the village school and a pleasing melange of houses. A book called *Buriton and its People*, produced by the Petersfield Area Historical Society, enables you, as the best local histories do, to see the place as it was through the place that it is there today. 'The change in village populations over the last hundred or so years and the disappearance of old ways of life', writes Dr Edward Yates, 'have been frequently described and lamented. In Buriton restrictive planning policies (particularly since Buriton is a conservation area) and the high prices of "period properties" have completed a social re-organization of the village.' Elsewhere he says: 'the older houses in the older part of the village, many occupied in 1841 by labourers, are now in the hands of professional people or retired officers from the armed services, with a very marked reduction in the number of occupants.' He singles out the Poor House, an eye-catching building part way down the High Street, 'built for the village poor but now subdivided into four highly desirable residences. The social structure of labourers, tenant farmer, landowner, has gone.' We Londoners call it gentrification, lad.

The sense of a past now largely forgotten is enhanced by his inclusion of family names that used to be found here, many of which you would hardly encounter now. In the fourteenth century there were people called Conk, Crank, Flute, Muleward, Whitbierd and Vag; also a Mogge. Could this have something to do with Mogg's Mead, down in Petersfield? Probably not. In the seventeenth, Buriton, home to Sir John Billson and Mistress Anne Billson, also accommodated a Thomas Hogesflesh; in 1744, as well as a Jolliffe, a Mr Goodwife appears in the parish record, along with a Mr Minthin and two men called Tallman. Surnames are not what they were. The census returns of 1841 are dull by comparison.

The history of this village is intimately intertwined with that of the town. The child has become the parent. Buriton, which began as Mapledurham, is the older, and was for centuries the more significant of the two. Even in the days of the Jolliffes, St Mary Buriton was the mother church of St Peter's and remained so until the 1880s. In 1800, Petersfield had 2,100 people and Buriton 630, a ratio of three to one. Now Petersfield's population is about 15,000 and Buriton's 730: a ratio of eighteen to one.

The difference, of course, was the railway. Buriton might have been given a station, but the gradients were against it. So now Petersfield has a station, where Buriton is left with the Buriton tunnel, 487 yards long and not of much practical use for those wanting to get to London or Portsmouth.

Who came better out of the equation? Petersfield has prospered and become better known, but Buriton has the peace that thousands yearn for. In front of the flinty church with its stoic replacement tower (the original burned down in the eighteenth century, and the spire that topped its successor was lost in a storm) there's a pond, now a place of leisure and ornament but once an essential part of the working village. Horses were brought here to drink at the end of their working day. Today you can sit in the shade, watching the comings and goings of waterbirds and contemplating exactly the kind of gently soothing scene which so many seek in the countryside. There are walks in every direction. The Hangers Way runs past the pond and in front of St Mary's. Across from the church is an imposing building, even more appealing perhaps before they blocked up some of its windows, which may once have been the manor house, was then the Rectory and is now the Old Rectory, rectors being required nowadays to live in more modest billets. And then, alongside the church, is the Manor House, where the great historian Gibbon once lived with his difficult father and the stepmother whose arrival he first resented but of whom in time he came to be deeply fond.

One of the unintended consequences of the reign of William III was the enrichment of Edward Gibbon, grandfather of the Edward Gibbon whom the world knows. This first Edward was a defence contractor for King William's campaigns, making money enough to become a director of the South Sea Company, enabling him to buy Buriton Manor in 1719 – the year before the bubble burst. Even then, though coming close to ruin, he pulled himself round and was comfortably re-established by the time of his death in 1736. He was one of Petersfield's two main landowners; he and the Jolliffe family controlled one seat each in its parliamentary representation, which opened the way for the second Edward to become one of the town's MPs in 1734, three years before Edward the historian was born, the first of seven children of the second Edward and Judith, his wife. His six siblings all died in infancy.

In December 1747, Judith died in childbirth. Gibbon's father was devastated, and gave up much of his public life. As the son says in his memoirs, 'He renounced the tumult of London and the hospitality of Putney [previously his main home, in what was then a village just outside London] and buried himself in the rural or rather rustic solitude of Buriton from which during several years he rarely emerged'; to which he adds, in a subsequent version, that though his father said that he settled in Buriton to farm, 'I may not dissemble that it was precipitated by a motive of baser alloy, the increasing disorder of his circumstances' – circumstances that largely reflected his general improvidence and his losses at the gaming table.

The son had a fitful education, frequently interrupted by illness. He was for a time at Westminster, but was too unwell to continue there. Then, at around the age of fifteen, suddenly, for no explicable reason, he began to thrive. At this point his father dispatched him to Magdalen College, Oxford, where, he says, he learned little, misbehaved in ways that he does not specify, ran up debts and, most affronting of all for his father, converted to Roman Catholicism. Having first threatened to disinherit him, his father hit on a better way of purging the infection. He packed him off to Lausanne, entrusting him to the care of a Calvinist minister who duly brought him back to the Protestant faith.

Returning reconverted to England in 1758, he divided his time between London and Buriton. 'An old mansion,' he later remembered, 'in a state of decay, had been converted into the fashion and convenience of a modern house; and if strangers had nothing to see, the inhabitants had little to desire. The spot was not happily chosen, at the end of the village and at the bottom of the hill; but the aspect of the adjacent grounds was various and cheerful: the downs commanded a noble prospect, and the long hanging woods in sight of the house could not perhaps have been improved by art or expense.' Here his ambitions as writer and historian began to take meaningful shape. An essay on the study of literature, his first published work, completed at Buriton, had been written in French, a language he found came more easily to him than English after his long exile in Switzerland. But as he says: 'It was at Rome, on the fifteenth of October, 1764, as I sat musing amidst the ruins of the Capitol, while the barefooted friars were singing vespers to the temple of Jupiter, that the idea of writing the decline and fall of the city first started to my mind.'

Buriton, for all its virtues, was sometimes a good place to get away from. 'My father's residence,' Gibbon says of Buriton Manor House (though he always writes it as Beriton), 'where I have passed many light and some heavy hours.' The heavy ones came from his father's insistence that he join him at every meal, and his requirement that they read and discuss the newspaper together; also the occasional incursions of unwelcome visitors. There were parental lectures about what he should do with his life – I could find you a parliamentary seat, his father insisted, but Gibbon resisted (though in later life he did become an MP, he made not one speech in his years in the House of Commons).

More distractingly still, he was persuaded to follow his father in enlisting in the Hampshire militia, a kind of citizen army. 'A wandering life of military servitude' followed, though he found some aspects of service unexpectedly satisfying, and 'on every march, on every journey, Horace was always in my pocket and often in my hand.' In time, he was summoned no more. But the last years at Buriton were almost impossibly difficult. The son had to try to sort out the father's tangled financial affairs. 'Economy', he wrote to his aunt Hester, 'was not one of my father's virtues.' The strictures he'd addressed to his son about the dangers of improvidence would have been better addressed to himself. The old man became increasingly unwell and full of complaint, rebuking the son who was trying to rescue his fortunes for failing to trust him. In 1770, his father died. 'It is a melancholy truth', he wrote afterwards, 'that my father's death, not unhappy for himself, was the only event that could save me from a hopeless life of poverty and indigence.' Independent at last, he resolved to leave Buriton, and found a new billet in Bentinck Street, off Cavendish Square.

The manor house was eventually passed to the Bonham-Carters – an alliance of two families with brewing interests in Petersfield. The Bonham-Carters have a clutch of memorials in St Mary's Church, alongside such other local dignitaries as the Hanburyes and the Hugonins of Nursted and past rectors, notably William Lowth, of whom a slate panel says: 'Near outside of this wall lyeth the body of William Lowth, Rector of this church, who died May ye 17th 1732. And being dead desires to speak to his beloved parishioners, and sweetly to exhort them constantly to attend public worship of God, frequently to receive Holy Communion and diligently to observe the good instruction given in this place, to breed up their children in the fear of God, and to follow peace with all men and holiness, without which no man shall see God.'

In 2013, a couple called Bob and Marcelle Camping announced an entirely new era in the Manor House's history. From now on, the house would be staging 'the kind of wedding you've always dreamed of'. 'Our family', they explained on their website, 'was thrilled to move to the incredibly beautiful and tranquil village of Buriton. With our wedding day still fresh in our minds, we understand the experience that couples desire.' With so many guests likely to come here, they also acquired a pub called the Maple for a smart bed and breakfast for additional guests. They renamed it The Village Inn. Very soon, the village, which prized its tranquillity, was showing signs of alarm. The Campings' dream was becoming their nightmare. Complaints poured in of excessive noise and anti-social behaviour, with drunken guests said to be reeling about in the streets. At a public hearing in February 2016, East Hampshire District Council announced to loud cheers from Buriton villagers that the licence for the premises was being withdrawn. Even before this, Bob Camping had warned that the project had run into trouble, and some fifty weddings due to be staged there would have to be cancelled. The Manor House would be put on the market. The Village Inn had already gone into receivership. The imperious Campings were in retreat. Here, in Gibbon's old home, you might say, was a classic case of decline and fall.

20

THE WORLD BEYOND BRASSKNOCKER HILL

94 Bath–Freshford–Trowbridge

THE CITY OF BATH, a Unesco heritage site, to which in an average year well over three million people will come from across the world to admire and enjoy, is one of the thirty-nine county towns of England. Trowbridge, some twelve miles away to the south-east, twenty minutes by train but nearer an hour on the sort of buses I use, is a county town too; but there for the most part all resemblance ends. Few from overseas, and not that many from England, flock to see it. No heroine in Jane Austen is discovered all of a twitter at the thought of a visit to Trowbridge.

For the moment, though, I am in Bath, where it's such an unalloyed pleasure to be on this glorious late April morning, and where it's perhaps a relief to find that my bus does not start, as the timetable says it will, from a place with the unBathonian name of Bog Island. A name all the more surprising in that Bath is not built on a marsh. This site got its name from a popular night club that occupied the site of a former public lavatory. But now they have built a bus station close to the railway station, and the walk into town suggests an almost untarnished salubriousness. A sixteenth-century abbey, stately streets, elegant squares and crescents, fashionable arcades, suave hotels, and an incomparable coherence that comes from an almost uniform use of honey-coloured Bath stone; a river flowing under one of the most celebrated bridges in Europe, with the water cascading below; and on top of all this, the priceless natural asset of hills sealing the views to the north and south: these are the trademarks of Bath.

There are others too less immediately conspicuous: unexpected side streets, too easily missed, like Little Orchard Street, a modest cobbled street that turns off Danvers Street as you come from the station, which seems so frozen now in a past century that the sudden sight, in the street beyond, of a KFC restaurant comes like an insult. Some other such streets have been lost. Indeed, there were times when the nature of Bath seemed threatened. In 1973 Adam Fergusson wrote a suitably angry book, loaded with caustic photographs, about the fate the city council was busy imposing on Bath: *The Sack of Bath*, he called it, and John Betjeman contributed a poem that ended:

> Goodbye to old Bath. We who loved you are sorry
> They've carted you off by developer's lorry.

The people in charge – elected councillors, but the city's servants too – emerged from this indictment as people who too often seemed to regard the past as an impediment rather than an occasion for pride. The most passionate of Fergusson's complaints was over what had been done – and would continue to be done unless the world woke up to it – to aspects of Bath's heritage outside its famous showpieces, and especially to the streets of artisan housing where its less famous citizens lived. He quoted with near disbelief the words of the city architect: 'If you want Georgian artisans' houses, then you will have to find Georgian artisans to live in them.' As for the new replacing the old, he found nothing of distinction, and a great deal of what he termed 'packing case architecture'.

The furore which greeted this book strengthened the hands of the preservationists, who had for years been fighting this battle, and tilted the balance enough for other threatened streets to be spared and restored. There are plenty of people living there happily now, as there are all over Britain's best cities, who are no more artisans than they are Georgians.

And however many still-mourned buildings, some of greater eminence than any of these, have been lost in the cause of Improvement, enough survives to ensure that Bath is still Bath. The abbey and the square about it, with the Roman Baths and the Pump Room and spaces to sit in the sun with a coffee while listening today to some mercifully competent buskers, are still a happy space to be in, though the presence of notices banning the public consumption of alcohol suggests all may not always be quite so tranquil.

Some people will wonder at the restraint still practised in this city. There's a hotel on the far side of Robert Adam's Pulteney Bridge which in keeping with its surroundings seems shy about flaunting its name. Across the road this morning there's a furniture van painted in so garish a shade of yellow that one almost expects some kind of beadle to rush to the scene and have it removed.

And yet Bath likes to offer something to varied tastes, though not of course wishing to go so far as to accommodate every variety. The Guildhall Market, which I'd rather feared would be full of stalls owing more to twenty-first-century indulgences than to the robust essence of markets familiar from northern towns, is home to displays of buckets and pails and ironing boards as well to outfits that do not flinch from using the word haberdashery. Its 'delicatessen' offers not just the adventurous range of pies you look for in any market, but even pigs' trotters – as well as the kind of treacle tart that experts warn you against.

A sign at the top of William Street points you both to the ground, unusually close to a city centre, where rugby union is played, and, at the less boisterous end of the sporting scale, the Bath Croquet Club. At the far end of Great Pulteney Street, sealing it off and giving it a sense of completion, is the Holburne Museum, which today is staging an exhibition called 'Gwen John to Lucien Freud, Home and the World'. At the other end (where it's still Bridge Street) the Victoria Art Gallery is featuring Beryl Cook (once nicely described as a cross between Rubens and the deviser of popular 'naughty' holiday postcards, Donald McGill).

The Guildhall, Bath's seat of government, where in the sixties and early seventies the decisions were hatched that so dismayed preservationists, is one of the best of Bath's secular buildings, happily placed on the corner of what is now High Street (it was once the market place, with an earlier Guildhall right in its centre).

There's a building nearby, completed in 1891, which some have sometimes considered as ripe to join the trail of destruction: the Empire Hotel, on the foundation stone of which was laid another plaque that says, 'twenty three feet below, by the Mayor of Bath, RE Dickinson Esq MP, on December 8, 1899. God Save the Queen,' As God obligingly did for one year and forty-five days thereafter. The architect of this proceeding, Charles Edward Davis, lasted only a little longer, dying in May 1902.

Major Davis, as he liked to be known, was Bath's architect and surveyor for almost forty ever more turbulent years. By the end, his role was so much reduced that his only responsibility was for baths and markets. It had always been his dream to give the city a majestic hotel, but each of his previous ventures had failed because of lack of money, local resentments and envies, or rather more balanced doubts about his architectural competence. But now, when, though well past seventy, he was at last commissioned to build one (it was funded by an entrepreneur who said he would back it so long as no restriction was put on the height of the building), he really let rip. In the original *Buildings of England* series, published in 1958, Nikolaus Pevsner called it 'a monstrosity and an unbelievable piece of pompous architecture'. Pevsner is sometimes cast as humourless, which he doesn't deserve, but this does seem a slightly humourless judgement. (It was modified in a subsequent issue of Pevsner, and is now described as 'an enormous and eccentric Queen Anne Revival building'.)

Though it may seem a bit overbearing for a site so close to the river, I would gladly accept the Empire as part of Bath's rich pattern. Perhaps when you read accounts of the major's life it makes most sense as a tribute to a great, always undervalued, often ignorantly thwarted man, paid to him by himself. It's galumphing, and pretentious, but it's entertaining. And entertainment is most of all what this city's about. Close by the Theatre Royal is the home of Bath's one-time presiding genius, Beau Nash. I used to assume that Nash was little more than a fop, but he served Bath well, not least when appointed its Master of Ceremonies. That by noon on this April Tuesday so many visitors are beginning to clog the town – a lot of them young, unmistakably students, surging along full of bubbling chatter in various languages – is a mark of how Bath has sustained that history; and I haven't even mentioned its festivals and its bars and its upmarket shops and its pubs.

If Bath were a person, I would class it with the sort of people who are said to be comfortable in their own skin. It's expensive, of course, bordering sometimes on the prohibitive, and the kind of Bathonian who cannot afford to live nowadays in the former homes of Georgian artisans must too often feel relegated, excluded. You have only to look in estate agents' windows to pick up a sense of us and them. (My friend David Harvey, passing a Bath playground one day, heard a mother addressing her child with words you would never expect to hear in Trowbridge: 'Come here *immediately*, Atticus!') But this is a city that does what it sets out to do with effortless style and aplomb.

*****

'This bus', the driver of the Libra Travel 94 to Trowbridge warns me, 'goes round the villages;' but that's just what I want it to do. In the early stages at least, it's an enchanting journey, one of the most enjoyable routes in this book. You sail up from Bath towards Combe Down, past houses which rarely diverge from Bath stone. The road climbs past the University of Bath on Claverton Down (the city has a second university, Bath Spa) and the glorious Avon Valley opens up before you, just long enough to let you drink the sight of it in before the bus plunges down to sample the first of its villages: Monkton Combe, which is home to an Anglican public school, housed in solid buildings whose stone keeps up the sense of Bath. It must be a lovely spot to be schooled in, all the more so when the Avon flows so close by. Our road takes us down Brassknocker Hill, a name for which I have failed to find an explanation, though I do remember that back at Slaithwaite in chapter 7 a street where the more aristocratic families lived was known as Brass Handle Street.

By the time we get to the Wheelwright Arms, one of the principal themes of the run has established itself. It's a blissful route for passengers, but less so for bus drivers, for the roads round here are sinuous and narrow, and time and again we are brought to a halt by a confrontation which requires some nifty reversing, sometimes by them, sometimes by us. Where it isn't vehicles that materialize in front of us, it's clutters of cars parked both where it's permitted and where it isn't, which leave only a smidgen of space for a bus to squeeze through. The same is true when we get to Limpley Stoke, another favourite spot for those who'd made money in Bath but preferred not to live in the city. Here, somewhere near the Hop Pole pub and the Georgian house set in three acres of gardens that is now the Best Western Hotel, we become involved in the least resolvable of the day's encounters, which means that the bus has to mount what there is of a pavement, and finds itself crushed between parked cars and a wall; at which point there is an ominous scraping sound which suggests that our bus has been injured.

There are further succulent views over the peaceful valley as we head for the next attraction, Freshford. Freshford is a picture too, and in more than one sense. When Ealing Studios wanted to make a film about an idyllic village whose railway station was threatened with closure, they picked this one. T.E.B. Clarke, who wrote the screenplay, called it Titfield, having in mind Limpsfield and its neighbour Titsey, both near Oxted, where he lived.

Here buses appear in a role far removed from the friendly welcoming creatures to be found in the rest of this book. The bus in *The Titfield Thunderbolt* is a mean and predatory creature, intent on stamping the railway out of existence, only to be foiled by an earnest alliance of the local squire, a railway-besotted parish priest, and a local toper who happily puts up the money when he finds that on railway trains you can drink at any time of the day.

We've been travelling just over half an hour and are now approaching the biggest settlement between Bath and Trowbridge: Westwood. After these other villages this seems a disappointingly indeterminate place. It expanded through the twentieth century, with its population as recorded in the census of 1921 all but doubled thirty years later, in which process the once distinct villages of Upper and Lower Westwood became effectively one. As a place to get off and take a break in the journey, it has less immediate attraction than any before it. Yet if you're allowing yourself just one excursion, this is the place to choose.

There are at least three appealing distractions here – four if you count the kind of deserted medieval village that O.G.S. Crawford savoured in chapter 15 – in this case, Rowley, in easy walking distance of Westwood. Westwood Manor, on the southern outskirts, now belongs to the National Trust. The original building was medieval, but subsequent owners, the Hortons and Farewells, lovingly enhanced it, and that process was taken further by Edward Lister, a former diplomat, who bequeathed it to the Trust.

I have never seen it, but I doubt if it matches the magic of Iford Manor, south-west of Westwood, reached by a bridge over the River Frome. Few places do. In 1899 the architect and garden enthusiast Harold Ainsworth Peto visited Iford with his friend, the garden designer Avray Tipping, and knew at once that he wanted to stay there for good. He bought the house, originally medieval but cloaked out as classical at some time in the eighteenth century, and began to enhance its gardens with the architectural items he had acquired on his travels through Europe. He laid out the gardens on a series of hillside terraces and added a lily pond, a cool colonnade, and his particular delight, a shady cloister.

Peto, it has been said, was turning a dream into a reality, and to me the place has always been dreamlike. My wife, sitting one afternoon in the cloister, was astonished to see a figure in Elizabethan dress walking slowly towards her: which, given the prevailing atmosphere of Iford, made her somehow feel that she, rather than these Elizabethans, was in the wrong century. The explanation was sadly mundane. Iford stages plays, and operas even, before such audiences as can cram themselves into the little cloister, and this figure was talking a break from a rehearsal.

Go north out of Westwood, down the wooded hill that leads to the Avon, and another kind of vision appears. This is Avoncliff, a coming together of the river, the Kennet and Avon Canal, carried on an aqueduct built in the early years of the eighteenth century, and the railway, which has been here since 1847, though Avoncliff had to wait a further sixty years for a station. Back towards Bath, close to both Monkton Combe and Limpley Stoke, is the Dundas Aqueduct, constructed by the great engineer John Rennie to take the canal over the river. Avoncliff's Rennie aqueduct is not quite so celebrated, but it's still an essential ingredient in a very original scene. The canal again crosses the river, the railway, which still has its station, rattles along through the foot of the valley, and the picture is filled out by two buildings: one, a complex of weavers' cottages from the 1770s and now, renamed Ancliff Square, divided into apartments; the other, the Cross Guns Hotel, nicely placed for your recovery after a walk down the towpath.

And Westwood has a further claim on your attention, though not one you can now inspect. There used to be quarries on these hillsides, which in 1908 were judged unproductive and closed. Attempts were made to find a new use for them. One answer was the growing of mushrooms, but here ambitions were blighted by a persistent virus, amplified by earth tremors, and then by the call-up of workers to serve in the Second World War. But the War Office saw a use for the place. The tunnels promised to be a safe hideaway for making munitions. The Royal Enfield motorcycle company, diverting from its habitual purposes, duly moved in. Its workers had to be housed, and that was how Westwood began to expand into green spaces.

Yet others had eyes on the place as well. One urgent need as the bombing intensified was to move the treasures of London's museums and galleries into places of safety. There were offers from stately homes in the countryside, though some officials who fielded them did so with scepticism, assuming the motivation was less an overwhelming desire to protect the nation's collections than grabbing at an excuse to say no to having city children billeted on them. But the conditions they could provide for storing arts treasures were often far from adequate, and enthusiasm among landowners died when they realized they would not be paid.

It was thus, as Nick McCamley says in an exemplary account of those days, *Avoncliff: The Secret History of an Industrial Hamlet in War and Peace,* that the Westwood tunnels became one of the chosen repositories. Reconstructed by workmen from neutral Ireland – known as the Mayo men and legendary, McCamley says, for their hard working, hard living and hard drinking – they became the emergency home for a range of world-class treasures, perhaps the most famous of which were the Elgin Marbles, though the plane in which the Wright Brothers made their historic flight at North Carolina was another remarkable lodger. In lines much quoted since, though not always attributed, McCamley wrote: 'By the end of 1942 Westwood probably housed the greatest and most valuable collection of cultural and artistic artefacts assembled in any one location anywhere in the world.'

This whole operation, those involved were warned, must be carried out with the utmost secrecy, though that did not prevent a story about it appearing in what an official described as 'one of the less reputable daily papers'. Yes, there were a few of those even then.

At a not very memorable spot, which the timetable calls Westwood Turning Circle, we change drivers, and the new and the old muse for a while on the scrapes, like the one we have had this morning, that they've got into on this route. The new driver, who is dressed as if he has spent the morning auditioning for a part in some rustic drama adapted from a novel by H.E. Bates, has the easier half of this journey, since by now the countryside has shed the eventfulness of Bath to Freshford and become flat and empty with long horizons. And the roads once we've passed the New Inn at Lower Westwood are far more bus-friendly, wide and uncluttered.

Had this route been chosen by me rather than by Libra Travel (or rather, by the subsidizing authorities), the bus would have taken advantage of the opportunities frequently offered to stick close to the river and head for the sweet little wool town of Bradford-on-Avon. But the iron law of this zetetic enterprise requires that I stay on to Trowbridge, a town whose approaching industrial skyline, and the screams and flashing blue lights of emergency services, make Limpley Stoke and Freshford feel like something that happened to someone else. In a very few minutes, the 94 is putting us down where the Methodist church used to stand before it was demolished to make way for premises owned by the Cow and Gate dairy company.

Trowbridge, as I say, is some twelve miles from Bath, but socially, culturally and, in most of its phases, architecturally, they might be separate countries. Where Bath is all about civilized leisure and pleasure, Trowbridge is all about work. Where Bath is stone, Trowbridge is more often brick. 'We are practical people here,' the place seems to say. 'We don't go in for airs and graces.' Where Bath is chic, cosmopolitan, international, Trowbridge feels utilitarian and local – even if it now houses the largest Moroccan population anywhere outside London, attracted by the chance of work in a chicken factory, and a numerous Polish community too. The town grew up round the castle, which is thought to have been established by the first Humphrey de Bohun, whose descendant Henry subsequently became the principal force in the town until deprived of his territorial lordship by King John. The castle had gone by 1640, when John Aubrey described it as 'ruinated', but the shape of the town is its legacy: the curious bow-like shape of Fore Street follows the line of the castle ditch.

This was once a booming wool town whose speciality was making blankets, and houses still survive that reflect that time of prosperity. The group of Georgian houses on The Parade, at the bottom of Fore Street, was described by the *Shell Guide to Wiltshire* of 1968 as 'one of the finest collections of eighteenth-century town mansions in England', which would put them level with Bath. The trouble now is their context. Quite apart from the fact that some look a little weary, the drabness of some of the buildings on the other side of the road diminishes their sense of occasion. And of course they long ago ceased to be the family homes of rich manufacturers. Some have plaques that plot their provenance. The fine home where Thomas Cooper, clothier, could reflect in comfort on his success and local eminence is Lloyds Bank; that of John Watts is HSBC.

Higher up Fore Street, too, there is evolution. What was once the White Hart pub is W.H. Smith. Across the road is the entrance to what in terms of local importance is probably the nearest thing that Trowbridge has now to its castle: the Shires Shopping Centre, through which you can get to a mighty Asda. In a rather woebegone effort to keep hold of the town's continuity, earlier buildings, which must have given this space real character, have been incorporated in the precinct. What is now Boswell's Café parades the evidence of its earlier life as the headquarters of Samuel Salter and Co., established 1769, one of Trowbridge's principal clothiers; today rubbing shoulders in its new guise with the likes of Peacock's and Bon Marché. They keep the place clean and tidy – against the odds, perhaps: I think this is the only shopping centre I've seen where there's a bin at the doorway for parking your used chewing gum.

At the top of the hill and looking down Fore Street is Trowbridge Town Hall, a building of some extravagance, which might seem to carry a modest echo of Major Davis's Grand Hotel back in Bath. In fact it was the work of an architect called William White, whom we shall encounter again in the village of St Columb Major in Cornwall. Davis is indeed here – but next door; what he bestowed on the town was the old Market Hall, now a J.D. Wetherspoon pub, named for a man whom the company picked out as the town's most famous son: Sir Isaac Pitman.

*****

Though they ought not to make the claim that he 'invented' shorthand, the honouring of Sir Isaac seems wholly appropriate. Where Beau Nash, because of his commitment to leisure and pleasure, can stand as a suitable symbol of Bath, so Pitman, for his commitment to dogged hard work, can do so for Trowbridge. There's a kind of informational shrine to him in the windows of a disused shop in Silver Street, charting where he came from and what he became. It contains a version of Psalms 100 and 133 written in Pitman's shorthand. That system, rather than shorthand pure and simple, was his lasting gift to the world. What he did was to take a previous version and greatly improve it. He'd begun by working for his father, the manager of a weaving mill in the town (Isaac, born in 1813, was one of eleven children), and had stepped up, largely through schooling himself, to become at nineteen the head of a school at Barton-on-Humber, North Lincolnshire, transferring in time to a similar post in Gloucestershire.

Having perfected his system, he publicized it in a book called *Stenographic Sound-Hand*. Its main advantage – an imperative, this, for a man who did everything at high speed – was that it was far quicker to write than previous systems. Characteristically, too, he kept tinkering with his invention, hoping to make it even more perfect – that is to say, even faster. His second great enthusiasm, also demonstrated in the windows in Silver Street, was phonetic spelling. Yet Trowbridge has to accept that as his reputation increased, this great son of the town relocated himself and his business; and where else but to Bath, where he established a phonetics institution, whose name he spelled in phonetics, in Albion Place.

*****

It has to be said that while Trowbridge looks like a home to hard work, that is not the town's only addiction. A walk down Silver Street in mid-afternoon encounters a level of tattooed obesity, together with its popular variant, tattooed obesity plus a dog, which would horrify, perhaps even terrify, respectable Bath. If you begin to suspect that Trowbridge is no stranger to the awarding of ASBOs, the crime figures show you'd be right. Between March 2014 and February 2015, there were 1,539 cases of anti-social offences; all cases recorded as crime amounted to 2,218, of which more than a quarter were crimes of violence, and 15 per cent involved criminal damage and arson.

But all seems entirely different if you wander from here to the improbably named Bythesea Road – this in a town whose nearest available seaboard (in fact, the end of the Bristol Channel) is a good fifty miles away. That County Hall stands in Bythesea Road is explained by the prominence in the town of the Bythesea family: clothiers, of course, who, having bettered themselves by moving to Freshford, left this land to the town. The walk to County Hall takes you close to the back of the Asda, where across the road a further shopping parade has augmented the panoply offered by the Shires, adding Next and New Look and Argos and an all-night Boots. And Trowbridge has recently taken delivery of a spanking new eight-screen Odeon cinema.

That Trowbridge became in 1893 the headquarters of the county of Wiltshire seems when you look at the map somewhat surprising. This honour used to belong to Salisbury, but that was too far to the south of the county to be wholly convenient. So other contenders came into the reckoning. Swindon, perched on the north-east corner, was also deemed too inaccessible for much of the county (though in Swindon they smelled local jealousies). The natural choice, near the heart of the county, was Devizes, one of the best small towns in England. The great failing of Devizes was that it had no rail link with Salisbury and only a tenuous one with Swindon (on a line that would be abolished in 1966). Trowbridge, though so far to the west of the county that it seems in imminent danger of toppling into Somerset, had direct rail links to most of the county's sizeable towns.

And here, at last, is a case where Trowbridge scores heavily over Bath. It presides over the county that contains such momentous ingredients as Stonehenge and Avebury, Salisbury with its cathedral and plain, Wilton and Stourhead and calm reassuring Heale, the Marlborough Downs and the Vale of Pewsey. People have thought of themselves, identified themselves, through the centuries as Wiltshire women, Wiltshire men. They have fought and died with the Wiltshire regiment. But Bath? It was never the county town of Somerset. That honour belonged to Taunton, which though close to the border with Devon had more of the feel and taste of a Somerset town. In the great ill-fated reorganization of local government engineered in 1972 by a Conservative government, a new county was plucked out of Somerset and named Avon. Bath was a leading component; yet it was little more than an after-ran compared with mighty Bristol, which so dominated the new set-up that Avon people used to complain that Bristol came first and the rest of the county nowhere. So twenty years later another Conservative government scrapped it, along with such other resented concoctions as Cleveland and Humberside, and Bath found itself in yet another confected territory.

So where Trowbridge can proudly claim to be the capital of historic and meaningful Wiltshire, Bath is the principal town of something called Banes – Bath and North East Somerset, to give it its true and wretchedly cumbersome designation; sometimes reduced to Bathnes, but that's hardly a term commanding allegiance either. How many people in Bath ever say: Me, I'm a Banesian, born and bred and proud of it? Whereas in Wiltshire, such local pride is long-standing and ineradicable. You don't have to be a UKIP supporter to think such things matter.

21

NOSING AROUND

94 Plymouth–Newton Ferrers–Noss Mayo

'LET US NOW', the book of Ecclesiasticus bids us, 'praise famous men.' It's an exhortation to which congregations no doubt complied with unusual enthusiasm in the pews of the church of St Peter, Revelstoke, high above the waterside village of Noss Mayo, Devon: all the more because the homily goes on to single out as especially praiseworthy 'rich men furnished with ability, and living peaceably in their habitations'. The villagers of Noss Mayo must have felt confident that one such meritorious person lived close beside them and even worshipped with them: Edward Charles Baring, financier, chairman of Lloyds, lavish patron of the arts, who in time would become the first Lord Revelstoke. It was he who had provided many of them with their homes and all of them with this church, built to replace an original, now derelict St Peter's, a mile and a half out of the village.

Noss Mayo and its elder sibling Newton Ferrers on the other side of a creek which runs off the River Yealm are a mere five miles as the crow flies from Plymouth, though nearer ten if you take the 94 Tally Ho! bus on a route designed to cope with the jagged Devon coastline. Plymouth, a historic city of more than 250,000 people, has no shortage of famous men, even if the most famous, Sir Francis Drake, who sailed round the world and defeated the Spanish Armada, was born fifteen miles away in

Tavistock. Drake was mayor of Plymouth and for a time its MP, which makes him a kind of honorary Plymothian – or, in the local usage, Janner. His name is frequently evoked around the city. The famous story of how, as the Armada was sighted, he insisted on finishing his game of bowls on the Hoe seems to be taken as embodying the spirit of seafaring Plymouth – even if may have been pure invention.

Surprisingly, though, he fails to appear on a list of local celebrities recently put out by the city council. Those nominated include Charles Eastlake, painter and first director of the National Gallery; Joshua Reynolds, born in Plympton; Robert Falcon Scott, the explorer who died in the Antarctic; Nancy, Viscountess Astor, the first woman to sit at Westminster, born in Virginia, but an MP here; yet not Michael Foot, journalist, author, biographer, bibliophile, besotted supporter of Plymouth Argyle FC, who for nearly three years led the Labour Party, though not with much success. Did they think that he might be too contentious a choice? If so, why did they select Patrick Abercrombie, who with the city engineer, John Paton-Watson, reshaped the centre of Plymouth after the Second World War in a fashion that was controversial then and remains so now?

As a naval town, Plymouth was always vulnerable, and bombing raids, which reached their most devastating in the spring of 1941, left over a thousand civilians dead and more than 4,000 more injured, with almost 4,000 homes completely destroyed and as many as 18,000 damaged. Much of the city centre was left in ruins. Abercrombie was sent for, as he was for an even mightier assignment, the reshaping of London. He saw himself as an innovator. Not for him the solutions that post-war cities like Dresden and Leningrad would adopt, painstakingly reconstructing what they had lost. In any case, some of the stricken areas of this Devon city had been mean and unhealthy: better to sweep them away, and build something entirely new and wholly twentieth century. The essence of what was originally billed in Plymouth as the Watson-Abercrombie plan was a grid pattern alignment with straight streets running west to east and, bisecting them, a great new ceremonial boulevard, north to south from the station to Plymouth Hoe, to be called Armada Way.

That Plymouth remains, as the 1975 version of the *Shell Guide to Devon* rated it, 'superb' is indisputable. To the north is Dartmoor, to the west, the Tamar and Cornwall; and ahead, beyond the Hoe (which still has a bowling green), with its mighty seventeenth-century fortification the Citadel and a lighthouse transplanted from Eddystone Rock, is the grand and generous sweep of the sea, across which great ships make their majestic progress. Around Sutton Harbour ancient buildings and irregular winding streets recall the origins of the city. Abercrombie and Watson had a great deal to live up to, with the certainty that whatever they did would provoke discontents, especially from those who had known and loved the old Plymouth before the Luftwaffe struck.

Simon Jenkins delivers a familiar indictment in his *England's Thousand Best Houses* (he's extolling a house that survived both the bombs and the surgery, the sixteenth-century Elizabethan House in New Street): 'Poor Plymouth. It was badly blitzed in the Second World War and then subjected to slash and burn by its city fathers. The modern visitor will find it a maze of concrete blocks, ill-sited towers and ruthless road schemes. Much of this damage was done by one man, Patrick Abercrombie, in the 1950s.' Abercrombie has his devoted defenders, most recently Jeremy Gould of Plymouth University. The incessant TV presenter Kevin McCloud has called his creation 'beautiful', saying: 'It's rare that you get, out of something as devastating as the wholesale bombing of a city centre, the hand of genius.' The radical topographer Owen Hatherley, in his book *A New Kind of Bleak*, hails Armada Way as 'England's last great street'. Hatherley is a modernist, and for him central Plymouth is 'a reminder of just how necessary modernism was'.

Yet some people, perhaps many, who live in Plymouth or pass through it every day find less delight in it. The long unresolved debate over Abercrombie reignited in 2007 after the city council announced that because of the impossible cost of repairing it, it planned to demolish the Civic Centre built in 1959–62. Many people in Plymouth approved. Not so defenders of architectural modernism: the Twentieth Century Society urged English Heritage to prevent its destruction by listing it, provoking a torrent of local objections many of which, the society's website said, were couched in language that they could not decently republish. In 2015 it was bought by the revivalist developers Urban Splash for purposes still unknown as I wander round Plymouth.

I have been here several times before, on days when the wind seized its chance to blow vehemently down the grid pattern streets and a lashing rain became its accomplice, and the Armada Way and the streets running off it felt then like the bleak end of Bleaksville. Today in the sunshine it all looks welcoming and cheerful. Yet even on a day as benign as this one, the place still feels uneasy. The blocks which house the great shops are undistinguished and slabby (Abercrombie himself favoured breaking the street pattern more than the city then chose to do). And where it seems to be striving for symmetry, it has failed to achieve it. The commercial spaces on the east side of the Way are still largely occupied, where too many sites on the west side are empty.

It's as if the whole balance of central Plymouth has shifted further east than first intended, a process amplified by the success of the new, replacement, Drake Circus Shopping Centre. Even in today's sunshine Armada Way seems lifeless. I think they should now uplift it, perhaps by running modern trams down a central reservation. Plymouth station is one of those cases where a city would probably like to beckon its railway nearer. Armada Way was supposed to link the station with Plymouth Hoe, but the station is on the further downward slope of a hill which reaches its peak at a roundabout called North Circus. Glamorous trams which could whizz you down to the Citadel and the Hoe and the Barbican would be an unqualified boon to arriving visitors (if not to the taxi trade) and would add a needed air of excitement to Abercrombie's boulevard.

*****

It's astonishing to discover that when Abercrombie was summoned, Plymouth as we now know it was less than thirty years old. Until 1914 there were three separate townships: the Plymouth that had grown up over the centuries around Sutton Pool, where it had its beginnings, where the fishing trade began, and from where the Pilgrim Fathers said their farewells to England in 1620; Devonport; and a place called East Stonehouse that had grown up between them. Devonport was a place of real consequence in its own right, which became an independent borough in the year of Victoria's accession to the throne. The impetus for that came from the threat of French invasion. The naval defensive build-up which that required needed more space than old Plymouth could furnish, whereas Devonport – then known as Plymouth Dock or, more often, just Dock – had it in plenty. For a while, under the threat of war in the time of Napoleon, the population of Devonport surged ahead of Plymouth's – until Plymouth, having built a mighty breakwater that would make its harbour secure, became once again the dominant element in this trinity. The idea that they might be brought together had been around for more than a century. Union Street, built across Plymouth Marsh in the 1810s, was intended as a move towards it.

But it needed the threat of war to bring the three towns together. Devonport was still resistant, but the Local Government Board in London, which adjudicated in such cases, was clearly impressed by the testimony of the officer in command of South West coastal defences. In peacetime, he said, dealing with three authorities rather than one had been no great problem, but in wartime it would be a serious impediment. So at the close of October 1914 the three old authorities went out of business and on Monday 2 November a new united council was voted into existence.

Even away from Abercrombie's legacy, one is constantly aware in Plymouth of tensions between old and new, between change and continuity. Post-war Plymouth was a city bent on change – as indeed it still is, as attested both by cranes busy on development sites and notices promising more. Unusually, the blitzed parish church of St Andrew was restored to its former state. Yet nearby is Charles Church, a ruin contained in a roundabout, comprehensively shattered, grass growing on what was once its seventeenth-century floor. The city chose to preserve it in its ruined condition as a memorial to those who had died through enemy action, but the graveyard was swept away to speed up the traffic flow. It stands today, melancholy in a sense that goes beyond the city's good intentions, its isolation a monument to a deference to the supremacy of traffic that echoes Manzoni's in Birmingham or Smigielski's in Leicester.

Close to Charles Church is another building due to be sacrificed soon to the cause of improvement, but here less regrettably. The Bretonside bus station, where I've come to catch the bus to Noss Mayo, built in 1958, is a creepy place now, almost devoid of buses except for the National Express coaches which still call here to collect for places as distant as Edinburgh. Announcements in several languages play to an empty house. A man with a nose which looks as though it has spent many hours in boxing rings is sitting reading his newspaper. 'Has this place been abandoned?' I ask. He replies in a tone which may come from mere surprise but sounds more like a rebuke. 'Haven't you heard? It's being redeveloped. It's all been in the *Herald* . . . ' As it is again in the *Plymouth Herald* this morning, with reports that the city council planning committee is about to approve a £40 million plan to replace it with a new leisure complex. So the 94 to Noss Mayo will need to find a new place to start from. But this morning it still has its berth at Bretonside, and picks up the only passenger waiting.

There's a long trek out through the Plymouth suburbs, enlivened by the crossing of the boat-dotted River Plym, and the sense of the city only begins to abate when, twenty minutes on, we reach a place called Elburton. Thereafter it's a progress through decreasingly suburbanized villages. Yealmpton is distinguished by a church, thoroughly rebuilt by William Butterfield in 1849–50, which was a particular source of joy to John Betjeman, while at nearby Kitley Hall, the home of Squire Bastard, the pleasingly nonsensical story of Mother Hubbard who lived in a cupboard was dreamed up by Sarah Martin, sister-in-law to the squire. Even so, if I had time to get off and look at a village anywhere on this route I think I would opt for Holbeton. The roads here are a kind of assault course, narrow and irregular, though there is little to dispute the 94's right of way as it plunges into the village, down towards the church at the bottom and cottages even deeper beyond it.

The hedgerows around here are so high that there's not much meadow or pasture land to be seen, and only the occasional habitation. The route, which ran east before turning off towards Holbeton, is now running west towards Newton and Noss. The first intimations of Noss come at Membland, where Edward Baring and his family spent such time as his business could spare him away from Dartmouth House, their grand residence in Charles Street, Mayfair. The house has gone. The novelist Maurice Baring, son of Edward Charles, who grew up there, remembered it as 'a place of rare and radiant happiness'.

The place was never the same after the Baring business ran into potentially terminal trouble in 1890. There had always been fears about Edward Baring's impetuosity, and now he so far overcommitted his firm in Argentina that a serious crisis arose from which he had to be rescued by the Bank of England. Thereafter everything had to go: houses, furnishings, pictures, along with Lord Revelstoke's reputation. Only in the memories of its people was Noss Mayo still a Baring village. The house passed into other hands and then into such neglect that in 1945 it was taken down. Estate buildings still survive, now put to more relevant uses. From here the road dips down to a place called Bridgend. There's a choice of two roads beyond: one signposted for Newton Ferrers, the other for Noss. This morning's bus will leave Newton till later; it is heading direct for its advertised terminus, Noss Mayo (tennis court). The name of Noss Mayo, the village of which St Peter's is now effectively part, derives from a proprietor whose name was Matthew Fitzjohn, to whom Edward I gave the manor. Noss Mayo means Matthew's Nose.

The church clock is chiming ten. A gentle tennis match is in progress, but otherwise all is still. (Villagers say this would not be the case in summer, when hordes of visitors, too many of them bringing their cars, cram into constricted space.) Down the hill is a cluster of buildings that amount to the village centre – the village hall (Pilates today 8.30 and 10.15), which was once the chapel of ease when the parish church was still distant; the Tilley Institute (billiards and snooker) – but no shops: the last closed its doors a while ago. Noss Mayo and Newton Ferrers

observe each other across their creek off the Yealm, but Noss has its own
subordinate creek. Here you can choose: a street to the west will take you
to a pub called the Ship, or one to the east, to the Swan. The water below
on a day of such perfection is unimproveably blue, the houses nowadays
clean and neat and gleaming white, and apart from the occasional whine
of a saw from somewhere up on the hill, the loudest sound you are likely
to hear is the lapping of water.

The road past the Ship takes you on to a nine-mile route round the
headland that Edward Baring built to provide a scenic drive to delight and
impress his eminent visitors. On the other side of the creek is Pillory Hill,
from where twenty-seven steps take you to Baring's church of St Peter,
Revelstoke. (Stoke was the early name of this territory, until a man called
Revel acquired it in the twelfth century and celebrated his ownership by
tacking his name on to Stoke's.)

St Peter's was the work of an eminent London architect, Piers St
Aubyn, but the core ideas were Baring's. It was Baring who resolved
that the old church should be replaced on a more accessible spot on
land that he owned; he who ordained that this new church should be
the echoing counterpart, matching tower with tower, of the ancient
church of Holy Cross, high above Newton Ferrers. It was he who must
have commissioned the extraordinary wood carvings, one depicting
a battle at sea, attributed on one of the pews to 'Harry Hems and his
Merry Men' from Exeter. And you cannot look for long at this church
without being aware of Baring. Baring before his fall: the product of one
of the wealthiest and most influential financier families in London, run
by the descendants of an immigrant from Bremen in Germany, five of
whose members became hereditary peers. There are windows dedicated
to him and to his wife, who is interred with him in a family vault in the
churchyard. Another window commemorates two sons who died early:
Arthur, born 1862, died 1863; Rupert, born and died 1878.

Yet as the book of Ecclesiasticus does not fail to point out, the
unfamous deserve our remembrance too, not just the famous:

> And some there be, which have no memorial;
> Who are perished, as though they had never been;
> And are become as though they had never been born;
> And their children after them . . .
> Despite which:
> Their seed shall remain for ever,
> And their glory shall not be blotted out.

Drake humbled the Spanish, but he could not have done it without the assistance of hundreds who were then and remain now unremembered, uncredited, their glory blotted out. The lives of humbler Noss Mayo, its labouring poor, are part of the village's history also. And they too are commemorated, though more modestly than His Lordship, at St Peter's. Gravestones record generations of Roes and Kingcomes, Gileses and Fosters. On a plaque on the ground, a boy has recently placed some flowers. On a handmade card, he has written: 'Dear Grandma and Grandad, HAPPY EASTER. Lots of love from Eric.' Inside the church door there's a book that lists many whose names might otherwise have been lost to posterity as the inscriptions on their gravestones faded. Some were victims of the waves of infection which from time to time swept through such places, especially the cholera that arrived here in the 1840s.

What the records can't tell us is how these nineteenth-century families lived and how their livings were made. But the 1881 census, taken four years after Edward Baring bought the estate, gives a vivid picture of that. Most who work are engaged on the land or the water: thirty-nine agricultural labourers in a population of just over 500 (including outcrops such as Bridgend); eighteen fishermen, ten mariners, four more working with boats. After which, sixteen masons, fourteen carpenters and eleven general labourers. More than half the population was born in the parish of Revelstoke, most others in Newton Ferrers or closer to Plymouth. The 2011 census shows how wholly the picture has changed since Baring's day. The top occupations here are 28 per cent rated as professionals, 17 per cent managers, directors and senior officials, 13 per cent associate professional and technical; 12 per cent skilled tradespeople and 10 per cent corporate managers and directors. Not many fishermen there, nor many now who would qualify as the working poor.

It used to be the practice in Devon to lump incomers, whether holiday visitors or newly arrived permanent residents, with the unlovely designation grockles. On that basis, Noss and Newton today would be largely the products of grockledom. Some come here for a gentle retirement (the average age in these villages was 51 and the median 56, compared with a national median age of 39) and some are second home owners, supplemented by renters of holiday cottages.

*****

A signpost outside St Peter's alleges that Newton Ferrers is just one mile away. That is what is known in the trade as a euphemism – or at least that is how it feels once I've trudged all the way to Bridgend and am slogging in summery heat up the wooded hill into Newton. (There are, at times, alternative ways of getting across: the ferry or at low tide a walk across the sands, but not at the moment.) But suddenly, there's a hooting behind me, and here is the bus that brought me to Noss this morning and its cheerful driver is asking: 'Fancy a lift?' And I do, and it's rather more than a lift, since this bus embarks on a tour of this village before finally arriving at what seems like the centre of Newton: the top of the hill that leads down from the Co-op, past Quality Foods and Luscombe Maye estate agents and the community post office and D.A. Tubb Ltd, pharmacists (for Newton retains the magic ingredient that Noss no longer possesses: shops); and so down to the waterfront and the inviting sight of the Dolphin Inn. But the inn must wait for a while. First I need to seek out a famous local attraction and landmark, the River Yealm Hotel.

There's a road that takes you directly there, but this is a day for sticking close to the river, which you can do by descending a hundred steps known as The Doctor's Steps, perhaps because the doctor's was where many felt they should head for after climbing up them. At the foot I meet a woman walking her dog, and ask where the path is making for. That way, she says, pointing east, takes you back into Newton Ferrers; and that way (west) to the Yam Hotel. Just as Slaithwaite is usually Slawit in Slaithwaite, so Yealm is Yam on the banks of the Yealm. It's a delicious path, lush with bluebells, both blue and silvery white, daisies and celandines, borage, and those fine and unfairly disparaged adornments, dandelions. Again, the loudest sound here is the water plashing against the shore.

We're now close to the little harbour which serves the village, and from where you can take a ferry to Noss or to Warren Point on the Yealm. The path has now reunited with the road, and here is the Royal Yealm Hotel, built in the early years of the twentieth century. A sad sight now, forlorn and shabby and no longer open to visitors, yet with just enough of an aura left to evoke the days when people came here from places even further away than London, arriving by pony and trap from Steer Point station or by steamboat from Plymouth, to breathe in the summer evening air, to sit perhaps with drink in hand gazing out over the water, before settling down to summon attentive waiters to fetch them their steak Béarnaise, or a plaice, bass or mullet that only a few hours before had been swimming off Plymouth. But such times are gone, and one cannot expect their return.

The walk back by the path to the village from here is better still, for this takes you to Riverside Road, where a smorgasbord of white cottages, almost none of them identical with its neighbour, achieves a kind of natural spontaneous harmony that nobody could have designed. Quite a press of people have found their way now to the Dolphin. There is still a place or two left on the terrace, to which my lunch is brought by two barmaids. A woman who seems to know everyone, perched on a wall, benignly observes: 'Here you are, sitting in the sunshine, being attended to by two beautiful young women. I hope you appreciate that!' Yes, thanks for that, Newton Ferrers. I do.

But soon she, and the Newton people around her, are joined by a most important arrival. We're three weeks away from the general election and Garry, already much talked about, has appeared to join us. He's Garry Streeter, Conservative member for South West Devon for the past eighteen years and now fighting off a Liberal Democrat. He shouldn't, I suspect, have much trouble round here (and in fact he doesn't: on May 7, he trounces his challengers, with the Liberal Democrat finishing fourth). This feels like inherently Conservative and, in a deeper sense, conservative country. The managers, directors, senior officials, associate professionals and ancillary people, active or, perhaps more often, retired, who live in a place as blessed by nature and subsequent human endeavour as this have a lot to conserve, and they do not want it to change.

There is always a fear in such places that change will be for the worse. Notices throughout Noss and Newton are alerting local residents to what might prove to be a potent threat to the Tally Ho! 94. Headed 'Help Save our Local Bus Service,' they say Devon County Council are soliciting views on their plans to reduce the service. It looks as though these buses won't disappear altogether, but may be reduced from five a day to three.

Buses like these are incurable lossmakers, and to find oneself the only passenger for most or all of a journey is a sign of how vulnerable they have become. Sooner or later, if cuts in public spending continue, as they seem certain to do, there must be a danger of losing this bus altogether. The least cost in that would be inconveniencing mere trippers like me. Even so, looking out from here over the dazzling Yealm, how sad to think I might never again be able to travel on such a morning from the fine, if flawed, city of Plymouth to the beautiful, peaceful, water-lapped villages of Newton and Matthew's Nose.

22

SAINTS THROUGH THE CENTURIES, SUMMERS OF SIN

94 Wadebridge–St Columb Major–Newquay

CORNWALL is *in* England certainly; but not *of* England. The world west of the Tamar is physically, culturally, some would even say spiritually, different from that to the east: calmly, not (for the most part) defiantly, yet still proudly different, intent on preserving and cherishing its sense of otherness. The legacy of its Celtic origins is never all-pervading, and in places along today's journey it hardly exists at all. But the black and white flags of St Piran and Cornwall flutter alongside that of St George and outnumber them; there's a saint's day, 5 March, unobserved outside the county except by its exiles, which is Piran's celebration, and Cornwall's; there's a Cornish language, once near extinct, now revived and advancing, with bilingual signs at the border.

In 2014, the Conservative–Liberal Democrat government recognized the significance of these distinctions by awarding Cornwall the status of a national minority, established under rules laid down by the Council of Europe that already applied to the Scottish, Welsh and Irish, promising protection against discrimination and a right to have its people's views given a proper attention by government. There's a Cornish political party, Mebyon Kernow, which demands recognition of Cornwall's differentness, though not – so far – calling for independence. It wins seats on the county council, yet its impact remains marginal: at the 2015 election its leader and most successful candidate, Dick Cole, took only 4 per cent of his constituency vote, suggesting a Cornish electorate that does not want to take difference too far.

And though these may be minority preoccupations, there are other signs that travellers over from England cannot miss: the prevalence across the county of granite; the gleaming white and cream of so many buildings as you come in from Plymouth, even those which closer inspection shows to be basically brick. There is also here a persisting sense of wariness about the non-Cornish English. Philip Marsden, whose book *Rising Ground: A Search for the Spirit of Place,* published in 2014, is full of profound evocations of Cornwall, recalled in a *Guardian* article how when he first drove down to live in Cornwall in the 1990s he was greeted by a message chalked up on a railway bridge near Truro: 'Go home, English!'

Devonians still rail at invasion by those they call grockles; the Cornish resent the same process, though their word is emmets. That resentment is rarely vindictive, but it is there.

And this sense of us and them must surely be heightened by the striking contrasts of affluence and poverty: the gleaming limousine sliding into a parking space in front of the food bank. When the convenient distinction is drawn between comfortable south of the kingdom and the struggling north, Cornwall on the south-western edge of the country belongs unequivocally to the north.

Yet nothing perhaps signals this sense of separate identity more immediately than the county's place names, so many derived from saints of whom even many in Cornwall know little or nothing – and whose record of sanctity, even their very existence, remains a matter of doubt. I counted more than seventy communities named after saints in the *Ordnance Survey Gazetteer of Great Britain*; some of these holy souls famous, like Mary and Margaret and John, others almost unheard of in all other contexts: Cadix and Clether, Day, Erme and Erney and Ewe, Issey and Keyne, Levan and Loy, Mewan and Minver, Pinnock, Ruan, Teath and Veep, Wenn and Winnolls and Winnow.

Sabine Baring-Gould, that immense but not always reliable scholar, disparaged those who wrote off so many as mere legend. He himself felt quite able to plot the saints' family networks. Winwaloe and Wethenoc (or Winock), he tells us, were brothers, sons of Fragan and Gwen of the Three Breasts, which is not a physiological condition but meant that she had married three times and had children in each marriage. St Wenn, he says, was really another, less allegedly multi-breasted, Gwen, aunt of St David, mother of St Cuby (not every saint has acquired a place name). Despite this sage's enthusiasm, it is clear that some of the saints owe such celebrity as they still have to corruption. The leading authority O.J. Padel has established that some whose names are now enshrined on road signs appear to owe their existence to accidental recycling: St Allen began as an apple tree (the Cornish word *avallon*), and St Teath as a pagan corn goddess (the Cornish *ith*).

But why should the names of saints have been adopted here on a scale in Cornwall unmatched anywhere else in England? It happened because the standard Saxon practice of clustering together in villages never took root in Cornwall. Across the border in Devon, place names are more likely to reflect the presence of some great family. In Cornwall, the pattern was one of small hamlets and farmsteads where, no noble family being available, the name of a saint was the best way to differentiate one settlement from another.

That's not to underestimate the glorious diversity of place names where even the most assiduous hagiographer could not sniff out a saint: names like Baldhu, Bugle, Praze-an-Beeble, Probus, Providence, Quethiock, Quoit, Rame, Tredrizzick, Zelah and Zennor that you'd never find anywhere else, reflecting the fact that when these names were coined the predominant language was Cornish. The Cornish historian and topographer Charles Henderson, a recognized polymath even in his teenage years, destined to die on honeymoon in Rome at the age of thirty-three and wonderfully evoked in Philip Marsden's book, knew of fifteen places called Penquite east of Par and at least eleven west of it called Pencoose. If you see a signpost such as one I saw on this journey offering Tregore, Tresithick, Trevithick, and Tregaswith, you will know you're in Cornwall.

This journey was to have taken me from Wadebridge in the mid-west of the county through to Truro, the cathedral city that succeeded Bodmin and Launceston as county town, and on to the seaside mining village St Agnes, a route that would also come within genuflecting range of other saints from St Breock, just outside Wadebridge, down to Saints Erme, Clement, Allen and Enoder, close to Truro, and finally to St Agnes herself, martyred when only thirteen, the hagiographies say, for refusing the ardent advances of a Roman governor's son. But in March 2015, the independent bus company Western Greyhound, whose cheerful, green, and not always reliable buses operated this route, abruptly shut down. Drivers reported for work one Friday morning to be told that the firm had gone bust.

Cornwall Council came to the rescue and arranged for two other operators, First and Plymouth Buses, to introduce routes through most of the villages which the Greyhound's demise had left stranded. One of these, which it now becomes my fate to embrace instead of the route to St Agnes, was a 94 from Wadebridge through two St Columbs, Major and Minor, and on to Newquay.

*****

Wadebridge belongs to the Cornwall of agriculture, one of the three great industries which over the centuries has sustained – or too often failed to sustain – the county's economy. There were other, lesser industries, too, some celebrated in novels of Cornwall, especially those of Daphne du Maurier, who wrote *Jamaica Inn* and *Rebecca*, and Winston Graham, whose Poldark stories were revived on television in 2015: smuggling, piracy, the gleeful looting of wrecks, and robbery on the highway at dead of night, as well as legitimate enterprises like the quarrying that has left such bleak and scarred legacies on places like Delabole. But the greatest, apart from agriculture, were mining and tourism, nowadays intertwined. The mining industry has gone, living on now only on the tourist trails, in preserved remnants and museums, and above all the abandoned sites, with their ruined engine houses and chimneys, spread across so much of the landscape.

Wadebridge is different. It's the home of the annual Royal Cornwall Show, which for three days in early June each year pulls in thousands who come to exhibit, or buy, or just gaze at what has been brought here, while outside, drivers and passengers in their cars and on buses like mine fume at the endless inching forward to which they are condemned till the show is over. The tourist trails which celebrate Cornwall's traditional industries – copper, tin and china clay – have no occasion to trouble themselves with Wadebridge: round here they hardly existed.

Through much of the county the effects of recession were calamitous. Some who had worked in copper and tin found work in the china clay sector, though to make that change seems to have been taken as relegation. Many fled to places they hoped might offer relief. The census returns of mining communities in places like Cleveland and Lanarkshire in the 1850s and 1860s show an abundance of birthplaces in stricken Cornwall. A great many went abroad to America, Brazil or South Africa. Frequently these emigrants left their families behind; some sent them the promised remittances, but others left them to starve.

Even Wadebridge, though indirectly, felt the effects. In the tough year of 1831, at the start of a decade in which Chile would supersede Cornwall as the greatest world producer of copper, impoverished miners marched on the town to try to prevent the export of corn to other parts of the kingdom. In the next decade, the miners of Luxulyan converged on it to demand that the export of corn be ended and that grain should be sold at prices they could afford. Thereafter miners from Delabole arrived with the same demands, but agreed to leave after each was awarded half a loaf of bread. Agriculture in Cornwall, its second industry, did not enrich the county as much as it should have done. The land was less productive than it was in much of the kingdom. There were various reasons for that: the terrain and the weather created inescapable problems, but experts in distant London deplored the conservatism of Cornwall's farmers, suspicious of innovation and of wise advice such as their own.

Of this once essential trinity, the one that counts for most nowadays is tourism. Cornwall was effectively discovered as a tourist attraction in the eighteenth century, but the journey there from much of the country was daunting. From 1840 onwards, the easiest route was a train from London to Bristol, and then a steamer to Hayle. Brunel's bridge across the Tamar, which changed everything, was not completed until 1859. And though today it's been boosted by such innovations as the walking and cycling trails across the old copper kingdom, the hugely successful Eden Project created by Tim Smit, and Rick Stein's recreation of Padstow as a gastro paradise, none of this has come anywhere near to making the county prosperous.

Alone in the UK it has qualified for what the European Union calls Objective One funding, reserved for areas where gross domestic product is three-quarters or less of the EU average. Now, as in the dying days of mining, the greatest hardship is to be found in the west of the county, around failing towns such as Redruth. Yet Truro, the county capital, a mere ten miles to the east, comes behind only Oxford and Winchester as a town where the gap between the cost of buying a house and the resources of its townspeople is hardest to bridge. The chances of local people buying a home in St Ives are now so negligible that in May 2016 its people voted by 83 per cent to 17 for new homes to be reserved for full-time residents; the final decision will lie with the county council.

*****

Wadebridge is hungry for tourists. It can't hope to be a St Ives or a Padstow (and indeed, given the tensions in St Ives, probably wouldn't desire to be), but it wants to offer temptations potent enough to coax people who've hardly heard of it into the town. One such attraction is the ancient bridge across the Camel, with seventeen arches, which links Wadebridge with the older, long superior town of Egloshayle. The rector of Egloshayle, Thomas Lovibond, concerned at the number of drownings of people crossing the Camel at low tide, built it in 1468 in the reign of Edward IV. The Cornish term for it was 'pons war gwlan', which means bridge on wool. According to local legend, bales of wool were used as part of its foundations as a defence against the shifting demands of the tidal river, but it may mean, rather more prosaically, that sheep farmers provided the money. The other lure is much newer. There used to be a railway link with Padstow, a line that warmed the easily warmable heart of that great devotee of Cornwall, John Betjeman. He had come by the 'windy, single line' from Launceston:

> We round a bend and there is the flat marsh of the Camel, there are the little rows of blackish-green cottages along the river at Egloshayle and we are at Wadebridge, next stop Padstow. The next five and a half miles beside the broadening Camel to Padstow, is the most beautiful train journey I know. See it on a fine evening at high tide with golden light on the low hills, the heron-haunted mud coves flooded over, the

sudden thunder as we cross the bridge over Little Petherick creek, the glimpses of slate roofs and a deserted jetty among spindly Cornish elms, the wide and unexpected sight of open sea at the river mouth, the huge spread-out waste of water with brown ploughed fields coming down to little cliffs where no waves break but only salt tides ripple up and ebb away. Then the utter endness at the end of the line at Padstow – 260 miles of it from London. The smell of fish and seaweed, the crying of gulls and the warm, moist, west country air and valerian growing wild on slate walls.

The old station at Wadebridge is now the John Betjeman Centre, where a notice in the window deplores Dr Beeching's butchery as 'a desecration of our national railway system'. Its closure seemed all the more sacrilegious, no doubt, because the Wadebridge to Bodmin was one of Britain's earliest railways, opened in 1834. And yet had Beeching not passed his death sentence, there would not today be a path for people on foot and on bicycles (there are plenty of places to hire them close to its start) to make their own journey along the glorious River Camel, stopping as those on the trains could not, to take note of birds and waterfowl of many varieties, possibly otters, perhaps even seals. Padstow to Wadebridge is a little more than five miles and on a day like today it's irresistible.

Maybe this tourist incentive is the reason why Wadebridge today looks so much brighter and more invigorated than it did when I last came here a decade ago. Betjeman, though it celebrates him, was not a great fan of the town; he found little to savour in its principal street, which along with a lot else round here is named for the Molesworth family. Part way up Molesworth Street you find the Molesworth Arms; at the top of the street beyond the Churchill Bars and the Windsor Restaurant (the Molesworths have competition now) it transmutes into Higher Molesworth Street. Though some of the ancient family shops have gone, there are new ones that vary the pattern. I don't think I noticed before the Elixir Health Foods Therapy Centre, displaying specialities of a kind unknown to Sir William, or the Rainbow Spirit Crystal Shop – 'providing coping stones along life's path', which is just what I need after the loss of my bus to St Agnes and the prospect of having to go instead to Newquay. Molesworth Street has a bookshop. I'd expected the window to be packed with Poldark, given that the BBC series is the biggest new tempter of tourists to Cornwall since the dawn of the Eden Project. But the window makes as much of Daphne du Maurier as it does of Poldark, a further indication that Wadebridge was never a mining centre.

*****

The 94 is due to leave from a bus station just beyond the Betjeman Centre, where a small group is waiting. A Woman Who Knows is explaining the fate of Western Greyhound and what has been done to replace it. The bus arrives and parks in a kind of siding: some would-be passengers try to get on, but the Woman Who Knows tells us they won't be allowed to; passengers cannot be picked up except from the stand where we are dutifully stationed. This sounds like authoritative advice – until the bus pulls out of the siding and makes purposefully off for Newquay. At which point the Woman Who Knows sets off in raucous pursuit, waving her walking stick. Fortunately there are one or two illegal alighters on board who spot her and tell the driver. So thus reprieved, we swing out past the end of the Camel trail. Soon we are in green meadowland, now ornamented with whirring huddles of wind turbines.

*****

Discounting the elusive St Jidgey, who lurks down a lane off this road, we are on our way to the day's first saint, since this bus is now due to run first to St Columb Major and then to St Columb Minor. It's hard to judge from the route of the 94 if the pecking order between Major and Minor ought to be otherwise, for as it arrives at the edge of St Columb Major the bus shies away and contents itself with exploring an industrial park beyond the St Columb Major Academy. But more important even than these is the former RAF base subsequently converted into Newquay Cornwall Airport, part of it now reconstituted as an enterprise zone known as the Aerohub. In 2014 the UK Homes and Communities Agency and the European Regional Development Fund agreed to put £6 million into a project designed to provide a general uplift for this part of Cornwall, exploiting the chance of good air links: an estimated 2,500 new jobs might result.

We are now quite clearly entering, if not Newquay proper, at least its sphere of influence, most perceptibly so when we get to what road signs say is St Columb Minor, where again this bus sticks rigidly to the main road and shuns the original village. All, at first, on this utilitarian road is subtopian, but then thrillingly we get a great wide glorious view of the essential sea.

*****

Just as Cornwall is *in* England but not *of* England, so Newquay is in Cornwall but not really *of* Cornwall. It's a construction that might have stationed itself almost anywhere, but you find it in Cornwall because of the lavishly available sea on this northern coast. Baring-Gould, writing on Cornwall in the final years of the nineteenth century, wastes little time on it. 'Uninteresting to the last degree', he says of the town, though commending its fine coastal scenery and bracing air. After which he honours the man who in essence created it, one of those ingenious and restless local entrepreneurs who keep cropping up on these journeys. 'It was projected', he says, 'by Mr J.T. (Austin) Treffry, of Place House, Fowey, a very remarkable man, far in advance of his time, to whom not Fowey only, but Cornwall generally owes a debt of gratitude.' The name Treffry, to which Austen (not Austin) converted in his middle fifties, was the maiden name of his mother, and of her brother from whom in his mid-twenties he inherited the family estates. In their home town of Fowey he built a quay for the export of tin; he developed a harbour at Par and added a smelting works, built railways and tramways and a great viaduct to carry his railway and canal across the Luxulyan Valley, to which he attached the family name. All of this was part of a wider network of enterprises; he acquired and controlled some of the county's most significant mines.

It was Treffry above all who created Newquay. His eye was on industry rather than leisure. He bought the pier and harbour to ship lead, china clay and stone from his mines and quarries. It was not until a quarter of a century after his death that the first passenger train ran into Newquay. It took some time thereafter for tourism to become the town's main priority. When in 1897 work began on the Headland Hotel, planned and designed by the leading Cornish architect Silvanus Trevail, who had hoped to create a chain of expensive hotels in the area, riots broke out. This land had been used before for grazing livestock and the drying of fishing nets, and farmers and fishermen tried to prevent development. Some of the work was wrecked, and Trevail himself was bombarded with eggs, apples and violent abuse. Some on the construction team refused to return, and unemployed miners had to be brought from hardy Redruth to replace them. But Newquay's future would be more in line with Trevail's ambitions than with Treffry's.

So the first place to head for when you get to Newquay – though you've glimpsed quite a bit already, including the Headland, on its grand clifftop site – should be the harbour ('the historic working harbour', as it's nowadays billed), which still has an old-fashioned air of Treffry's times about it. This used to be a hotspot of the Cornish pilchard trade, so much so that pilchards were given a place in the town's coat of arms. From there a climb of ninety-nine steps takes you up to the town and straight on to Fore Street, where you will find Stardust Amusements and the Cornish Fudge Shoppe and a surf shop called Smile that's been there since the end of the sixties. This is not the last surfer haunt you are going to see. Here's

another: it's called Surfing Life; a notice on the side wall announces Old
Guys Rule, which is not the impression you get from the front windows.
Much of what they are offering is for practical waterborne use, though I
sense this may not apply to a product called Dr Zog's Original Sex Wax
('best for your stick').

Today's Newquay appears from what I have read to be one of two
identically situated towns of this name. As the summer progresses it will
more and more welcome stag parties, hen parties and exuberant young
people celebrating their escape from school exams; a few, a very few, of
those who have come here for wild adventure will never go home again. All
these proceedings will be lubricated by drink. By then some of Newquay's
vital statistics will be shifting. The town will be far fuller than it is now,
and its crime figures will soar, while intending upmarket visitors will take
their custom elsewhere. As I understand it, your really superior surfers are
not drawn to Newquay. They prefer to convene at Rock, a spot with a high
built-in millionaire quotient four miles out of Wadebridge and just across
the Camel Estuary from Padstow – a place on which the additional deluges
of the well-to-do converge in very expensive cars on their fairly expensive
holiday billets, credit cards at the ready, prepared for a spell of waterborne
adventure and high-powered extravagance.

Some of Newquay's high-season afflictions seem to have eased in recent
years. The town is able to claim there's less crime than there was despite
greater numbers of visitors. Less, but still too much, with anti-social
behaviour topping the charts with violence and sex offences second. That
drink is a regular contributor is underlined by notices in the centre banning
public drinking along with public skateboarding and roller-skating.
Barechestedness among men displaying formidable tattoos is not, however,
proscribed. Domestic Newquay – that's the Newquay that actually lives
there – has to take what it gets and enjoy the much needed revenue in a
town that scores fairly high on assessments of deprivation in coastal resorts.

The beaches, of course, are magnificent, and here and there, there are
tranquil seats for old guys and gals who have never surfed or who've
put their surfing behind them to gaze out over the sea undisturbed.
Construction and demolition are thriving; near Towan beach, a hoarding in
front of what's destined to be the Towan Heights development announces:
one day all homes will be built like this.

· The appeal of Newquay's beaches – Fistral, Harbour, Towan, Great
Western, Tolcarne – remains as potent as when Baring-Gould surveyed
them. There's another a little way east of them called Lusty Glaze, which
seems wonderfully appropriate for a place so devoted to sea, sun and

sex, but the name, to my disappointment, is simply a corruption of the Cornish 'lost an glaze', meaning a grey-green promontory. For a relative puritan (as you may have noticed) like me, this is a charmless town, with few buildings, aside from Ninian Comper's church of St Michael, worth stopping to look at, but that, of course, is not the point of the place. Even if you are staying in one of the grander hotels, don't bother to bring Dr Pevsner. If gentle civilized charm and visual distinction are what you want on your holidays, better to stick to somewhere like Sidmouth.

*****

There don't seem to be many saints in the history of Treffry's creation, but there's still a couple of chances to stop and pick one up on the route back to Wadebridge. The first requires you to get off the bus near the Co-op in St Columb Minor and follow the street that leads off towards the church. Newquay was once part of the parish of St Columb Minor, but has now largely devoured its offspring. But this village street is in no way Newquay, even if the older world to which it belongs is in some ways fading. Here is a Methodist chapel, dead I would guess for some time, looking as abandoned and as ripe for conversion as some of the people Wesley founded his church to save. The Anglican church of St Columba, still it seems in good heart and condition, has, fringed around it, attractive cottages (the further you get from the Co-op the more the place's appearance improves) and a pub right outside called the Farmers Arms.

Back on the 94 bus once more, and now for St Columb Major. How strange, as Cole Porter nearly wrote, the change from Minor to Major . . . Where Minor, so subsumed in Newquay, is a disappointment, Major, overall, is a delight. There's a long single street at the heart of it, which begins as Fair Street and then, at the parish pump, narrows down still further to form Fore Street. It's a glorious jumble of buildings perched above vestigial pavements. Here is a dead Nonconformist chapel that's now a youth club; and here, another, now in the hands of an organization whose name might once have caused the faithful distress: Evolution Engineering. And here is a third, squeezed in behind the main line of the street, now a printer's shop, which still bears the sign of the Bible Christians, a sect that began in Cornwall, extended to Devon, and featured a charismatic preacher called Billy Bray, a long time drunkard and by all accounts solid ASBO material who put those days behind him and preached a message of hope, interspersing his sermons with singing and dancing. Beyond, just past the Rose and Crown pub, is a strange, exuberant, irreverent building, all but blocking the street, that until recently was Barclays Bank. Now it's empty and 'for sale or to let'.

Here the road divides, opening on to two squares, the Market Place and Union Square, in one of which the old Conservative Club, divided into apartments, confronts the old Liberal Club, now for sale. Here is another former bank, now Bank House, this one by William White, builder of Trowbridge Town Hall; unlike the joyful concoction that used to be Barclays, it seeks to epitomize dignity and sobriety, those exemplifications of what in those days people expected their banks to be – honest, industrious, God-fearing, and above all trustworthy. It's not a bank any more, of course.

There's a stolid town hall, a modest collection of shops, some unostentatiously handsome houses and some pleasingly odd ones, and one which, despite ecclesiastical windows, has the silhouette of a witch on a broomstick on its street wall. And equally irreverent, as if stationed there to dispel any notion that St Columb is over-solemn, a tattoo parlour – which should save you a trip to Newquay. At the heart of the village, where Fore Street gives way to Bank Street, is the majestic church of St Columba, which seemed for a time when the Truro diocese was created in 1876 destined to be the cathedral of Cornwall, but Truro, which required the building of a wholly new cathedral, was chosen over it.

And who was St Columba, patron of these two places? Not in all probability the celebrated sixth-century saint of that name, an Irishman, one of the founders of Christianity in Scotland, but a Cornish martyr of about the same time, whom the eminent historian William Camden logged as a man – as did Baring-Gould, until persuaded by the writings 300 years earlier of the Cornish hagiographer Nicholas Roscarrock that a gender reassignment was necessary.

And now, as if to insist that St Columb has still more to offer, there's a road at the northern end of the village whose signpost offers St Mawgan – the name of a delicious village in the valley of the Menalhyl river, a place that scarcely seems to have left the nineteenth century, let alone come to terms with the noisy, thrusting, headline-infected twenty-first. Even saints have their imperfections, of course, and even the aura of its martyred saint cannot spare St Columb Major some patches of shabbiness, the most notorious of which seems to be a long disused shop known as the Cabbage whose dilapidation moved one of its neighbours to cut out a piece from the local newspaper condemning it as an eyesore, frame it, and stick it up on a wall. But that doesn't diminish that unpremeditated charm which will sometimes make a village seem beguiling in a way that no amount of confection could ever contrive.

That applies, in my eighty years' experience, to people, too.

23
ALL CHANGE!

594 Edinburgh–London

THREE O'CLOCK IN THE MORNING; moonless, pitch dark and we're not yet even half-way to my final destination. Yet that destination has in a sense been the background accompaniment to the whole of this book. So much of the destiny of people living on Teesside, in Atherton, Tyldesley or Huddersfield, in Cupar, Fife, Colchester, Petersfield or Noss Mayo, is determined by what is decided in mighty, intimidating, glamorous, exhilarating, oppressive, convivial, sometimes painfully lonely London. 'The flower of cities all,' the poet William Dunbar called it some 600 years ago, 'gem of all joy, jasper of jocundity, most mighty carbuncle of virtue and valour.' 'The great wen,' said contemptuous Cobbett when William IV was king. Both judgements still apply.

There should have been a less taxing way of bringing this book to a close. There's a 94 London bus that pursues its blameless course from Acton Green west of the city to Piccadilly Circus and, almost, Trafalgar Square. But that was the route I took at the end of a previous book, and though the buses look different now, the journey is much the same. But then I discovered – from a notice board in the condemned bus station in Plymouth – that there's also a 594, one of a group of National Express services that leave Scotland by day and night for destinations as distant as Penzance. For the 594, the gateway to London is Edinburgh. And as I shall suggest in a moment, Edinburgh is a suitable place to depart from, since it is here that the revolt against London and all its works has been most powerful and most decisive. That is how I come tonight, among passengers most of whom have long been asleep, to be watching the road signs flashing past in the rain somewhere south of Barnsley.

The rain has been with us since Edinburgh where, as it has been for so much of 2015, the weather is what the Scots call 'dreich'. Around six o'clock, I join a small crowd assembled around the imposing Gothic memorial erected a decade after his death to the talismanic Scottish writer Sir Walter Scott. The great man is holding a book and looking preoccupied. The tilt of his head suggests that he's keeping an eye on Jenners department store, established in 1838, six years after he died, and today festooned with advertisements for their 50 per cent Big Brand sale. Fortunately for Scott, he is sheltered under a canopy, unlike his immediate neighbour David Livingstone. A gull is perched on the head of the celebrated explorer and the legacies of previous visits by gulls and pigeons are streaked down his rugged Scots face.

I watch the crowds heading for homebound trains, buses and nowadays once again trams, and wonder what Sir Walter would have to say of the choices so many of them must have made in the Scots' independence referendum and the following year's election. 'Breathes there the man with soul so dead,' he muses in *The Lay of the Last Minstrel*, 'who never to himself hath said, This is my own, my native land!' But though Scott was a super-patriot, who not only celebrated, but in some cases even invented, the country's traditions of Highland ways and Highland dress, that was always in the context of a continuing unswerving allegiance to the London-based Union. To be proud that one was a Scot did not diminish one's Britishness. That was for centuries the default position in Scotland. But it isn't now, Sir Walter; it isn't now.

*****

The coach for London leaves at a quarter to ten. Long before then, passengers clutching their tickets, most of them young or youngish, one or two couples lulling small children, are gathered to await its arrival. Eventually it appears and settles beside a companion coach about to embark on the even longer run to Penzance: by the time you have taken a break of an hour and fifteen minutes at Plymouth, a twenty-hour journey.

'Enjoy your journey,' says the disembodied voice on the intercom, which, since the journey is timed to take the best part of nine hours, may be easier said than done. It's raining hard as the coach eases out through drenched city streets, and one envies the passengers we pass on their 26 buses for Musselburgh, Prestonpans and Tranent, who'll be home and safe and watching the late evening news long before we reach Berwick. There's a teaching I have always cherished since I first found it in a now forgotten book called *The Unquiet Grave* by 'Palinurus' (Cyril Connolly): 'No city should be so large that a man cannot walk out of it in a morning.' Edinburgh passes that test. It's just twenty minutes, possibly less, past the dark hulk of Arthur's Seat, which looms above the southern side of the city, before we are over the boundary and into East Lothian, and though much of what follows is still in essence Edinburgh, the sense of the city soon begins to abate as roads hive off to the eastern suburbs.

We are out on the A1 trunk road; it's another suspected testimony to London's habitual disregard for Scotland that it's never been upgraded to a motorway. The houses dwindle and die away and we're into an eerie, empty ten o'clock landscape through which menacing pylons stalk. A baby at the front of the coach, howling only five minutes ago, has settled to sleep.

From this point, buildings are rare. And now, some thirty miles on, here is the sea, washing into a bay, beautiful and mysterious in the almost-darkness. At eleven o'clock we come over the multi-arched bridge into Berwick-on-Tweed. In England. Ideal Carpets, I see, is having a rug sale; there's a pub, the White Horse, and a Kwik Fit, and some good-looking houses, and a bookshop: all now locked away for the night – though even now you could still, if you wished, pick up a pizza. Now and then an event looms up on the roadside: a roadhouse called Purdy Lodge, near Belford, Northumberland, looks to be buzzing. The young woman who's sitting beside me seems to be fast asleep, though now and then she stirs and sighs – and out straightaway comes her mobile phone to be examined silently, and silently texted on. Sometimes these days smartphones seem to be part of whoever's using them. My skimpy understanding of evolution suggests that one day children may be born with some kind of natural smartphone in hand.

And then, as we come into Alnwick, something extraordinary happens. A castle looms up before us, floodlit, dreamlike, magical. Worth being awake for; almost, as I'd say to the girl in the next seat had she not fallen asleep again, worth making the journey for. Then a long blank patch before our travelling dormitory comes at one minute to midnight to Morpeth, where we stop at the bus station and, breaking the monotony, new people come aboard. The rain is heavier still: roofs and tarmac and pavements glisten.

Onward again. The lights of the bus illuminate road signs, but they're hard to read, especially in this weather. But now again a name looms up that brings memories of these travels flooding back. Carlisle, where my bus ran only to Crosby and I learned about catechism technique from William Pinnock. Newcastle – gateway, as I now disrespectfully think of it, to Gateshead. Gutsy, struggling Middlesbrough, which has fallen on even harder times since I was there. At ten to one, a little distance from the surviving bright lights of goodness knows where, we change drivers. Then, a huge lorry park, line upon line of them, all safely tucked up for the night.

Around twenty past three we pull into a service station: Trowell in Nottinghamshire, a stop promised on the timetable, complete with a little image of a coffee cup. About a third of the passengers climb out and head for the café. It's closed. There are people inside, and some of the bolder or

more affronted spirits among us bang on the door hoping they'll let us in.
They take no notice. Perhaps they are used to this sort of demonstration.
We traipse back, uncoffee'd and unimpressed. Time to resume our sleep.

But I'm making this journey a couple of days after midsummer night, in
the hope of seeing as much of the route as one ever could, and now as we
pull away the first hint of daylight is infiltrating the sky. Some seasoned
travellers seem to be able to sleep, or semi-sleep, for much of the journey.
Those less used to spending nine hours on a night bus are not so fortunate.
Still, it's very soon bright enough to catch all the signs pointing to
destinations down lesser roads, and now they begin to offer some sense of
hope. Huddersfield (change here for a wonderfully entertaining evening in
Slaithwaite) – that means we're more than half way. Here's Leicester (town
of Richard III and Konrad Smigielski): only 102 miles to London! And now
there's a turning for Birmingham, town of Joe Chamberlain and Herbert
Manzoni; and another for Oxford, where the people of Otmoor marched
down St Giles to rescue the heroes who'd fought enclosure. And here is
the even more cheering intelligence that we're closing on Milton Keynes.
Never had I suspected that the imminence of Milton Keynes would inspire
such delight. It's not that we see very much of this home of straight lines,
only a coach station. But what matters is the sign that clearly confirms
that we're now only 55 miles from London. More encouragements follow,
Luton is signalled; then Watford; and here, already thundering away at ten
past six, is the M25.

The sense of London only really sets in at Mill Hill, where the road that
has swept past the beginnings of London comes down alongside Mill Hill
Broadway station, where local trains rumble past and the first red buses
appear. 'Breathes there a man with soul so dead . . .'? I was born at Mill
Hill, and I have to say that contemplating its huddled homesteads as their
lights come on for the morning I don't feel the slightest twinge of emotion.

After a brief submission to taste the North Circular Road, we move into
a suburb where the bus will stop – and those who cannot wait for the
day's first coffee will not this time be denied it. Golders Green. Its *raison
d'être* is its Underground station. When it opened in June 1907, it was
out almost alone in green fields. Once it was there, the houses would pile
in around it and a built-in supply of passengers would be assured. The
main street here picks up a characteristic feature of the city into which
we are heading: its great cosmopolitan mix of distinctive communities.
Here the keynote is Jewishness. There are people even at this hour dressed
in the impeccable garb of observant Jews, and the names on the shops,
interwoven with all the usual Subways and Paddy Powers and Bootses

and Corals and Sainsbury's Locals, tell the same story. Menachem's Glatt Kosher. Shefa Mehadrin (also a kosher butcher); then, beyond the King Solomon Hotel, Jerusalem the Golden Ltd (a gift shop) and something I never remember seeing before, a kosher Indian restaurant. Barnet, the borough of which Golders Green is a part, was home at the time of the 2011 census to almost two-thirds of all Jewish people in London. The same strong sense of identity is evident in particular places across the capital: Indians in Southall and Wembley; Pakistanis in Tower Hamlets and Newham; Greeks in Enfield, Palmers Green and Cockfosters; Turks in Enfield and Haringey; Poles most of all in Ealing; Koreans clustered in New Malden.

What you also notice now are the footprints of the capital's affluence. On the hill east of Finchley Road there are tree-lined streets through to Frognal where in September 2015 there were houses for sale at £17 million, and a two-bedroom flat on offer at £3 million. And here at the end of the Finchley Road, beyond Swiss Cottage, is modestly notorious St John's Wood, where rich men famously kept their mistresses; kept them in stylish villas which are still to be found off the main road, though no longer on it, where they have given away to apparently respectable apartment blocks. On the western side we skim past the private (and reputedly far from cheap) Wellington Hospital; just beyond is Lord's Cricket Ground, less exclusive, though it may still cost you a bomb to get the best seats for a test match. To the east is Regent's Park.

And here is Baker Street. Before long, crowds will be gathering, many with cumbersome backpacks, at the door of a building which claims to be number 221b, the address for much of the time of Sherlock Holmes. The traffic steadily thickens. Now in the final stages there's a growing impatience aboard the bus. We edge into Oxford Street, then westwards to Marble Arch, then south between Hyde Park and a range of expensive hotels. This is Park Lane, on the edge of Mayfair: two names that symbolize wealth, as they did even before they became the two costliest squares on the Monopoly board. The Dorchester, established in 1931 on a site where a notable house had been, was reported in the autumn of 2015 to be charging up to £5,500 night for a top-notch suite; down in the Promenade bar you could pay £770 for a 50g portion of Beluga caviare.

Across the width of Park Lane, once penned behind a high wall, now screened only by trees, is Hyde Park – one of London's great playgrounds. Again, that typical London duality: a place for ostentatious aristocratic indulgence (horses on Rotten Row) and for political agitation (radical gatherings that sometimes frightened Authority into banning them). Then

the traffic whirlpool of Hyde Park Corner, and beyond it the garden wall
of Buckingham Palace.

Among arriving travellers, London has always been a place to wonder
at – most often for its glories, its prosperity and its renown, but sometimes
for its desperate inequity and squalor. 'Sovereign of cities,' wrote William
Dunbar in the sixteenth century, when the population, on today's best
available estimates, had only quite recently topped 150,000:

> Seemliest in sight,
> Of high renown, riches and royalty;
> Of lords barons, and many a goodly knight;
> Of most delectable ladies bright;
> Of famous prelates, in habits clerical
> Of merchants full of substance and of might.

Throw in a welter of celebrities, especially from show business and sport,
and constant arrivals from lands which Dunbar could never heard of,
some to visit and others to settle; cut back a bit on the prelates – and much
of the rest still applies.

Yet Dunbar's flower remains Cobbett's wen. Close to great affluence you
may still find hardship and squalor – not on the scale of past centuries,
but grievous nonetheless. Many will have gone cold and hungry in the
London of William Dunbar. And alongside the warm gregariousness you
find in Dickens's London, it could also be what George Gissing called it: 'a
wilderness abounding in anchorites, voluntary or constrained'.

You may also sense in these streets what must have been there in the days
of Dunbar's glittering congregation, though it reached a new peak in the
great reconstruction after the Fire of London a century later: the constant,
restless impulse for change, far ahead of anywhere else in the country.
Defoe, in *A Tour through England and Wales*, written in the 1720s after
travels compared to which a night bus from Edinburgh is a day on the beach
at Copacabana, looked about him in wonderment. 'New squares and new
streets rising up every day', he reported, 'to such a prodigy of buildings,
that nothing in the world does, or ever did, equal it, except old Rome in
Trajan's time, when the walls were fifty miles in compass, and the number of
inhabitants six million eight hundred thousand souls.' 'Whither', he asked,
'will this monstrous city then extend? And where must a circumvallation or
communication line of it be placed?' It's a question that echoes still.

But again, newcomers were also struck by the sudden jarring contrast
between one set of streets and the next. If they leave the tourist track,

they still are. And in that sense, what I see as we come into London on this midsummer morning confirms the impression of Britain that I've accumulated travelling some 3,000 miles to make these journeys. This brilliant, exhilarating, often extremely beautiful, horribly overgrown, and at times and in places desperate city embodies the nation which it so dominates. London: the disunited capital of an ever more disunited kingdom. That sense is already inescapably plain well before the spectacular evidence of the Brexit vote that will come a year later.

*****

As I've said, in this context Scotland may have been the appropriate place from which to advance on London, since Scotland in 2014–15 seemed to catch and to magnify a growing set of assumptions about the excessive, even outrageous, dominance of the capital: the sense elsewhere in the land that Britain is run by the people, for the people, of London. None of this is exactly new. Defoe notes time and again how much of the nation's activities are shaped by the needs of London. His amazement is a match for that of any occasional irregular visitor who has seen through the last three decades the transformation of the London skyline by Shard and Gherkin, Cheese Grater and Walkie Talkie and their thronging associates. Other cities in Britain build high and glamorously and daringly, but none on the epic scale of this one.

It's a sight which immediately says Big Money, and that is part of the problem. Days before the general election of 2015 the relationship between London and the rest of the country was described by Tony Travers of the London School of Economics, perhaps the supreme authority on the workings of modern-day London, as 'a bit like a relationship between a grumpy couple. They know they've got to be together, but they always sort of see each other's weaknesses more clearly than anybody else would.' Yet already by then there were many thousands in Scotland whose feelings had moved way beyond grumpy, who had come to see the relationship as a kind imprisoning bond that no longer made sense and was best thrown off now that constitutional divorce had become an option. As the social geographer Danny Dorling wrote at the time of the Scottish vote: 'the referendum . . . is at heart, not a vote about Scotland. It's a vote about London . . . London largesse, London decision-making, London hegemony.'

Yet that kind of resentment was by no means confined to Scotland. 'The election', wrote David Goodhart, former editor of the magazine *Prospect*, analysing Labour's defeat in May 2015, 'was a decisive vote against metropolitan liberalism – against mass immigration, further European integration and the high-churn society that discomforts so many people. It was also a vote against London – the city that most represents those things.' Because UKIP took only one seat, there was a tendency to think that Nigel Farage and all his works had been banished now to the sidelines. That was to overlook some telling signs of the dislocation of much of Britain. Many of the seats where UKIP took a fifth or more of the popular vote in 2015 were the kind of coastal constituencies, like Clacton, Boston in Lincolnshire, and Grimsby, where the sense of London having lost touch and lost interest had long been greatest. But others were out in the sleeping shires through which my bus has travelled this morning: Rotherham, Rother Valley, Wentworth, Doncaster Central and Doncaster North, Bradford South, Barnsley East and Barnsley Central, Don Valley, Hull East, Sheffield Brightside and Normanton in Yorkshire, Mansfield and Bolsover in Nottinghamshire, Blyth Valley in Northumberland, South Shields and Houghton South and Sunderland South in County Durham. Such outcomes too may have been, at least in part, a rejection of 'London decision-making, London hegemony'.

The post-2007 recession made the disparities worse. Walking round London, even at the height of it, the signs of a city retreating into its shell were surprisingly hard to discern. The construction industry's cranes still punctuated the skyline. The crowds on pavements outside cafés and restaurants and bars seemed scarcely less animated, scarcely less numerous, than they had in the fatter years that preceded it. Every January the Centre for Cities think tank draws on official statistics to compile an account of the state of our cities (including big towns which have yet to be given city status). Their findings in 2015, like those of the years before them, showed London, followed by its attendant south-east region, pulling even further ahead of the rest. London accounted for 79 per cent of all new private sector jobs between 2010 and 2012; and where new public sector jobs did appear, in education and health, London took by far the greatest share. And among new jobs in London the majority were full-time. That wasn't the case in the rest of Britain.

The pattern for jobs was replicated elsewhere. The shopping trade in cities and towns of the South (here defined as London, the south-east, the south-west and the eastern region) had expanded at double the rate elsewhere. In the summer of 2014, a cross-party House of Commons committee condemned the over-provision of arts subsidies in the capital. In London, they had been told, arts spending was running at £68.99 per head of the population; elsewhere the level was £4.58. At about the same time, a sister committee made the same point about public transport. Contemplating a pattern of investment that had seen spectacular sums spent on Crossrail, the upgrade of the Underground network, and the special provision that had to be made for the Olympic Games, the committee noted that passengers in London and the South-east were being treated to new and better trains while the rest of the country had to make do with reconditioned old ones. Anyone travelling Britain by train will know what that means. It's a system where a journey from London to Birmingham (125 miles) takes a shade over an hour and a half, while those who aspire to travel much the same distance from Hull to Liverpool must allow two hours forty minutes, including a change at Huddersfield. Those who travel across much of the North must do so on tin-can trains which London and the South-east would never tolerate.

The strikingly lopsided nature of modern Britain, London and its satellites against the rest of the kingdom, is nowhere more powerfully demonstrated than in housing. In this case, though, much of the capital's population numbers among the disadvantaged. Relentless house price inflation enriches the haves, with thousands who never expected it discovering they're now, technically at least, millionaires, but it slams the door on have-nots. For the great bulk of working people, their right to be part of that property-owning democracy which Margaret Thatcher classed on taking office as an essential part of 'the British inheritance' is no longer attainable.

The 594 bus passes through four of the ten postcodes rated by the property website Zoopla as the most expensive in London – with average prices in Kensington W8, half a mile or so off the route and the priciest of the lot, coming in at £2.9 million in 2016. London is the city where so many, from so many parts of the world, long to be. For all the renaissance of cities like Birmingham and Manchester, there remains that feeling with which I grew up in Leeds (a city which itself has been spectacularly transformed since those days) that London was where things happened, and where you had to be if you wanted to grab the best opportunities.

But it's not just those aspiring to live well in London who have pushed up property prices and made the prospect of purchase impossible for so many Londoners; it's also the certainty among people who have shedloads of money to spend that the London property market is a fail-safe way to enrich yourself. That is why, until uncertainties over Brexit began to undermine the top of the market, buying to let had become one of the city's growth industries and buying to leave – letting the place stay empty while it appreciates – had blossomed beside it.

All of which, in its various permutations, has been good for those with first-class seats on the gravy train, but leaves those who have no hope of climbing aboard with a sense of helplessness, sinking to hopelessness. Many who once would have dreamed of owning a home in the capital have had to accept that their destiny is to rent. And renting in London is phenomenally expensive too. According to the Council of Mortgage Lenders, in 1970 the age of the typical first time buyer was twenty-five; now a mere 8 per cent of this age group own their own homes. Local authorities that once provided homes for the poorer people on housing lists find themselves no longer able to do so. Instead they look for properties outside their boundaries and move their most vulnerable tenants there, a process described by Jeremy Corbyn during his campaign for the Labour leadership as 'social cleansing'.

*****

The glaring imbalance between London and the rest of the land is matched by the wild imbalance within London itself, which contains, as well as the richest postcodes in Britain, many of the very poorest. The 2010 Index of Multiple Deprivation listed the boroughs of Hackney and Tower Hamlets as among the most deprived in the country. Just off my route, just west of the salubrious sector of Baker Street that is famous for Sherlock Holmes, there's an area which runs westward across to the Edgware Road. This is the Church Street ward of Westminster, down the centre of which runs a once-notorious street (crime, excessive drinking, prostitution) called Lisson Grove. It was developed in the early years of the nineteenth century to attract respectable households who couldn't quite make St John's Wood, but it failed in that ambition and rapidly degenerated into a slum.

That eased in the twentieth century, but still in the two decades from 1990 on, the Lisson Green sector had a dire reputation for robbery, violence, drugs and gang warfare. It was also a place of notable poverty. But here is what at first sight looks like good news. New deprivation figures issued in the autumn of 2015 showed a marked improvement, as indeed they did across much of the capital, with London's four most deprived boroughs, Hackney, Newham, Tower Hamlets and Haringey, no longer at the top of the national charts.

But why has there been this improvement? That's less reassuring. The main reason seems to have been the use of the right to buy legislation which Margaret Thatcher's Conservatives introduced in 1980, with provision for discounts of up to 50 per cent, according to how long you had lived there, on the purchase price. It was also stipulated that those who bought would have to repay part of the discount if they sold up in less than five years. Thereafter they could do as they pleased. Many fancying a life in some better location sold up and moved out. Sometimes they sold direct, but often they dealt with property companies who refurbished the properties and either sold on at a much higher price or rented them out. In either case, the cost of accommodation became much more expensive.

What this means is tellingly demonstrated in a dissertation successfully submitted for his MSc degree at King's College, London, by Achim von Malotki, a Church Street ward resident. The kind of poorly paid people who could once have afforded to live in these streets, he shows, can no longer do so: 'If they do not already own a house, the vast majority of Church Street residents has effectively been priced out of their own neighbourhood.' And that must inevitably mean the loss of that neighbourliness, rootedness and sense of community which had long existed here. It's the kind of process which explains why the London boroughs that were high in the national deprivation league even five years before now look to be moving out of it.

For all its enhancements, Church Street ward remained in 2015 one of the most deprived wards in the capital. Life expectancy in Church Street ward on these figures was 79.1 for men and 82.6 per cent for women. Far better than it used to be, but four or five years worse than in Regent's Park ward, through which the 594 runs, and ten years worse than in Knightsbridge and Belgravia ward, half a mile to the south. Across Westminster, two-thirds of the sixteen to sixty-four age group have work; in Church Street ward, it's less than half. The estimated median household income in Church Street is £27,000. In Regent's Park ward it is 75 per cent higher; across Westminster as a whole, it is three times as high. And in Knightsbridge-Belgravia, it's higher still: a difference of over £88,000 a year.

The discrepancy in the cost of housing is just as spectacular: £440,000 in (rapidly appreciating) Church Street, but well over twice that across the way in Regent's Park ward, and almost eight times as much in Knightsbridge-Belgravia. Hardly surprising when Knightsbridgers have so much more space around them: there are more than ten times as many people crammed into a square kilometre of Church Street as are accommodated in the equivalent space in Knightsbridge-Belgravia. Almost three in ten households in Church Street need housing benefit to get by on, against one in ten in Regent's Park. In Knightsbridge-Belgravia few would even know it existed.

*****

So what could be done about these imbalances – these injustices – the nation's, and London's? In the case of the nation, some voices (mostly in London, of course) insistently say: why do anything? Lie back and enjoy it; London's riches enrich us all! According to this analysis the humblest homesteads in the back streets of Felling and Tyldesley benefit from London's success. (Here I remember that vast advertisement I saw on the wall in a downtrodden street in Gloucester: 'Expand Heathrow, and the benefits will extend all over Britain.' Really?)

Londoners, it's been calculated, are 69 per cent more productive in terms of gross domestic product generated per head than others around the UK. London's boisterous former mayor Boris Johnson claimed towards the end of his tenure that the capital was 'a gigantic undersea coelenterate' that sucked in talent from all round the world and harnessed it to create economic activity and dynamism around the country. The sucking-in's indisputable. But to sceptics elsewhere – and in London too – this all sounds like the discredited 'trickle down' theory, or the convenient doctrine that 'a rising tide lifts all boats'. You only have to walk a brief distance from City Hall to detect the unreality there. If that were true, surely the battered boats of Tower Hamlets and Hackney would have buoyed up in line with the high rewards and incontinent spending of the City of London.

By 2015, something seemed to be changing. George Osborne, then Chancellor of the Exchequer, one of the few senior ministers representing a northern constituency, had announced in his budget plans to create what he called a 'Northern Powerhouse', essentially based on bringing together cities on either side of the Pennines, effectively linking Liverpool on the western coast to Hull on the east to form an economic and political entity that could match and complement – rather than rival, he emphasized – magnetic London. He promised a substantial devolution of power and financial resources to the cities that it might incorporate, though only on condition that each agreed to install the kind of elected mayor already established in London – something Manchester, allowed to express a view in a referendum, had earlier declined to do. In the political crisis that followed the Brexit vote, however, Osborne was swept away, and the North began to sense that Theresa May's successor regime had doubts about this whole enterprise. Even so, especially after the Brexit vote, there seemed now to be a realization in the commanding heights of the party likely to be in power for the next decade that something would at last be done to peel back the over-centralization of Britain.

*****

This rejection of London-based politics and London-based government is a theme that is nowhere more relevant than in the London borough that the 594 has now reached: the eight miles square super-powerhouse that is Westminster.

The city of Greater London contains its own subsidiary cities: the financial centre known as the City, now amplified by a kind of towering secondary City around Canary Wharf; and this one, which does for political power what the City does for money: the two houses of the nation's Parliament, the homes of the great institutions of its civil service, many of its finest cultural assets – museums and galleries, cinemas and theatres – and the gleaming headquarters of great business companies are congregated here.

For decades it has been argued that while so much power is concentrated in Westminster, no other region can ever come close to competing. While it stays where it is, central government, it is often claimed in the regions, will always tailor policies to the world it knows best, ordering them in ways that suit London but are out of place everywhere else. A skewed politics is always likely to make for a skewed society. The Labour cabinet that left office in 2010 had a sizeable northern contingent (five of them from Yorkshire alone and four from Scotland), but only two represented seats in London, with one from the South-west and none from the eastern or East Midlands regions. Theresa May's first cabinet in 2016, like David Cameron's before it, was overwhelmingly southern. Ten of its members came from the area close to London loosely categorized as the Home Counties, including three each from Surrey and Kent. They include the Prime Minister herself and her Chancellor. Three more represented seats in the outer suburbs of London. There were four from the Midlands, but only one from the northern counties, one from Scotland and one from Wales. The great cities of Glasgow, Edinburgh, Newcastle, Manchester, Liverpool, Leeds and Birmingham had no voice at all in the cabinet. And this was scarcely odd, because these places no longer elect Conservatives.

The urgency and the difficulty of reuniting this toxically disunited kingdom could be read line by line in the results of the referendum of June 2016. Outside London and Scotland, there were only nine referendum constituencies where 60 per cent or more voted to stay in the European Union: Gibraltar (where the vote for remain was 95.9 per cent), Cambridge, South Cambridgeshire, Oxford, Brighton and Hove, St Albans, Bristol, Manchester and Cardiff. It would not surprise any recent visitor that Newcastle voted to stay and Gateshead to leave, that Middlesbrough and Redcar and Cleveland were leavers, along with Stoke-on-Trent and even Newcastle-under-Lyme, and Wigan, which takes in Leigh, including Tyldesley. Cornwall, too, despite its heavy inflow of EU subsidies, voted to leave.

There are those who say that London (like Oxford, Cambridge and Brighton) is simply surging ahead into what will become standard twenty-first-century life – adventurous, cosmopolitan, wide open to new and unconventional patterns of living – and the rest of the kingdom is lagging behind. Change is the city's essence. Ever since its humiliation at the hands of Colchester's cherished Boudicca, London has constantly been adapting, developing, incontinently growing. (Defoe's question again: 'Whither will this monstrous city extend? And where must a circumvallation or communication line of it be placed?') Today, as the night bus comes close to Victoria Station, the signs of renewal are everywhere. Towering new palaces of steel and glass are taking shape to join the legion of earlier ones, with familiar buildings, serviceable but drab, razed to make room for them. Change *is* continuity here. Merely to read the account of the capital's transformation from 1800 onwards in Jerry White's superb *London in the 19th Century* leaves one feeling in need of a rest. The coming of the railway (London's first terminal, London Bridge, opened in 1836), the replacement of horse-drawn transport by the mechanized kind, new bridges, new sewers, new hospitals (and new public health systems), new schools and libraries and museums, new theatres, new prisons, new docks and industrial sites, new great parks for public enjoyment, new imposing buildings (some praised, some mocked and too many later destroyed) – all helped to rewrite the experience of London as it grew to be an economic and financial hub around which the world now turned; the biggest city yet known to man. 'It seemed', says White, 'as though the whole living edifice was a creation of the past 100 years. To a great extent it was.'

At times, London's recurring waves of elimination and replacement have been a response to some kind of disaster, such as the Fire of London which opened the door to Wren, or the twentieth-century Blitz; at others, as through most of the nineteenth century, they were born of a thirst to innovate in the name of the irresistible cause of Progress and the equally compelling cause that went with it, Profit.

So here, as ever, as we come to the end of this journey, are the boardings-up and the hoardings, the relentless drone and moan of machinery, the construction workers striding about in hard hats and safety jackets, the pedestrian diversions pointing you in the opposite direction from the one you want to take. It is twenty past seven – we're around an hour late (there were roadworks impeding our progress though northern England) – and the 594 has finally come to rest at Victoria Coach Station.

Here too you can't fail to see how the world is changing. Alongside the coaches marshalled for early departures to Penzance and Bristol and Bath, Totnes and Dover, Wolverhampton and Cardiff, there are nowadays services advertised for Paris, Milan, Poland and Romania, and no shortage of people ready to take them, some of whom are asleep on the ground, cushioned by such devices as several copies of *Metro*. Out on the general streets the people are going to work and the coffee shops are dispensing the morning's caffeinated ambrosia. And familiar red buses are conveying the world to Chelsea and Fulham, ultra-expensive Knightsbridge and Kensington, and less favoured (though more favoured now than they used to be, when so much closer in is so pricey) locations like Tooting.

There's a reassuring sense of continuity in these 11s and 44s and 170s and 211s. Where outside the capital the service buses are clad in company colours, proclaiming that they belong to Stagecoach, Arriva, GoAhead and the rest, in London they're still, whichever outfit provides them, uniformly red. They announce an allegiance not to some big commercial company but to the great world city they serve, much as they did when George Orwell, returning from the war against Franco in Spain, numbered them among the sights which brought him some kind of peace: 'the huge peaceful wilderness of outer London, the barges on the miry river, the familiar streets, the posters telling of cricket matches and Royal weddings, the men in bowler hats, the pigeons in Trafalgar Square, the red buses, the blue policemen'.

So many of them, so reassuringly, to be seen even now, as I leave the night bus from Edinburgh and walk back at last into the routine day of the busy resuming city.

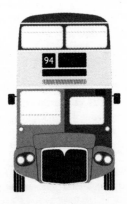

NOTES ON SOURCES

This account has relied throughout on the *Oxford Dictionary of National Biography*, Wikipedia, *Who Was Who*, Pevsner's Buildings of England and its counterparts for Scotland and Wales, and on Shell guides and Victoria County Histories for relevant counties. Also on local newspapers, new and old, including those accessible through the British Newspaper Archive and the Newsroom at the British Library.

Introduction
John Harris, 'Buses are a vital requirement', *Guardian*, 24 August 2015.

Chapter 1
For Blewbury and Didcot, Edward Thomas, *The Icknield Way* (London, 1913). Brian Lingham, *The Railway Comes to Didcot: A History of the Town 1839–1918* (Stroud, 1993), and *A Poor Struggling Little Town: A History of Didcot 1918–45* (Didcot, 2000). For Oxford's resistance to the railway: Jan Morris, *Oxford* (Oxford, 1987).
For Middlesbrough and Grangetown: a characteristically brilliant account of the town is in Asa Briggs, *Victorian Cities* (Harmondsworth, 1968). Middlesbrough Central Library found me several instructive books, notably: Minoru Yasumoto, *The Rise of a Victorian Ironopolis: Middlesbrough and Regional Industrialisation* (Woodbridge, 2011); chapter by Tony Nicholson in *Middlesbrough Town and City 1830–50*, ed. A.J. Pollard (Stroud, 1996). Maurice E. Wilson, *The Story of Eston* (self-published, 1972); and Vera Robinson, *Grangetown Remembered* (Redcar, 1990), where I found Julie Outhwaite's poem. Vera Robinson wrote several histories of the area, published locally; she died in 2015 aged 101. Disapproving visitors to the town include C.F.G. Masterman, *The Condition of England* (London, 1909); J.B. Priestley, *English Journey* (London, 1984); Douglas Goldring, *Gone Abroad: A Story of Travel, Chiefly in Italy and the Balearics* (London, 1925). More sympathetic is Florence Bell (Lady Bell), *At the Works: A Study of a Manufacturing Town* (first published 1907; Newton Abbot, 1969), The *Teesside Gazette*, formerly *Evening Gazette, Middlesbrough*, was another useful source. The overblown claims for Middlebrough's worldwide fame, usually attributed to H.G. Reid, occur in his book *Middlesbrough and its Jubilee* (Middlesbrough, 1891), though here they are assigned to a 'shrewd observer' of some twenty years earlier.

Chapter 2
Much material here comes from files held at the Oxford History Centre, Cowley. *Jackson's Oxford Journal*, especially editions of 11 September 1830 and 18 September (piece contributed by 'An Otmoor Proprietor'), is essential for the events of 1830–35, as are John Dunkin's contemporary histories of Oxfordshire and Bernard Reaney, *The Class Struggle in 19th Century Oxfordshire: The Social and Communal Background to the Otmoor Disturbances of 1830 to 1835* (Oxford, 1970). Earlier, J.L. and Barbara Hammond surveyed events at Otmoor for their

book *The Village Labourer 1760–1832: A Study in the Government of England before the Reform Bill* (first published 1912; Stroud, 2005). See also M.G. Hobson and K.L.H. Price, *Otmoor and its Seven Towns* (self-published, 1961).
The testimony of the 'farmer called Thornton' is quoted by Reaney.
For the M40 route and its thwarting, see Hugh Clayton, *The Times*, 4 July 1983; James Lees-Milne, 'Otmoor and the M40', *The Times*, 8 February 1973, also quoted in Joe Moran, *On Roads: A Hidden History* (London, 2009).
George Orwell's broadcast on pubs was printed in the *Listener*, 21 January 1943.

Chapter 3
Much in this chapter is based on material held at the Gloucestershire Archives, Gloucester. For Goldsworthy Gurney's invention, see Dale H. Porter, *The Life and Times of Sir Goldsworthy Gurney: Gentleman, Scientist and Inventor, 1793–1875* (Bethlehem, Penn., and London, 1998); also David Beasley, *The Suppression of the Automobile: Skulduggery at the Crossroads* (Westport, Conn., 1988) (rev. edn, *Who Really Invented the Automobile*, Simcoe, Ont., 1997). For Cheltenham, John Betjeman, *First and Last Loves* (London, 1952); Thomas Rudge, *The History and Antiquities of Gloucester* (Gloucester, 1811); and the Revd Thomas Fosbroke, *An Original History of the City of Gloucester* (London, 1819).
For GCHQ, Robert Hannigan's outburst was reported in the *Financial Times*, 3 November 2014, and reaction to it in the *Guardian*, 4 November 2014; more irreverently, Bob Dormon, 'Geek's Guide to Britain – Inside GCHQ: Welcome to Cheltenham's Cottage Industry', 24 May 2013, http://www.theregister.co.uk/2013/05/24/geeks_guide_gchq/.
For Gloucester: John Britton, *The History and Antiquities of the Abbey and Cathedral Church of Gloucester* (London, 1828). Ian Nairn, 'The city with the hole in it', *Sunday Times*, 22 February 1981. David Verey comes to much the same conclusions in his *Gloucestershire: A Shell Guide* (London, 1970). For Finzi, see Stephen Banfield, *Gerald Finzi: An English Composer* (London, 1887). For Ivor Gurney, *Selected Poems of Ivor Gurney*, ed. Patrick Kavanagh (London, 1997); Michael Hurd, *The Ordeal of Ivor Gurney* (Oxford, 1984).

Chapter 4
Asa Briggs, *Victorian Cities* (Harmondsworth, 1968), is again essential here – as are his volume of the *History of Birmingham: Borough and City, 1865–1938* (Birmingham, 1952), and its successor volume by Anthony Sutcliffe and Roger Smith, *Birmingham, 1939–1970* (Birmingham, 1974). The *Birmingham Post* marked the fiftieth anniversary of Manzoni's retirement with 'Herbert Manzoni: The man who changed the face of Birmingham', by Stacey Barnfield, 8 March 2013, which includes the assessment of Manzoni by Carl Chinn. Also useful: Elizabeth Frostick and Lucy Harland, *Take Heart: People, History and Change in Birmingham's Heartlands* (Beverley, 1993), where I found the description of life in a Nechells household. Andy Beckett, *When the Lights Went Out: Britain in the Seventies* (London, 2009), has a good brief account of events at Saltley.
For Chelmsley Wood, see Lynsey Hanley, *Estates* (London, 2007); also her ' A Waitrose state of mind', *Guardian*, 5 April 2014. For how it came about, R.H.S. Crossman, *Diaries of a Cabinet Minister*, vol 1 (London 1975).

Chapter 5
Local newspapers: the *Western Mail* (consistently sympathetic to Cardiff and to the Butes, who owned it along with so much else); the sympathies of the *Barry Dock News* were the reverse. Nowadays, the *Barry and District News*, for the renascence of the Pleasure Park. *The Times* ran an obituary of David Davies on 22 July 1890. More generally: Peter Howell and Elisabeth Beazley, *The Companion Guide to South Wales* (London, 1977), and Stewart Williams, *South Glamorgan: A County History* (Barry, 1975), which contains a chapter on Penarth by Patricia Moore. Also – first published in Welsh but reprinted in English by Penguin in 1974 – John Davies, *A History of Wales*.

Chapter 6
Paul Johnson, *The Vanished Landscape: A 1930s Childhood in the Potteries* (London, 2004), has a very good feel for this territory. Arnold Bennett's *The Old Wives' Tale* (1908) and *Clayhanger* (1910) are both republished by Penguin. Margaret Drabble's *Arnold Bennett: A Biography* was also republished by Penguin (London, 1985). For the source of the Trent, see Tom Fort, *Downstream: Across England in a Punt* (London, 2008). For the oatcake scandal, the *Sentinel* (Stoke), 9 March 2014. For Tunstall Town, Barney Ronay, *Guardian*, 14 March 2014, picking up on a leader comment the previous week.

Chapter 7
For Huddersfield: *Roy Brook, The Story of Huddersfield* (London, 1968). For its station, Ian Nairn, 'The towns behind the teams', *Listener*, 28 August 1975 (based on a TV programme). For Slaithwaite: Penny Wainwright, 'Slaithwaite: A prime candidate for redevelopment in West Yorkshire', *Yorkshire Life*, 14 February 2010. For Colne Valley politics, David Clark's *Labour's Lost Leader – Victor Grayson* (London, 1985), and *Colne Valley: Radicalism to Socialism* (London, 1981).

Chapter 8
A key local historian here is John Lunn, whose books include *The Historical Past of a Lancashire Borough* (Leigh, 1958). For rugby league, see Geoffrey Moorhouse, *At the George and Other Essays on Rugby League* (London, 1989); for sport and its former snobberies, Derek Birley, *A Social History of English Cricket* (London, 1999). Though Leigh failed to reach the Super League in 2015, they did so one season later.

Chapter 9
For the circumstances in which this ridiculous route was created, Peter Findlay, 'Cumbria bus service shake-up comes into force today', *Express and Star* (Carlisle), 3 November 2014. Ian Nairn's strictures on the city came in a TV feature called 'From Leeds into Scotland', part of a series called *Nairn Across Britain* transmitted 28 September 1972 (try http://www.bbc.co.uk/programmes/p01rwh55). William Pinnock's *The History and Topography of Cumberland* was published in London in 1822. For an earlier exploration, see Thomas Benton's *A Perambulation of Cumberland 1687–88* (Woodbridge, 2003).

Chapter 10

For a comparative history of twentieth-century housing in Glasgow, see Miles Glendinning and Stefan Muthesius, *Tower Block: Modern Public Housing in England, Scotland, Wales and Northern Ireland* (New Haven and London, 1994, and at http://towerblock.org/TowerBlock.pdf). Sean Damer's view is given in *From Moorepark to 'Wine Alley': The Rise and Fall of a Glasgow Housing Scheme* (Edinburgh, 1989). See also Carol Craig, *The Tears That Made the Clyde* (Argyll, 2010). For Red Road, Ian Jack, 'Demolishing Glasgow's Red Road flats could leave the city's reputation in rubble', *Guardian*, 12 April 2014, which also includes planners saying, 'don't consult the frogs'; also Robert Booth, 'Glasgow 2014 scraps live "celebration" of flats demolition', in the same paper two days later. The photographer Chris Leslie had a further account of the Red Road process in the *Guardian*, 22 April 2015.

For Maryhill specifically, Guthrie Hutton, *Old Maryhill* (Ochiltree, 1994). I.R. Mitchell's 'Unlocking Maryhill – A history of its places and people' is in *Pat's Guide to Glasgow West End* (www.glasgowwestend.co.uk/unlocking-maryhill). For a seminar on Scottish devolution (one of many), see *Renewal*, 2015, 'The Scottish referendum: What happened and what next?' (http://www.renewal.org.uk/articles/the-scottish-independence-referendum-what-happened-and-what-next).

Chapter 11

For Kilmore church at Dervaig, see http://www.undiscoveredscotland.co.uk/mull/kilmorechurch. There are introductions to Calgary and Dervaig in Julie Davidson's accounts on the *Daily Telegraph* travel website, 26 June 2001 and 13 July 2001, http://www.telegraph.co.uk/travel/destinations/europe/uk/scotland/718952/Isle-of-Mull-Weekend-to-remember.html; also www.theguardian.com/travel/2014/jan/13/best-beach-camping-sites-readers-tips. On the edge of Tobermory harbour there is a town clock incorporating a memorial set up by a Mrs Bishop to her sister Henrietta Amelia Bird. The story of these two Victorian sisters, one (Henrietta) devoted to Mull, the other an intrepid world traveller, is too long to accommodate in this book, but if you have never come across them, it is splendidly told in two books: *A Curious Life for a Lady* by Pat Barr (London, 1985), and *Letters to Henrietta*, ed. Kay Chubbuck (London, 2002), where in effect the remarkable Isabella addresses the reader direct. They also give the flavour of life within the constricted confines of nineteenth-century Mull and the totally different life a very few of its people discovered outside it.

Chapter 12

For St Andrews and almost everywhere else on this journey, Glen Pride, *The Kingdom of Fife: An Illustrated Architectural Guide* (Edinburgh, 1999). For Cupar, Paula Martin, *Cupar: The History of a Small Scottish Town* (Edinburgh 2006). For Jimmy Shand, his obituary by Brian Wilson, *Guardian*, 27 December 2000. John Junor's daughter, Penny Junor, published a book she called *Home Truths: Life around my Father* (London, 2002), which is dedicated to her long-suffering mother.

Chapter 13
F.W.D. Manders's *A History of Gateshead* was published by Gateshead Corporation
in 1973. See also Nick Neave, *Gateshead through Time* (first published 1934;
Stroud, 2010). J.B. Priestley's baleful view of the town comes from *English Journey*
(London, 1984). See also John Stevenson and Chris Cook, *The Slump: Society and
Politics during the Depression* (London, 1977). A recent assessment is in Grace
McCombie, *Newcastle and Gateshead* (New Haven and London, 2009). The Owen
Luder–Rodney Gordon shopping centre, demolished, is championed in Owen
Hatherley, *A Guide to the New Ruins of Britain* (London, 2010), where he calls the
Get Carter car park 'one of the most visceral architectural experiences available
in Britain, in terms of sheer physical power, architecture that both hits in the gut
and sends shivers down the spine'; also in Jonathan Meades, 'Bunkers, Brutalism
and Bloodymindedness: Concrete Poetry', available on Vimeo in a sector called
MeadesShrine, established by one of his fans (https://vimeo.com/93963469).
Hodgson Casson is the subject of Allan Steele, *Christianity in Earnest, as
exemplified in the Life and Labours of the Rev. Hodgson Casson* (London, 1853). The
account of the Booths's Gateshead meeting comes from *Newcastle Daily Chronicle*,
21 May 1879. Wesley's experiences are quoted in Manders's book.

Chapter 14
For Selby, W. Wilberforce Morrell, *The History and Antiquities of Selby* (York and
London, 1867), and Patricia Scott, *The History of Selby from the Earliest Times to
the Year 2000* (Pickering, 2005).
For William the Conqueror and his northern ravages, David Douglas, *William
the Conqueror: The Norman Impact upon England* (London, 1964). Orderic Vitalis,
The Ecclesiastical History of England and Normandy, vols 4 and 5, translated with
notes by Thomas Forester, Bohm edition (London, 1853–6). David Smurthwaite,
The Ordnance Survey Complete Guide to the Battlefields of Britain (Exeter, 1984), has
a section on Towton. See also Edmund Bogg, *The Old Kingdom of Elmet* (London,
1902). Alan Bennett's diary for 2013, when he visited Lead church on 4 February,
appeared in the *London Review of Books* in January 2014: http://www.lrb.co.uk/
v36/n01/alan-bennett/diary.

Chapter 15
Maurice Beresford, *The Lost Villages of England* (first published 1954; Stroud,
1998), and Richard Muir, *The Lost Villages of Britain* (London, 1982), are key texts
here. Also W.G. Hoskins, *The Making of the English Landscape* (London, 1956). For
Abraham de la Pryme, *The Diary of Abraham de la Pryme, the Yorkshire Antiquary*,
ed. C. Jackson (Durham, 1870). For Crawford, Kitty Hauser, *Bloody Old Britain:
O.G.S. Crawford and the Archaeology of Modern Life* (London, 2008). His own *Said
and Done: The Autobiography of an Archaeologist* was published in London in 1955,
but *A Tour in Bolshevy* and *Bloody Old Britain* were left unpublished.

Chapter 16
For the city and county: Jack Simmons, *Leicester Past and Present*, 2 vols (London,
1974). Siobhan Begley, *The Story of Leicester* (Stroud, 2013). Richard Hoggart,
An Imagined Life, part of his 'Life and Times' trilogy (Oxford, 1991). W.G. Hoskins,

Leicestershire: An Illustrated Essay on the History of the Landscape (London, 1970). Entries for 24 February 1950, 9 March 1950 and 2 September 1954 in Harold Nicolson, *Diaries and Letters, 1945–1952*, ed. Nigel Nicolson (London, 1971). Ian Nairn, 'Places where the heart takes off, on its own', *Sunday Times*, 6 January 1974. Adrian Jones and Chris Matthews, *Towns in Britain* (Nottingham, 2014). For Konrad Smigielski and his legacy, Simon Gunn, 'Between Modernism and Conservation: Konrad Smigielski and the Planning of Post-war Leicester', in *Leicester: A Modern History*, ed. Richard Rodger and Rebecca Madgin (said in September 2016 to be 'coming soon' from Carnegie Publishing); Rebecca Madgin and Edward Morgan, 'Konrad Smigielski: A visionary and a victim?', http://www. rtpi.org.uk/media/9857/spectrum-158.pdf. For Glenfield: Jonathan Wilshere, *Glenfield: A Considerable Village* (Leicester, 1984).
For Richard III: *Leicester Mercury* throughout 2015. Maev Kennedy, 'Thousands line Leicester's streets for glimpse of Richard III's coffin', *Guardian*, 23 March 2015.

Chapter 17
The old spelling Boadicea is now rejected in favour of Boudicca or Boudica. The *Oxford Dictionary of National Biography* uses the former. For this warrior queen, *Tacitus Agricola and Germania*, ed. H. Mattingly (London, 2010); *Annals of Imperial Rome*, ed. Michael Grant (London, 2003); Cassius Dio, *Roman History*, ed. Michael Grant (London, 1914–27); H.E. Marshall, *Our Island Story* (London, 2014); Antonia Fraser, *Warrior Queens: Boadicea's Chariot* (London, 1988); Richard Hingley and Christine Unwin, *Boudica: Iron Age Warrior Queen* (Hambledon and London, 2005); Charlotte Higgins, *Under Another Sky: Journeys in Roman Britain* (London, 2015).
For East Bergholt: C.R. Leslie, *The Letters of John Constable* (London, 1931).
For Hadleigh and Tesco: Jonathan Glancey, 'Outrage revisited: Save Hadleigh from Tesco', *Guardian* video, 10 June 2010. Judi Bevan, *Trolley Wars: The Battle of the Supermarkets* (London, 2006).

Chapter 18
For Delius and Limpsfield: Peter Vernon and Norman Cameron in *Delius Society Journal*, no. 57, October 1977 (www.delius.org.uk/journals/uploads/journal57.pdf). Eric Fenby, *Delius As I Knew Him* (London, 1948). Michael Kennedy, *The Works of Ralph Vaughan Williams* (London, 1980). Michael Tippett, *Those Twentieth Century Blues: An Autobiography* (London, 1991).
For second-hand bookshops: www.inprint.co.uk/the bookguide/shops.

Chapter 19
Gibbon's memoirs (he wrote six versions) are distilled in *Autobiography of Edward Gibbon*, ed. Oliphant Smeaton (London, 1948).
Edward Yates, *Buriton and its People* (Petersfield, 1976).

Chapter 20
Adam Fergusson, *The Sack of Bath: A Record and an Indictment* (London, 2011). Barry Cunliffe on Major Davis is at https://www.bathspa.ac.uk/Media/CHC%20 Images/Vol%2001%20-%2002.%20Cunliffe%20-%20Major%20Davis%20-%20 Architect%20and%20Antiquarian.pdf.

For Westwood: Nick McCamley, *Avoncliff: The Secret History of an Industrial Hamlet in War and Peace* (Bradford on Avon, 2004).
For a sympathetic account of Trowbridge: Ken Rogers, 'Out and about in Trowbridge', *The Historian*, summer issue 2010. Rogers is a retired county archivist.

Chapter 21

For Plymouth: W.G. Hoskins, *Devon* (Chichester, 2011); Simon Jenkins, *England's Thousand Best Houses* (London, 2003); also his 'Let's restore and rebuild, not fetishise the ruins of conflict', *Guardian* 18 April 2014; Jeremy Gould, 'The architecture of the plan for Plymouth', *Context*, September 2006 (http://www. ihbc.org.uk/context_archive/96/gould/jeremy.htm); Owen Hatherley, *A New Kind of Bleak: Journeys through Urban Britain* (London, 2013). *Nairn's Towns* (London, 2013) by Ian Nairn, edited, updated and introduced by Owen Hatherley, includes a chapter called 'Friendly Plymouth'. Hatherley, a thoroughgoing modernist, considers Nairn too critical of the remodelling of the city.
For Noss Mayo, Maurice Baring, *The Puppet Show of Memory* (London, 1987).

Chapter 22

For Cornwall generally: Sabine Baring-Gould, *Cornwall* (Cambridge, 1910).
O.J. Padel, *Popular Dictionary of Cornish Placenames* (Penzance, 1988). Philip Marsden, *Rising Ground: A Search for the Spirit of Place* (London, 2014); also 'Cornish identity: Why Cornwall has always been a separate place', *Guardian*, 26 April 2014. Emily Dugan, 'Cornwall: A land of haves, and have nots', *Independent on Sunday*, 27 July 2008, For the county's industrial history, John Rowe, *Cornwall in the Age of the Industrial Revolution* (Liverpool, 1993); I gather the definitive work is A.K.H. Jenkin, *Mines and Miners of Cornwall* (Truro, 1961–78), but it's in sixteen volumes. The lost Wadebridge–Padstow railway line is remembered in John Betjeman's *First and Last Loves* (London, 1952).
For St Columb Major: 'St Columb Major: Character appraisal and management proposals', Cornwall Council, 2010. Also the *Cornish Guardian* newspaper.

Chapter 23

Edinburgh: on Scott and Scottish traditions, Hugh Trevor-Roper in Eric Hobsbawm and Terence Ranger, *The Invention of Tradition* (Cambridge, 1994). On London as seen from the rest of Britain: Danny Dorling, 'The London problem: Has the capital become too prominent?', *New Statesman*, 4 September 2014, at www.newstatesman.com/2014/08/London-problem; Stephanie Flanders, 'Should Britain let go of London', at http://www.bbc.co.uk/news/business-21934564; David Goodhart, 'Labour has lost its cultural connection with the people it claims to represent', *Guardian*, 29 May 2015. See also the annual Cities Outlook published by the Centre for Cities. For inequalities within London, accessible via ResearchGate – https://www.researchgate.net/profile/Achim Malotki.
For London history, Daniel Defoe, *A Tour through England and Wales*, vol. 1 (London, 1928). Jerry White, *London in the 19th Century: A Human Awful Wonder of God* (London, 2007).

INDEX

ACKNOWLEDGMENTS

My main debt here is to George Miller, who edited this book and who steered me through the daunting process of reducing it to its predestined size. Many others have helped to shape it too: some whose names I shall never know, by talking to me on my travels – from fellow passengers, and sometimes drivers, on routes numbered 94, to proprietors and guests of the bed and breakfasts I stayed in, especially on the Isle of Mull, to librarians in many places I visited, through to people attending the monthly coffee mornings at St Peter's, Limpsfield. Others are acknowledged by name in these pages. Ewen MacAskill, Penny Wainwright, Pat and Jon Hartridge and Bryan McAllister offered valued guidance, and Alf Young and Carol Craig gave me both their advice and their warm hospitality. Becky Clarke gave the book its splendid green buses, and Hilary Bird its index

Lynsey Hanley's Estates is quoted by permission of Granta Books; Tower Block: Modern Public Building in England, Scotland, Wales and Northern Ireland by Miles Glendinning and Stefan Muthesius, published by Yale University Press, 1994 (© 1993 by Yale University); Alan Bennett on Lead church, Yorkshire, taken from his 2013 Diaries, by permission of the London Review of Books; and Simon Jenkins on Plymouth, from his England's Thousand Best Houses, by permission of Penguin Random House. I have made every effort to trace copyright holders and to obtain their permission for the use of copyright material. I apologize for any errors or omissions and would be grateful if notified of any corrections that should be incorporated in future reprints or editions of this book.

Finally, my particular thanks to my daughter, Annabel Matthews, who put the idea of this book into my head, and to my wife Beryl, as watchful detector of errors, asker of thoughtful questions and source of useful ideas, but above all as an essential sustenance through the writing of this as of all my previous books; to whom this one, which could be the last, is dedicated.